Disobedient Theatre

Related Titles

Applied Theatre: Aesthetics
By Gareth White
ISBN 978-1-472-51355-7

Impro
By Keith Johnstone
ISBN 978-0-713-68701-9

Introduction to Arts Management
By Jim Volz
ISBN 978-1-474-23978-3

Popular Performance
Edited by Adam Ainsworth, Oliver Double and Louise Peacock
ISBN 978-1-474-24734-4

Reader in Comedy: An Anthology of Theory and Criticism
Edited by Magda Romanska and Alan Ackerman
ISBN 978-1-474-24788-7

Script Analysis for Theatre: Tools for Interpretation,
Collaboration and Production
By Robert Knopf
ISBN 978-1-4081-8430-1

The Art of Rehearsal: Conversations with Contemporary Theatre Makers
Edited by Barbara Simonsen
ISBN 978-1-474-29201-6

The Story of Drama: Tragedy, Comedy and
Sacrifice from the Greeks to the Present
By Gary Day
ISBN 978-1-408-18312-0

Disobedient Theatre

Alternative Ways to Inspire, Animate and Play

Chris Johnston

Bloomsbury Methuen Drama
An imprint of Bloomsbury Publishing Plc

B L O O M S B U R Y
LONDON · OXFORD · NEW YORK · NEW DELHI · SYDNEY

Bloomsbury Methuen Drama

An imprint of Bloomsbury Publishing Plc

Imprint previously known as Methuen Drama

50 Bedford Square	1385 Broadway
London	New York
WC1B 3DP	NY 10018
UK	USA

www.bloomsbury.com

BLOOMSBURY, METHUEN DRAMA and the Diana logo are trademarks of Bloomsbury Publishing Plc

First published 2017

© Chris Johnston, 2017

Chris Johnston has asserted his right under the Copyright, Designs and Patents Act, 1988, to be identified as author of this work.

British Library Cataloguing-in-Publication Data

A catalogue record for this book is available from the British Library.

ISBN: HB: 978-1-350-01453-4
       PB: 978-1-350-01454-1
       ePDF: 978-1-350-01455-8
       eBook: 978-1-350-01452-7

Library of Congress Cataloging-in-Publication Data

A catalog record for this book is available from the Library of Congress.

Series: Performance Books

Cover design by Clare Turner

Cover images: (top) *Festival Three* © Chris Johnston; (middle) *Guerrilla Girls* © Christian Sinibaldi; (bottom) *Megaphone* © mheim3011/iStock

Typeset by Fakenham Prepress Solutions, Fakenham, Norfolk NR21 8NN
Printed and bound in Great Britain

To find out more about our authors and books visit www.bloomsbury.com. Here you will find extracts, author interviews, details of forthcoming events and the option to sign up for our newsletters.

For Maggie

© Joseph Giordmaina

Chris Johnston (1951–2017)

Chris was protean, initiating and sustaining an ever-evolving mix of socially therapeutic and dissident arts initiatives. Like an inventor from a bygone age he was usually the guinea pig for his own experiments, perpetually thrusting himself into the most uncompromising situations. In prisons, schools and amidst communities he made awkwardness the spur to creativity, dissonance the basis for, not harmony, but rather the much more valuable utilities of resonance and resource. A perpetual (but assiduously anti-colonialist) Crusoe, he fashioned tools from found material and tested theories from first principles, through experience and by listening (he was a forensic but constructive prober of others' assertions, always avid to learn). His books form a unique legacy to emerging and established theatre makers, workshop leaders and performance activists. He will be remembered by those who knew him as a saturnine and quietly subversive theatrical polymath of huge compassion, endless curiosity and a kind of wisely skeptical idealism; a great facilitator who learned how to build structures within which others could invent, flourish and have their voices heard; a perpetual oppositionist and contrarian, but a discreetly cherishing and sensitive one.

This book was completed in the throes of a final illness he resisted with characteristic determination. Would that there were more like him. Perhaps through his writings and through the cherished memories of those many who came into direct contact with him, there will be.

Colin Ellwood
London, 2017

Contents

List of Games and Exercises

Acknowledgements

There are many to thank in the creation of a book such as this – not least all those who gave up their time to sit and discuss their working lives with me. Their names you will find throughout the book as interviewees. Besides these, there are several who have read and commented on draft texts, or who lent suggestions to the scope and range of the book. In particular I'd like to thank Colin Ellwood who did a great deal in both respects. Anders Alterskjaer should also be highly commended for his incisive suggestions. Thanks also go to Jack Cole, Simon Day and Jeff Thompson for their support. I'd also particularly like to thank Marcus Markou whose continuing support for a range of projects discussed in the book has been both influential and generous. Finally I would not have been able to complete the work without my wife and partner, Maggie Gordon-Walker, whose patience and consideration has been the glue holding the flakier parts of myself together while working on it.

Acknowledgements

Introduction

We always say that we are not here to show or reflect life. We are here to form our tomorrows

Gilbert and George, *Guardian* 2014

Disobedience, in the eyes of anyone who has read history, is man's original virtue

Oscar Wilde

There was never a better time to be disobedient. When cultural momentum is so blighted by consumerism and the widespread mistaking of material success for morality, it's time to go to the back of the class. From there, mobilization is possible. If we can't take over the school we can at least quietly disrupt things while cannily smuggling out our scrawled manifestos about how it could all be different. Meanwhile, in a spirit of prefiguration, we can mount small pageants of elegant protest or rough-hewn plays of humorous defiance that point to another way of learning. And when the teacher's out of the class we can move all the chairs round.

This argument for a measure of cultural disobedience hopes to find you receptive. If so, this book sets out some propositions you may find engaging. But be warned; it offers performance and theatre – one a subset of the other – as useful modes of operation towards a greater end: the nudging of society into different, better, political and social health. Further, it attempts to answer some key questions such as: If so-called radical theatre has a role as a means of social action, then what exactly is that role? And what is it that makes this radical theatre radical, exactly? (For the purposes of the book I take the word radical to mean actively promoting humanist values: combating injustice, promoting equality and taking pride in creative mischief. It has nothing to do with that other sense of 'being radicalized' for an extremist cause.)

So why disobedience? The answer is both simple and complex. Simple because the term points to an unbridled spirit of impulsiveness, which is the fount of theatre creativity. Complex because in the often protracted business of negotiating a practice which is genuinely effective as social action, there will be merit in remembering just how many conventions within the theatre world are predicated on an entirely different set of assumptions about what theatre, indeed entertainment, has for its purpose.

It would do my self-esteem considerable benefit to assert at this point that this book is all about trumpeting the existence of a new movement called Disobedient Theatre. I would therefore be following in the footsteps of others who have trumpeted In-Yer-Face Theatre or Theatre of Commitment or even – most disarmingly – Applied Theatre. In this way, I could impress a scholarly readership by grouping together a number of productions and planting a big label on them. Others might pick up the term and get labelling themselves, which would be especially rewarding. But it would be a conceit. For unfortunately there is no such school or movement. It doesn't exist. I unscrupulously borrowed the term from an exhibition at the Victoria and Albert Museum in 2014 called 'Disobedient Objects'.

And yet, perversely, it does exist. Not exactly or even partially as a movement or school but as a spirit, an eclectic enterprise fuelled by imagination, political passion and creative innovation. And where it does, it exists as it were in fragments, in fragmentary moments: in a play's subject matter here, in an activist theatre-on-the-street there, in an argumentative drama workshop there, even somewhere else again in a leap across the footlights at a West End show. It exists not in any uniform, easily identifiable way but as a multitude of initiatives across various forms and across geographical and cultural boundaries. It's the task of this book to try and identify some of these initiatives even though what are pursued are as slippery as fish. I see these signifiers of disobedience in a multitude of places but most evidently where the familiar tramlines of theatre orthodoxy are being pulled up or redirected. And in such haulage work, it becomes evident just how tenuous are the holds of cultural conformities. The tramlines come away more easily than you might imagine.

Were this Disobedient Theatre to have a manual, it's as if all the pages had been removed and shared out between different practitioners. Each practitioner is therefore operating without knowledge of what the others are up to. Were this manual reassembled, however, we might just be looking at a robust, significant and potentially powerful arsenal of ideas and techniques.

Such work as this book examines does nevertheless have identifiable features: it is often more facilitator- than director-led. It often breaks down some traditional, revered distinctions: between performer and audience, amateur and professional, community and public. It places politics centrally, which means not just having an attentiveness to the values implied by any theatre content but also to how the company manages itself and how key decisions are made. Here, disobediently, 'the show' isn't always 'the thing'. In fact it's very often not 'the thing'. Instead, it is merely one facet of a practice that flows around what the writer Chantal Mouffe has proposed as being 'art that foments dissensus, that makes visible what the dominant consensus tends to obscure and obliterate'.[1]

Such principles or strategies as we can identify should not be considered immutable, however. These are not ideological pillars of wisdom expected to survive political hurricanes. Rather they should be considered lodestones with varying degrees of permanence. They are certainly ripe to be reassessed periodically, and then adapted or changed as the social context within which they hope to be dynamic itself changes. So while some principles can be reasonably assumed, yes, to be perennial, others will alter, at least in their expression and perhaps even in their nature, as society continues to rumble into different shapes and patterns. To take an example, any society pitched into civil war may well require less the call of 'Revolution Now!' than a carefully managed process of preventing life-preserving cultural traditions from being lost in the fog of battle.

It follows therefore that this book cannot be entirely about principles or ideas; it also has to discuss tactics. Nor for the same reasons is it intended as an examination of any particular field of work, perhaps 'community theatre', 'live art' or 'socially engaged art'. Instead it attempts to run through and between these different traditions, ignoring complaints from offstage while identifying connections between some very unlikely bedfellows: perhaps a live art event at Tate Modern and a drama workshop in a young offenders' institution, a clown show in a street market and a monologue on Shaftesbury Avenue. It does this in the interest of finding common factors, common strategies, common ideals, which are shared across the different contexts.

In an attempt to justify this approach, I can only protest my status as a practitioner rather than a scholar who, over forty years or so of stumbling through rooms, has wrestled constantly with the relationship between theory and practice, and, too, between the joys of performance and the demands of movements for social change. I admit therefore to a preference for advocacy over true scholarship, which may be neither fashionable nor even-handed. Yet to site this book within the busy field of theatre scholarship would be like entering a Shakespearean quotes competition with Trevor Nunn. Not that my own work is the sole field within which the digging for fragments has taken place, very far from it. I have, as in previous books, talked to colleagues and peers about their experiences, especially those whose ratio of success to failure is better than mine and whose ability to summarize the challenges of a disobedient culture is so much more evident.

If I had to state what personal beliefs sit backstage of my advocacy, I'd point to a conviction that there is always a struggle going on over culture – and artists lie within that struggle. This is not a struggle between classes or indeed between any two forces assembled as binaries. Rather it is made up of a multitude of smaller struggles that take place in the tiny crevices of culture as well as in the high plateaus. And my assertion is: the value of what takes place in the former should never be underestimated while sitting in awe of the latter. It's our job to bring to critical and evaluative consciousness what the dominant consensus tends to ignore – pushing up through the cracks in the floor all those stories and understandings that mainstream culture tends to dismiss as trivial or not worthy of attention.

Further to this, I don't believe it's an outrage to aver that theatre makers live and practise within these struggled-over contexts irrespective of their acknowledgement of it. Who gets what money, which sectors of our citizenry thrive while others shrink, which values are applauded and which derided – all these are aspects of our culture with which we are engaged and from which we draw our material for performance. I don't believe it is sustainable to allege that the creation, production and sharing of art has no political resonance or implications. Even if you produce a song and dance show in the West End entirely for entertainment, it employs people, it makes money, it organizes lines of command, it gives power to some and not others, it pays people disproportionately, and its narrative is constructed around certain values that are given a blessing or denied one. This is not some bitter excoriation of West End musicals; rather it's Sybil Fawlty's alleged specialist subject, the bleeding obvious.

Clocking this is therefore essential for any artist, I would advocate, even if you line up in a different part of the room from me. Especially if you line up in a different part of the room from me. Or even in a different building. (While achieving just this is very much part of the struggle, I'm afraid.) We need to acknowledge this important assertion if the artist – and the performer, director or writer should be included here – is not simply to become one small operational unit in games designed and managed by others who may not share the same social objectives. Or as Jonathan Kay succinctly puts it, we need to get wise; it's time to 'create or be created'.

We all have different responses to political initiatives that aim to keep capitalism alive, observing as we do that it's the poor who carry the greatest weight of sorrow. Some of us – perhaps the more disgruntled – choose to convert the resulting, incipient sense of political unease into a conversation with the rest of society, through art. It's the artist/activist's way. Disobedience therefore is just one line of defence/attack among many tactical manoeuvres that are available. Hence our positioning at the back of the class. In defence, we might also usefully borrow from Martin Luther King, who argued that 'the world is in need of a society of the creatively maladjusted. It may well be that the salvation of our world lies in the hands of such a creative minority.'[2]

As implied earlier, I've spent much time in small rooms. Part of me feels resentful about this as if it indicates a failure to move into larger ones with seats that don't move. Yet another part of me recognizes that in here in the scruffy basements there is more intimacy, less pressure and more chance of personal discoveries than elsewhere. And that counts for something, and may deliver something to pass on, for example in this book, where small-room experiences are prized not because they give birth to greater wisdom, but rather to correct the imbalance that exists in theatre commentary in favour of examining what happens in the bigger spaces. Small rooms have no less scope than larger ones to articulate and transmit values that can change the world, after all. Finally in my defence, I hang on gamely to the popular belief that in sharing these reflections, BETTER THINGS WILL HAPPEN. Others will be emboldened. This may come across as an aspiration borrowed from Winnie-the-Pooh via Karl Marx but even he – that's Pooh (but also Marx) – got things right sometimes.

To argue a case for a small-room culture with conviction therefore means deconstructing what happens when we, as creative practitioners, commit ourselves to these modest places. It means examining what are the values and ideas that motivate us there. It means looking at the techniques, the formats, the exercises and the strategies that bring values to life and life to values. This alliance of theory and practice, taken together, represents what might be seen as a disobedient practice, presenting a case for us to keep returning to those little rooms, time and again, in hope of great reckonings.

Structure of the Book

The book is divided into two parts. The first deals with some of the key principles that might inform disobediences within any number of theatre practices. These principles are often found brewing within the hearts and minds of artists who take the less-travelled route; artists who are right now testing new templates for what happens when performers and audiences meet. This part is therefore largely theoretical, but sometimes flows into practical issues when I can't quite tear them apart. The final few sections in Part One are, increasingly, more strategic, looking at the role of the facilitator or director in community contexts. Last of all come some observations around making allies and finding ways to survive as a creative practitioner.

The second part is more hands-on and informal, identifying some tools or skills that show the aforesaid principles in action. Here, in what is often a small-room context, an imagined devising task holds together different perspectives on pushing back against those rules of theatre that coax default thinking. Finally, games and exercises are also included for those who like to take away some concrete disciplines – not that these should be taken as substituting for the necessary work of reinterpretation and remaking that is a core part of any disobedient theatre practice.

Affordances

One definition of 'affordance' is that it refers to a capacity to achieve a certain function. For example, a handle affords turning, a cord affords pulling. So what does a disobedient theatre practice in the interests of social change make possible?

First, it can take the opportunity to question how we live.

> Questioning the ostensibly unquestionable premises of our way of life is arguably the most urgent of services we owe our fellow humans and ourselves.
>
> Zygmunt Bauman

What else, specifically?

- It has the capacity to operate as an independent, thoughtful, autonomous activity not reliant on outside agencies for permission to be.
- It cultivates the implementation of a socially useful, rough democracy, thereby proposing to the world a model of people working together in acts of prefiguration.
- It is not reliant on technology or material resources but on a simple equation of actor+space+time+audience, making it accessible, portable and immediate.
- It is fluid and ephemeral; its makers can monitor, reimagine and correct its outputs. Can pack up quickly and run away.
- Theatre offers a chance for collective ownership of content in a way no other art form can quite achieve, bridging the gap between invention and execution.
- Because of its capacity to present 'other worlds' and establish narrative progression within those other worlds, theatre can use metaphors to provoke disquiet around commonplace, everyday assumptions.

Part One

In the World

1. Some Principles

Which are those drivers that characterize a rebellious, subversive theatre practice?

1. Defiance

Definition in this context: An active stance taken in opposition to a prevailing power.

On 4 April 2011, an unidentified gunman waited outside the Freedom Theatre in Jenin refugee camp in Palestine. At around 4.00 pm, out of the theatre walked the director, Juliano Mer-Khamis, who got into his red Citroen along with his small son, Jay, and a babysitter. He started up the car and began to drive away. At this point the gunman emerged, his face covered with a balaclava, and called out for Mer-Khamis to stop. The gunman shot him five times. Mer-Khamis died immediately. It was an utterly devastating blow for the theatre company and all its supporters. It brought home just how dangerous was the simple act of making theatre in the way that the company had. Possibly the company should close down the theatre and walk away, either into the armed struggle, as previous actors had already done, or into passivity. After a period, the company met, discussed the options available and decided to start work on a new play.

Striking a defiant stance against the prevailing dispensation has been 'the identifying signature of avant-garde art'[1] throughout contemporary times, according to the scholar Christopher Innes. While we now understand the term 'avant-garde' as a tad outmoded – after all, the term originates from an army context – nevertheless 'standing up and speaking truth to power' is a distinct feature of any theatre that addresses social injustice. In this context, defiance may mean no more or less than simply asserting the democratic right to free speech through performance. It is a right often denied by repressive regimes where civic laws are used to repress artistic expression. Two young students in Thailand hardly expected to be imprisoned for mounting *The Wolf Bride*, a satire on Thai politics and written in only three days. But they were.

For the Freedom Theatre actors, robbed of their director, to carry on making plays was merely to observe a core tenet of their profession: to keep going despite the dangers. While still free to perform, perform they would. Having made this decision, it was then a question of 'Which play?'

In the same way, albeit under siege in a different country, the members of the Free Theatre of Belarus made a similar decision. They also decided to defy the violence against them perpetrated by the authorities, and to carry on with their theatre programme. This was a company which, even at the moment of its formation, was told by the Belarusian authorities that productions of any kind would be forbidden. No programme of work would be acceptable, not even opting for Chekhov, which was their first intended production. The authorities knew of the individuals behind the project and simply didn't trust them to generate any production that would not be subversive of the state.

In defiance of such hostility, the company adopted a policy of moving swiftly from building to building to avoid their programme of work being closed down. Performances would take place in garages, private rooms, in woods, offices, anywhere that could be occupied out of sight of their oppressors. It was a tactic only made possible by their allies and friends. Only when their friends were in turn harassed and threatened did the company turn outward to seek international support.

Nor is it the case that defiance only arises within situations of overt political repression. What characterized much of the progressive theatre in the UK in the 1960s and 1970s was the spirit of assertive rebellion. As Steven Berkoff told Richard Eyre: 'There were groups from America – La MaMa, The Living Theatre – and from Europe – and Grotowski, of course. People were in love with Antonin Artaud. Peter Brook was doing the Theatre of Cruelty.'[2] The experimentation was fuelled by anger at the Vietnam war, contempt for corporate business and enthusiasm for utopian and idealistic visions: 'Everywhere there seemed to be some kind of almost millenium fervour: they were getting rid of the old theatre.'[3]

As I emerged from drama school, what was so exciting – and still is – was the very means of defiance. There was a real drive to use theatre to make a difference. Recently when I spoke with women theatre pioneers in the Argument Room – an online debate forum – about their agenda back then, there was no denying how ambitious they were: 'We wanted complete transformation of all social systems,'[4] said Siren Theatre's Jane Boston, a point cheered by those round the table.

For any young theatre enthusiast, it was impossible not to resist the charming, witty, campaigning force that was blowing through theatre. I simply wanted to be part of it. I'd been taken to *Hair!* and while I knew this wasn't exactly the cutting edge, I understood that on smaller stages I might find it. And did, initially in the radical Charing Cross bookshop, Better Books, where the People Show were breaking the rules of theatre more flamboyantly than a karate master breaks bricks. Looking back, I can identify the theatre vocabulary of those times as comprising some very distinct elements:

- Improvisation onstage.
- Talking directly to audiences and them answering.
- A rough, muscular language that didn't rely on lights or technical wizardry.
- An energy that was bigger and more raucous than any more 'traditional' acting style.
- Talking openly about current politics.
- A sexiness and an intellectual smartness onstage.
- Equality between men and women performers.
- Use of irony and satire.
- Use of 'double-ness' or allegory.
- A playing of same status as the audience.

What's notable is how much of this vocabulary is still evidenced today in the work of companies like Forced Entertainment, Ontroerend Goed, Punchdrunk, Blast Theory, Fluxx, One Zero One, Gob Squad, Tim Crouch and many others. The crucial difference is that targets have shifted. No longer present are easy assumptions about the ills of the world and what is required of the audience to remove them. There are instead more intellectual and reflexive elements in play. Audiences are encouraged into a more playful set of responses. Even the idea of an activist theatre itself, so fervently championed in this earlier period, is itself under examination. This is how Matt Adams of Blast Theory argues the point:

> To be an activist is to be someone who can boil something down to a position that can be acted upon ... but good art is doing something that's the opposite. If you know what you're being told about, it's already bankrupt.[5]

So there's a recognition that the business of contributing to social change is far more complex than was imagined forty years ago. The old targets can't be lined up in the crosshairs like before. Adrian Heathfield puts it like this:

> Opposition is evidently still part of artists' vocabulary as they articulate what they do in their work, and it allows you to create resistances between you and something else. But it's not the predominant organizing mechanism. The way people make work is more complicated; a mix of compliances, resistances, peculiar relations and perversities and

amorous relations, desirous relations – opposition is only one kind or mode of thinking.[6]

One aspect of this recalibration is the way in which theatre makers are addressing their own professional culture, for it's the professional culture that's often – and rightly – perceived as sharing infrastructural priorities with a patriarchal mode of value dissemination. For a radical theatre show to establish an authoritarian relationship with its audience is surely to wreak havoc on its own express intentions. The writer and performer Tim Crouch puts it thus:

> Most of my adult [theatre] work – and also the children's work as well – has been about challenging the orthodoxies [of theatre] that I experienced when I was a dispossessed, disenfranchised actor … in my teaching I became more and more passionate about the things that had fucked me off about theatre.[7]

This attitude points to the heart of the matter, displaying a determination to revisit and remodel the apparatus of production. By so attacking the orthodoxies, one carves out new territory. It was no less the same for Brecht, whose first play, *Baal*, 'became a classic demonstration of the contrary Brecht's assumption of antagonistic positions to existing works', according to his biographer.[8]

To summarize then, one aspect of our contemporary practice has shifted to changing the world in the room, not always using the room to try and change the world.

The thinking goes further, however. In the business of re-examining what takes place in the room, the aim is to create performance work that not only looks, feels and sounds different, produces different resonances and perhaps animates an audience in new ways, but operates according to different priorities. Many of the pioneering productions of the 1960s and 1970s still relied on the authoritarian male as an organizing template. Witness the establishment of women's companies like Monstrous Regiment, Siren and Beryl and the Perils as counteracting initiatives. The process of deconstruction continues. Now, today, it's about acknowledging that how a work is made is as important as the content. So the target beam of political awareness, so characteristic of early political theatre, is now being directed into the rehearsal room as well as onto the stage.

It's therefore no longer just about the song, it's the singer and the concert room as well. And the contract. And the role of the technician and the tea-maker. All aspects of the work are being considered for their implications in terms of their power structures, their economics and their gender politics.

The relationship with the audience is a vital part of this re-examination: the how and where and when of that. Examining even whether there should be such a thing as an audience. Or a theatre building. All of this points to the clearest of arguments that theatre artists need to operate with sufficient independence to allow any results of this re-examination to be acted on.

For we live now in a more cynical – or knowing – age. In this Age of Irony, it has become clear that any display of rebellion within promotional literature or any waving of banners onstage does not necessarily indicate that these hearts and minds are inclined to any activist intent. Rather the reverse: sometimes this posturing for effect simply reinforces a pessimism about social progress itself. Perhaps there's a parallel here with a trend in the visual arts identified by Grayson Perry in his Reith Lectures. In this trend, he argues, 'striking a defiant note' through the art can be no more than a career strategy at times:

> Revolution and rebellion, these are no longer defining ideas. When I started at art college, that idea of rebellion and change and revolution was almost the DNA of art. One of the delightful traits of the art world now is that idea of revolution and challenge – we encourage it. Along comes the young artist, talented, angry; he shakes his fist at the establishment ... and the art world looks down at him and goes 'Nice rebellion, welcome in'.[9]

Tate Modern loves rebellion and eats it for breakfast. (Unless the rebellion is directed against the Tate itself of course – see later for the work of Platform and Liberate Tate.) It welcomes in apparently discontented artists such as Tracey Emin, Damien Hirst, Gillian Wearing and Michael Landy. For such as these and many others, entry into the cultural citadel perhaps represents a longed-for blessing. For others, any such 'welcome in' may not be the desired objective. The implications may be felt to be too compromising or too restricting. Consider the attitude of the artist and musician Billy Childish against that of his former partner Tracey Emin. Childish, co-founder of the Stuckists, a movement created in opposition to conceptual art, would probably wince at such an invitation. Refuseniks such as Childish and Jerry Sadowitz or Kim Noble feature more prominently on the fringe and around the edges of culture. And the edge is usually a livelier place to be. The Fringe has always been where it's at.

Yet to argue that disobedience is only found there would be false. There are artists aligned with an activist view of life who successfully hover between the centre and the edge. Improbable has worked at the National Theatre with a full-scale show (*Theatre of Blood*) but still creates improvised puppetry shows in tiny venues like the Little Angel in Islington, London.

DV8 and Robert Lepage's Ex Machina have created strong, resonant work in the largest venues without any sense of compromise.

It can be said, however, that such relatively sophisticated iterations of the principle of defiance have less traction where theatre artists are confronting oppression on a daily basis. Here the idea of a rebellious stance as some sort of fashion statement would be absurd. A defiant stance is likely to be forced on the artist quite unwillingly; it's an outcome of the daily experience of trying to function as a theatre maker in the context of an oppressive state. When the gunman assassinated Mer-Khamis, he was attacking a theatre that had been built on the work of Juliano's mother, right in the centre of Jenin refugee camp. This theatre had been established specifically to give opportunities to the young people, using theatre as a model for social change. His murder followed the deaths of a number of former actors who had previously quit the theatre to join the resistance. All but one of these former actors had subsequently been killed. After the murder of their director, the company had a very real and difficult choice quite unfamiliar to UK artists: to be a fighter or an actor. Rabea Turkman had previously given up being a resistance fighter to join the company, although crucially he saw this as maintaining the same set of ideals. 'This play', he said, of the work begun after Juliano's murder, 'is another kind of resistance'.[10] In the meetings, he argued to continue with theatre making. The murder of Juliano was 'a catastrophe for us',[11] said Nabil Al-Raee, the current director. Not only had they lost their key figure but others also; a board member, an actor and a technician were arrested and detained. After discussing among themselves and with their supporters, the decision was made: 'We decided to lock ourselves on the stage and create a play'.[12] They created a dramatization of *Animal Farm*. I asked Nabil about this and the resonance this would have for the audience. Who were the pigs? The Palestinian Authority, he replied. Did the audience realize this? Oh, yes. 'Our audience are always asking – what are you wanting to say?'[13]

At the time of the murder the Freedom Theatre had only four young men in training and many in the community considered the project to be failing. But two years later, because of the respect the company had earned from these decisions, when they advertised a new training season fifty young people applied.

Whether in Jerusalem or Jesmond, campaigning for free speech through performance may require not just considerable effort and personal commitment, but very real personal risk as well. While clearly these risks remain very different in different parts of the world, creative practitioners everywhere have to constantly argue and mobilize when their work is seen 'not to fit'. It may be when this happens, they are pushed towards adopting a defiant stance which otherwise they might not have taken. If the artists in question are unprepared to take this position, however, and their practice is cribbed, suppressed or disappears as a result, surely the spirit of theatre dies a little that day?

2. Provocation

Definition in this context: The conscious stimulation of an external party for the purpose of a reaction

Social life is ordered for good or ill by sequences of routines, transactions and procedures of ownership. When a performer walks into the street and places down a hat, the action signals an interruption to such procedures. You may resent the cheek, annoyed at having to steer round, but we need that maverick. Arguably even the most anodyne musical theatre stops routine and establishes activities according to different rules. When performance does more – when it determinedly and effectively disquiets, unsettles assumptions or coaxes thought – it can urge reassessment of our ethics, our social management, our systems of justice and our ideals. It can move us on. None of this is against entertainment. The desire to provoke is an essential of entertainment. Ewan MacColl, the founder with Joan Littlewood of Theatre Workshop, argued that by taking on social themes in a society such as ours, theatre even had an obligation to be unsettling. Others such as Alan Read argue it's almost inseparable from the business of being a performer: 'It would not appear too far-fetched at the outset to suggest that a capacity for performance is a capacity to irritate.'[14]

If 'unsettling' the audience is simply part of performing, arguably all performance work is at some level provocative. For even if a theatre intends primarily to be a reassuring balm to its community, it still has to work with provocation. As the director Colin Ellwood put it to me: 'To reassure, you first have to generate anxiety; the baby has to be thrown in the air before it can experience the reassurance and pleasure of being caught.'[15] It's a fair assertion; if the hero/ine never gets into trouble, arriving home safely feels far less rewarding. Yet there are traditions within performance where theatre makers do more; they harvest this aspect of provocation consciously and for a deliberate social purpose. The baby gets thrown a little higher in these cases. The focus in this book is on just such strategies as these.

In his book *Theory of the Avant-Garde*, Peter Bürger set out what distinguishes work of this kind:

The organic work of art seeks to make unrecognizable the fact that it has been made. The opposite holds true for the avant-gardiste work: it proclaims itself an artificial construct; it calls attention to the fact that it is made up of reality fragments; it breaks through the appearance of totality.[16]

Instead of safeguarding the audience – perhaps with a fourth wall to insulate the stage action rather like a fire curtain – the exercise is often deliberately unvarnished. It has an exposed atmosphere. It is more than porous; it cultivates porosity. It is perhaps even to be completed by forces outside itself – either by the audience immediately or possibly by their actions beyond the theatre. The director Chris Goode argues that such a resistance to 'wholeness' is to be welcomed and there will be many like him, who 'prefer to seek a theatre that, in its hospitality to a difference which is not ours to "know" or subsume within the expanses of our authority and privilege, guards vigilantly against any suggestion of wholeness or completion for the sake of its viable life.'[17]

So what then are the techniques that grant this kind of work its provocative force? They might include:

- A distancing effect which helps to inhibit the immersion of the spectator in the event.
- A generated sense that the spectator is a potentially active agent in relation to this event.
- An ethical or philosophical critique of the status quo, visible within the material content of the work.
- A style of presentation which avoids any implication that what occurs as dramatic action is 'natural' or 'inevitable'.
- Performers appear often as themselves; any 'character' display is worn lightly or not at all.
- Distinctions between performers and spectators are likely to be deliberately challenged or even dissolved.

But there are many ways to throw a spanner. It may be useful to look at how these provocative tactics manifest themselves. Arguably they do so primarily in two ways. First, there is the dramaturgical approach; here the provocative component exists within the staged drama. For example, there are scenes of disturbance, strong language, nudity, violence, quarrelling, or conflict – in other words, the provocations happen within the play. Second, there is the disruptive event that takes place outside the theatre building. It might be referred to as a site-specific event – one which has no familiar performance frame. It's possible the audience has not even signed up to be an audience for such an event since it's often 'happened across' rather than visited.

In the first of these traditions, it's quite likely that the efficacy of the provocation relies paradoxically yet necessarily on a stable and reassuring dramatic frame. The purpose of this frame is to settle the audience down into a bed of familiar signifiers such as the building/the seats/the programme/ the ice cream/the convenient start time, etc. and only then to pitch it into a state of partial helplessness via use of content that will induce alarm. An early example would be John Osborne's *Look Back in Anger* which Osborne himself described as something of an 'old-fashioned play'. What generated its shock value was the nihilistic attitude of its protagonist. Witness more recently Sarah Kane's *Blasted* in which the first act is clearly naturalistic while the second catapults the audience into visions of horror and tragedy.

Activist playwrights do often seek out established forms within which to smuggle their disobedient content. Perhaps we can look to Dario Fo's plays as offering examples. For 'while Fo is a revolutionary in politics, he is conservative in theatre',[18] as Joseph Farrell has written. Fo's play *Can't Pay? Won't Pay!* is relatively orthodox in its dramaturgy yet its hoped-for impact is hardly less than insurrectionary. To take another example, when the playwright John McGrath wrote *The Cheviot, the Stag and the Black, Black Oil* he consciously took the form of the ceilidh – 'one truly popular form of entertainment ... a gathering at which all, or most, of those present, with or without the aid of the whisky, sing a song, tell a story, play an instrument – and tell through it the story of what had happened and is now happening to the people';[19] specifically, how the Gaelic language had been suppressed and how the Scottish people had lost their land and their oil during the Clearances.

In researching such examples, I began to wonder how this issue of provocation within theatre plays worked in terms of younger audiences. So I talked to the children's playwright Mike Kenny about this and in particular how he uses provocation. He told me how he's learned from those stories and plays that deliberately create jeopardy for audiences: 'In *The Winter's Tale*, you begin with the catastrophe. Leontes is mad with jealousy from two minutes in.' But he argues this is not about just hooking the audience in, although it palpably has that effect. There is something else too in terms of the nature of that engagement: 'The audience is much less interested to know how he, Leontes, got into the shit, than how he's going to get out of it.'[20] Presented with a situation of peril, Kenny argues, audiences, especially children, seek in their mental reflections solutions to the trouble they see onstage. How does the hero survive is what concerns them. What caused the trouble is of less concern. This argument, at least as it refers to children, is supported by an examination of children's literature. Let's take one of the classics: *The Tale of Peter Rabbit*. It's clear that the first five pages are spent on the set-up: the hero Peter Rabbit's error in going into the farmer's garden. The next ten are then spent on Peter running around hither and thither trying to escape from the farmer. Even this book for young children, it seems, is predicated on the notion that most of the story should be given over to unsettling the reader – the chase, in other words.

Placing the protagonist in peril is a way of provoking in the spectator/reader feelings of empathy, concern and protectiveness (feelings that are capitalized on in Forum Theatre to nudge the spectator into intervening). I'm remembering Richard Curtis's maxim, offered I believe after working on *Four Weddings and a Funeral*: 'First hit your hero with a small stick, then hit him with another small stick, then another small stick, and then finally a very big stick.'[21] Examples of stick-wielding in film are unsurprisingly more numerous than plankton in a village pond. My personal favourite is *The Killing of Sister George*, which incidentally is based on a stage play by Frank Marcus; here the lesbian heroine actress first loses her sobriety, then her job as a leading soap performer, and finally her girlfriend, before being brought to a professional low by being asked to voice the part of a cartoon cow.

But playwrights have many provocative strategies beyond tormenting the hero/ine. It's likely that many of these can be identified as social context-dependent. In other words, they reflect an awareness of the manners and sensitivities of the time. They are constructed to unsettle or challenge these. For what disturbs and unsettles one year may be greeted with indifference a decade later. Reading through Nicholas de Jongh's book *Great Moments in the Theatre*, you're reminded of just how many established classics began life in a howl of outraged critical indignation, with critics protesting about quite 'unnecessary' attacks on the audience's sensibilities. Twenty or thirty years later, such attacks have been warmly adopted by the general public, with the plays concerned becoming staple fare of theatres across the land. De Jongh writes: 'A sadly familiar sign of the arrival in Britain of an original dramatist is a critical mauling. It happened to Ibsen, Beckett, even Chekhov.'[22] The process continued well into the twentieth century. The now lauded playwright Sarah Kane had to see her work described as 'naïve tosh' and 'like having your whole head held down in a bucket of offal'.[23]

The other route is to instal the provocation not within the drama's content but within the performance frame. By dismantling the pillars, beams and joists of the traditional theatre show and then rebuilding them elsewhere, a different kind of event becomes possible. Audiences can be engaged in new ways. Detachment from the cultural glue helps to make actor–spectator interactivity feel less awkward. Many companies and artists have in the last few decades elaborated a vibrant and continually shifting set of experiments that overturn all previous assumptions about 'where theatre should be located'. Station House Opera, Mem Morrison, Platform, Oreet Ashery, Nic Green, Forkbeard Fantasy, Joshua Sofaer, Tehching Hsieh and Graeme Miller, to mention only a tiny few, operate or have operated in non-theatre spaces in a multitude of playful iterations. Yet the key fact, as Lois Keidan, director of the Live Art Agency, put it to me, is that while much of this work is intentionally provocative, its attitude to spectators remains respectful, using the opportunity of being away from theatre buildings to engage them without compulsion.

Not that there aren't more confrontational approaches. With considerable insouciance, the Clandestine Insurgent Rebel Clown Army (CIRCA) create playful provocations at public events. Their practice is to turn up unheralded at key political conferences, for example the G8 Conference at Gleneagles, and perform clown routines that satirize and challenge the conference business. They neither issue invitations nor have they received one. The group, colourfully costumed, employ a tactical approach to performance in what they describe as 'collective creative disobedience', operating largely in the street but sometimes ducking in and out of shops and eating-establishments with routines that, following the Iraq invasion, included a 'searching for weapons of mass destruction' piece of play. Operating in a similarly activist register, members and supporters of the organization Liberate Tate smuggled a 1.5-ton wind turbine into Tate Modern in 2012 to protest about the Tate's relationship with BP. Given the size and weight of the thing, it wasn't easily removed by the museum authorities. This may have been in part because the group made sure to create good relationships with the ground staff and cleaners. This was just one part of a series of initiatives by Liberate Tate and the organization Platform, which led finally to the Tate reassessing its funding sources and in fact declining any further BP sponsorship.

Such provocative tactics, whether inside or outside a theatre building, inevitably have to contend with the deep-seated, reactionary conservatism that lies within UK culture like a grumpy lion. Such conservatism is often both the target of the provocation and the octopus-like inhibitor of it. To help negotiate a pathway through this minefield, there are the theatre touring agencies who broker relationships between theatre companies and non-theatre venues such as church halls or community centres. However, a widely supported safety-first approach is observable throughout the agencies' programming. So while the goal is estimable – these touring shows are for many rural audiences their 'way in' to performing arts culture – it's often a narrow doorway. To give a flavour of this preference for caution over risk, and the conservative approach to programming, here are the concerns of voluntary promoter Cate Latchford, which she expressed on the Rural Touring Network's website:

> We worry if we'll sell the tickets, fill the seats, please our audience and win them back. A light-hearted drama, some gentle music, a bit

of comedy or occasional exotic dance. Give our audience a pleasant
evening, choose something that won't rattle them too much, that they
can bring a friend to, have a cup of tea to or tap their feet. It's a bit nerve-
wracking, choosing, deliberating, will they, won't they?[24]

Such anxieties are understandable but misplaced. The English countryside
has a long tradition of robust, peculiar and surreal folk practice. The
Atherstone Ball Game, the Ottery St Mary Tar Barrel Race and the Cooper's
Hill Cheese Rolling are annual events, all of which have ambulances standing
by. The countryside is where issues of disparity of land ownership are most
acute. It's a place where, as the writer Malcolm Sinclair commented, 'You're
turned outdoors into something more savage than you are, and you know
something terrible is going to happen'.[25]

My own attempt to enter the rural touring circuit was to confirm the
existence of this proprietary cautiousness. The musician Rex Horan and I
created a show entitled *Billy the Kid - His Life in Music!*. It was accessible,
comedic, partly improvised and with its social critiques lying discreetly
beneath the surface (as we thought). It was initially approved by a touring
scheme's representative who saw it in Brighton at the Nightingale Theatre
and then wrote a laudatory report. However it was then disapproved by the
scheme's chairman, who hadn't seen it but had watched a video of the same
performance. This chairman deemed it unsuitable for rural audiences not on
quality grounds but on those of unsuitability. Leaving aside questions raised
about the validity of judging theatre on the basis of video - a questionable
tactic at the best of times - there also remains clear evidence that over-
protectiveness was in this case triumphing over risk.

Inside such paternalism lie curious assumptions about the delicate
proclivities of rural audiences. The impression given is that rural audiences
cannot cope with provocative material. The writer Claire Bishop points out in
her caustic critique of well-meaning performing arts projects, *Artificial Hells*:
'An over-solicitousness that judges in advance what people are coping with
can be just as insidious as intending to offend them'.[26] As a result, audiences
and plays are held back from each other. Bishop argues that this over-
protective attitude 'self-censors on the basis of second-guessing how others
will think and respond'.[27] This second-guessing of the audience's response is
precisely what took place in respect of *Billy the Kid*, a disobedient outsider if
ever there was one, still mysteriously causing tremors in the shires.

The views of administrators and directors I've spoken to, however,
suggest that what audiences don't like is not so much provocative material
as thoughtlessly made pieces of work that fail to respect that audience's
capacity for independent thought. Audiences are not predisposed to dislike

what they don't know. It's my suspicion the Gatekeepers of Middle England are confused about the difference between provocation and offence. They would doubtless react with alarm to a proposed play in which there were several murders, a rape and eating of children. But these events all occur in Shakespeare's *Titus Andronicus*. It's a matter not of the dramatic action itself but how that action is presented that determines the likely capacity of the material to be offence-generating. We know this from the way in which the most appalling crimes and brutalities are contained within folk tales. As Marina Warner writes: 'Uttering the fear, describing the phantom, generally scaring oneself and the audience, constitutes one way of dealing with the feelings that giants, ogres, guzzlers, ghouls, vampires, cannibals, and all their kind inspire.'[28] Indeed the death of children has been a theme of our folk tales for centuries, a fact well exploited by Roald Dahl.

Audiences are not unhappy with provocation – rather the reverse. They seek it. This is Peter Bürger's assertion: 'Shock is aimed for as a stimulus to change one's conduct of life; it is the means to break through aesthetic immanence and to usher in (initiate) a change in the recipient's life praxis.'[29] In other words, folk do like to be woken up. It's only mild shock that can shake them from their complacency. Amber Massie-Blomfield of the Albany and Camden People's Theatre is also clear on the point. She argues that despite everything the more protective Gatekeepers aver, the idea that 'more experimental, formally innovative work' and non-theatre-going audiences should be kept apart is a 'complete misconception.'[30]

Civic wariness about the nature of provocation, however, extends further – to include a muddle over ethics and aesthetics. The default position of civic authorities is often to pay for art only when it has an ethical basis that conforms to civic values. When the art is delivering appropriate messages, it's welcome. But such civic authority thinking is invariably short-term. It reflects immediate political imperatives born of social policy directives, encouraging 'good behaviour', rather as if the arts were an extension of the Public Relations department. But I would dare suggest that in the long term, rather than support arts work on the basis of its ethical 'fit', it might be better to programme with a clearer understanding of how the arts operate differently to PR. For to make the demand that performance should primarily reassure and emolliate is neither fair on artists nor does it reflect a sound understanding of how creative practice functions. Performance work, especially when interactive, is more complex, nuanced and much less instrumental than its purchasers sometimes assume. Further, while it may be the case that, especially in interactive work, the more dynamic community artists will bring issues to the surface that cause disagreement, in the long run this may serve community cohesion better. After all, what is nestling beneath the surface, be it racism, gender prejudice, forced unemployment, poverty – these concerns won't disappear by being avoided. It's therefore for theatre practitioners to negotiate intact their own creative authorship and argue the benefits of more provocative, yet more relevant, material to be programmed. For to fall in line with a doctrine that is entirely about 'good messages to the community' leads ultimately, I'm afraid, to an infantilization of audiences and a diminution of theatre's potential for vibrant community engagement.

3. Transgression

Definition in this context: Using performance to cross the line of what's socially acceptable

Until 1968 the United Kingdom state had a particularly archaic way of determining whether theatre makers were transgressing; it gave a group of ex-military men power to approve plays. It seems curious, looking back, that men who spent their time discussing who walks behind who at Parliament's State Opening should be tasked with the business of theatre censorship. But that's how it went. I know because my father was one. Johnnie Johnston was the last theatre censor. What he and his friends did was pass round the scripts, striking out what appeared seditious, scurrilous or vulgar. If the theatre profession ever had a yardstick by which to measure compliance with the normative, this was it. However, negotiation was possible. Sometimes chats would be organized between civil servants and directors or authors and they'd work out levels of acceptability between them. The lodestar for this work of censorship was simple. Nicholas de Jongh summarized it as 'plays that threatened the stability of class and rank had to be prohibited'.[31]

The establishment has good reason to be wary of theatre. For it is the art form most suited, along with film, to confront society with its own prejudices. It has a capacity to test moral and ethical assumptions by acting them out. By so doing, the artist asks the audience if lines in the sand that divide acceptable from unacceptable have justification. If I cross them like this, is that so bad? Do you want to proscribe this, what I'm doing now? If I do this to him with this or that to her with that, are you outraged or delighted? As Arthur Miller observed, 'Theatre is the simplest way for one citizen to address other citizens. It is the least complicated, the most naked means for a society to address itself.'[32]

Such performance work has the capacity to challenge taboos. This would include those unreservedly and consistently condemned over centuries as well as those socially evolved. Matricide, fratricide and patricide would be examples of the former, while China's one-child policy, Nigeria's stance against homosexuals, and abortion or nudity in public places would be examples of the latter. All must be consistently open to examination. But it's the latter which are theatre's periodic concern. War and social conflict, for example, often lead to taboos of silence subsequently over what took place. When the writer Julia Pascal went to Germany to present her work *Theresa* about the Holocaust, older people there 'threw themselves into the arms' of the company. The reason was simple: 'no one dared present work of that kind about the Holocaust from a Jewish perspective.'[33] In Guernsey the play was banned entirely. During its life the theatre company Gay Sweatshop constantly tested the boundaries of acceptability in terms of presenting gay relationships onstage, but they were hardly the first. The play *Agnes de Castro* depicted what many understood as a lesbian relationship in the year 1695.

The UK has grown relatively comfortable with much of what the Lord Chamberlain previously banned. Performance acts such as Jane Horrocks urinating onstage as Lacy Macbeth, Franko B walking a catwalk while dripping blood, or Margaret Thatcher depicted in the West End while she lay dying off it, have been quietly tolerated. Yet laws to curtail theatre makers still exist in other ways, laying fresh challenges. Howard Brenton's 1980 play *The Romans in Britain* had a private prosecution brought against it for its acts of simulated gay sex; this is well known. What is less known is the way in which a theatre made a play of the trial proceedings, testing what is permissible to be performed. Nick Kent outlined:

> When I was at the Oxford Playhouse there was the *Romans in Britain* trial. And I conceived of the idea that we should do it day by day onstage. It had never been done before in that way, a court trial. On the first day, the Judge said: 'It has come to my attention that the Oxford Playhouse is intending to do this. I would warn any company or television company that to do this you will be in contempt of court. And if you are, I will come down heavily on you.' We took legal advice. And the advice was, this is dangerous. If you do it, you must have no set and you must use the transcripts only and tell the audience at the beginning that they must not laugh or applaud. Because if they do, they and you will be in contempt of court. You must just watch the proceedings in silence.[34]

However, the company persisted. The judge backed down. The show went on. Such an account illustrates the extent to which legal boundaries buried in the sand may only become visible when the tide goes out.

Theatre productions infringing the law are now few and far between in the UK, but they get into trouble in other ways. Who determines what is transgressive and requiring to be suppressed has been decentralized, trickling down to a minority of – to phrase them kindly – concerned citizens. *Behzti*, the play by Gurpreet Kaur Bhatti that according to the playwright was in no way intended to be transgressive, was closed after angry protests from the Sikh community. Prior to its opening, in anticipation of problems, given the rape scene in the play involving a Sikh elder, the Birmingham Repertory Theatre had invited Sikh leaders to discuss the play. The leaders had agreed not to oppose the play if the rape scene set in a gurdwara (Sikh temple) was relocated to a community centre. Bhatti refused, thereby identifying precisely the position of the transgressive line in the sand:

> I wanted to write a play about religious hypocrisy for which the setting in a gurdwara was non-negotiable. The attempt to establish a dialogue with the Sikh community was well-intentioned, but ultimately misinterpreted as an invitation to rewrite my play.[35]

Behzti went on as written. As a result, there were highly vocal protests made by the Sikh community that became widely publicized. Bhatti was told of a threat against her life and given police protection. She went into hiding. That the protesters' feelings were undoubtedly heartfelt was not disputed; however the self-censorship implemented by the Birmingham Rep perhaps reflected some misplaced priorities. Having set up a consultation and been given a line in the sand, they crossed it. But instead of holding fast to this decision, they crumbled. So it might be argued they made a mistake; having first stuck by their playwright they then abandoned her, awarding a small, vocal constituency the right to censor.

In a different case, the artist Brett Bailey's show *Exhibit B*, a 'human zoo' in which Africans sat in cages, was, like *Behzti*, also closed by those who had produced it in the first instance. In this case it was the Barbican that responded to extensive social media protests. Brett Bailey, accused of racism by his detractors, wrote subsequently in the *Guardian*:

> The intention of *Exhibit B* was never hatred, fear, or prejudice. It is about love, respect and outrage. Those who have caused *Exhibit B* to be shut down brand the work as racist. They have challenged my right, as a white South African, to speak about racism the way I do. They accuse me of exploiting my performers. They insist that my critique of human zoos and the objectifying, dehumanising colonial/racist gaze is nothing more than a recreation of those spectacles of humiliation and control. The vast majority of them have not attended the work.[36]

The final point is crucial, indicating clearly how censorship now operates differently; every owner of a mousepad is now one millionth Lord

Chamberlain. In this way, what is 'transgressive' has become a matter of ethics, with the business of its execution devolved from the few to the very many. Instead of legal statute as we had before, the new weapon of censorship is shame. What's more, such democratization of censorship allows a wider range of issues to be engaged with by our multitude, and a wider number of aspects of the theatre event to be subjected to examination. Is the artist exploitative of anyone? Have members of the community been slandered? Has advantage been taken of volunteers? Have they used people in films without their permission? It's time to fire up the laptop, load your preferred social media and let's get slanging.

The first of these questions was directed at Ursula Martinez, who had used in her show *My Stories, Your Emails* some letters she had received. These were sent by admirers of her previous show *Hanky Panky*, the video of which had appeared online. Trouble was, the video of the show in question, in which she appeared nude, was uploaded without her permission. Her objection to this theft was simple: 'The medium of the internet changed how the act was perceived.'[37] She no longer had control of the context in which the material was engaged with. Out of context, the piece could be viewed purely as porno-graphic: 'You can feed your obsession if you're watching it online but you can't do that if you're watching it live.'[38] So Martinez built a new show around letters and photographs she received from 'admirers' who'd viewed *Hanky Panky* online. It's hard not to see this new show as a kind of revenge, or at the very least a rebuke to those who had taken advantage. When interviewed on ABC RN in Australia, however, the interviewer Fran Kelly put some objections to her. The suggestion was, Kelly alleged, that Martinez had crossed a line:

> There has been some criticism of you and the way you've used this material. You've got pictures of these men, you're reading their emails and exposing what they have to say. Is that not a breach of faith, the same breach of faith that you were exposed to?[39]

Martinez answers in the best possible way that she's a 'provocative artist – and it's my job to be provocative.'[40] She's engaged in an ongoing conversation with her public, both the admiring and the dissenting. Martinez also points out that a man who had sent her a photo of his 9-inch erect penis, and had heard subsequently that it was in the show, wrote again saying he was 'pleased to know that I am on tour with you'.[41] So even some dissenters were joining the game. Her claim is legitimate: that as a performance artist, her transgressions have more legitimacy than any public howls of outrage, for 'it's my job to be provocative.'[42]

Bailey, Martinez and Bhatti all dealt with the censorship wielded against them in similar ways – by asserting the rights of the artist or playwright to operate freely within their chosen medium. The attacks against them appeared to deny them this right. Their attackers also denied by implication that art as a medium has its own sphere and its own sovereignty. While their distress was evident, it would have been preferable perhaps for the show to have enabled the arguments over religion and sexual violence to have taken place within the performance. (This would have meant creating an interactive piece which clearly wasn't what each writer had in mind.) If not possible, then the protesters should have acceded to the author's right to be authorial and instead used the play to raise debate within the community, rather than simply trying to close the play down. The artist should not be held accountable for offence caused by the work. It's this assumption that sends the writer into hiding. The point is made here by Sarah Kane talking to Aleks Sierz in respect of her own plays: 'What conclusions people draw are not my responsibility – I'm not in control of other people's minds and I don't want to be.'[43]

Of course it's understandable that galleries and theatres – which have to maintain a presence after the artist has gone – will be concerned about long-term social and local relationships. Yet handing over a curatorial role to a protest lobby is effectively putting curation in the hands of an unrepresentative minority. Other minorities are also likely to have an agenda and a set of PR concerns. Why can't they also influence the programme? This is not to suggest that communities shouldn't influence programming – quite the reverse. It's just that there are ways to expedite this that are infinitely better than operating reactively and initiating censorship.

4. De-identification

Definition in this context: The removal of a narrow or fixed identity in order for the performer to play with multiple identities

One principle that should be included within a disobedient theatre tradition is that of demoting the artist's personality in relation to the greater good of the work itself. The work, in other words, is not constructed to elevate the personality of the artist. That's the game of showbusiness. That's the game of celebrity theatre.

A managed process of de-identification allows the suspension of personal identities. Here, in a small-room context, be that a rehearsal or a workshop, the business of bestowing identities becomes a matter of play. In that moment therefore I'm no longer Chris, I'm someone else: Hamlet or Satan or Jill. Or all briefly, or none. Or I'm the Bearded One who stands for the

Enemy. Or maybe I'm 'Chris the performer', as Stewart Lee says he's 'Stewart Lee' rather than Stewart Lee. I have an identity granted by my altered function now that I'm standing in front of everyone holding their attention. I'm de- and re-identified.

By making identity something mutable therefore, it can be played with.

Come, woo me, woo me, for now I am in a holiday humour and like enough to consent. What would you say to me now, an I were your very very Rosalind?[44]

In performance and improvisation work it's possible to set up drama-based experiments that explore the impact of identity bestowal. These might include, for example, examining how human beings respond to status changes. What happens when a person is accorded high status; how does this change behaviour, attitude, relationships? What impact does this have on others around him/her? What if that person is from a minority culture; has a disability or is black, Jewish or outwardly gay? How do others respond? How should they? The process becomes a social laboratory in which we can simulate how these status and identity changes operate in the worlds of business, commerce, the services and the street. We can exaggerate, mock, celebrate, disabuse, unpick and protest this process of identity bestowal. But we can only do this if we treat identity as a result of social attribution, not as something innate. The work falters if, when we come to the act of performance, the performer has an identity so fixed in the minds of the spectators that playing outside it simply isn't possible. When Angela Lansbury walked onstage to play Madame Arcati in *Blithe Spirit* in the West End in 2014, the audience stopped engaging with Coward's play and simply applauded 'a star'. It's how the West End rolls. And should celebrity royalty marry into actual royalty and Helen Mirren gets to play the Queen as she did in *The Audience*, audiences get cranked up into an almost sexual excitement.

Artists such as Oreet Ashery, Lois Weaver and Wafaa Bilal have been making identity a subject for some time. Many of these experiments move far beyond the drama workshop. There are many who have taken the specific focus of gender identity, such as Orlan, Susan Bettle and particularly Genesis P-Orridge, who most dramatically altered his identity to be indistinguishable from that of his partner, Lady Jaye Breyer, who did the same, in order to 'physically manifest the "third mind"'.[45] Together they made a third identity: Breyer P-Orridge. By such alterations questions are raised about the solidity of those gender identities to which we default – husband, wife, boyfriend, partner, man, woman, heterosexual, bisexual, etc. – and about what it is possible to create rather than inherit. In this way, identity is promoted as a much more flexible, fluid construct than uncritical social thinking would have us believe. By so unlinking it from its perennial associations with, for example, 'being a husband' or 'being a wife', the idea of what it is to be human is extended – and for good measure, what it is to be a performer. For artists therefore who want to argue back against the way a capitalist economy anatomizes people and encourages compliance with an identarian culture, this dismantling of default thinking around identity seems necessary.

There are arguably two directions that have been adopted by artists who have recognized the importance of de-identification as a strategy. Each offers a different contribution and each carries a very different challenge. The first is about satirizing, mocking, inverting and upending orthodox thinking about identity, especially in the way it operates within popular culture. Here, artists set about exposing the mechanics of identity culture for its falseness and absurdity. This might involve, for example, satirizing the routines and procedures of the star-making machinery. You can see this in the work of Scottee, who ran a campaign to make his grandfather, Liam Gallagher, 77, an ex-miner living on a Camden housing estate, into a celebrity of the art world. Banksy's film, *Exit Through the Gift Shop* explored a similar idea on a much larger canvas, pretending that an unknown artist had fooled the art world. The artist Bryony Kimmings did something similar, albeit with a touring show. Her production *Credible Likeable Superstar Role Model* aimed to make a 'celebrity' out of Kimmings's nine-year old niece. 'In an audacious and provocative protest against the world's flagrant attempts to sexualise and commodify childhood, Kimmings and her nine-year-old niece, Tayler, decided to take on the global tween machine at its own game.'[46] A third example, Katherine Araniello, created an alter ego SickBitchCrips who has an 'inflated personality', a Facebook profile and other presences, this persona acting to challenge and overcome prejudice towards disabled people.

Or there is the second strategy. Rather than critique the shallowness of identity culture, this strategy involves working to establish a micro-counterculture that exists in quiet opposition to the dominant, prefiguring a hoped-for displacement of it. It involves developing an ensemble practice in an entirely different register, setting up camp in a different landscape, in what Chris Goode identifies as 'shelter mode'. It might be at peace with the dominant culture or it might be actively hostile to it, as the social activist Amiri Baraka argues black performers should be as a necessary and legitimate protest against the dominant white culture: 'White men will cower before this theatre because it hates them!'[47]

There is arguably a groundswell of young artists pursuing this separatist path. As John Britton said in the Argument Room:

I think there's a desire for artists – often young but not always – who look at the status quo and say 'OK fine but we want something else, we want some other way of being together, of communicating, of talking with our audiences, be that a local community, a gender community or a secular community – we want to find some other way of organising in opposition to or in difference to the status quo'.[48]

In other words, the aim is less to adopt a campaigning stance than to nurture a practice with a different ethic entirely. Here, any prominence of the individual is not the issue. It's the company that has the prime identity. It's the company that must be promoted because it's that which embodies the ethic of difference. And there's another point too: 'It's only with trust and confidence and experience of each other that you can move forward into the dangerous territories', as Simon Callow expressed it in another conversation.[49]

The exercise of bonding together, of melding talents alchemically into one group, has a long and varied history that carries at different times conflicting imprints of approval and disapproval. Joseph Campbell, who has been credited with providing the genesis of many classic Hollywood films, has observed how the subjection of the individual to the group was entirely normative in earlier society:

> The highest concern of all the mythologies, ceremonials, ethical systems, and social organizations of the agriculturally based societies has been that of suppressing the manifestations of individualism.[50]

Clearly this was to induce a kind of homogeneity considered essential to group survival; but what's instrumental for our argument here is how the use of trance and ritual, synthesized in a collective self-hypnosis, enabled individuals to see the same visions within what Barbara Ehrenreich refers to as 'collective effervescence'. It was seeing the same visions that granted the shared identity, the bestowing of collective solidarity under the wings of the lourie [African bird] or the strength of the buffalo. It was initially the shaman who broke down the doors of perception, who took the first steps into the unknown, who led the crazy dance as it were, but others followed behind in order to experience the same lessons; 'Certain rites and rituals are imperative for the acquisition of new knowledge – rituals whose very nature imparts knowledge in a way that no conceptual logic can duplicate'.[51]

In the contemporary world Freud was one of the earliest thinkers to articulate theory around the creation of something uniquely group-like: 'The higher the degree of "this mental homogeneity", the more readily do the individuals form a psychological group, and the more striking are the manifestations of a group mind'.[52] This was most probably one of the first conceptualizations of the idea of a group mind where there was a sharing of thoughts and feelings. However, Freud was not arguing that such group activity lifted its members to any higher understandings – rather the reverse. He was inclined to the view that the mob mentality was only a step away. Nor did Jung disagree with him about the limitations of collective sharing: 'A group experience takes place on a lower level of consciousness than the experience of an individual.'[53] Such a negative view reflected the general consensus within the burgeoning psychological community in the twentieth century. But as Barbara Ehrenreich acidly pointed out in respect of Freud: 'It is doubtful that he ever witnessed, much less experienced, anything in the way of collective ecstasy.'[54]

It is more contemporary thinkers who have rescued and articulated the benefits of group-ness in the modern world. One of these was Rupert Brown who, writing as recently as 1988, found himself still having to make an argument against 'this cultural and scientific bias against groups'.[55] For his argument he was able to draw on writers such as Mead, Sheif, Asch and Lewin, anthropologists and writers who 'have insisted on the reality and distinctiveness of social groups, believing them to have unique properties that emerge out of the network of relations between the individual members'.[56] Moving forward further still, the post-war creative upsurge generated many theatre companies and artists' collectives who began to argue for the potency of their group identity over that of individual members. The momentum has continued; there are currently many UK and US theatre ensembles struggling to evolve collaborative ethics in the spirit of a shared dream and against the general run of social pyramid-building. In many cases what is hoped for is a sense of extended, democratic ownership such as is modelled by Odin Theatre or Forced Entertainment. It's a prefigurative model of ownership that extends into a challenge of what art itself can be; no longer built around the Renaissance model of the lone genius but one created out of the hard work of several united in purpose. Membership of a collective such as this does not, however, obliterate a sense of self as might have been sought in a tribal context, but rather grants a new sense, one that is rooted in comradeship, the sharing of ownership of the creative treasure chest and a conscious sense of mission. The hope is this connectedness of souls becomes transferred into the work itself. In fact, the notion of a 'group mind' has now become a key tenet especially within the philosophies of many companies who use improvisation as performance. *The Comedy Improv Handbook* describes it as the state when 'all of the players on a team are working toward the same goal by opening their awareness and creating one group mind that encapsulates each individual; it is *e pluribus unum* exemplified'.[57]

Such a commitment to group working takes on particular meaning where the practice is sited in a countercultural tradition. Where the group members already have their backs against the wall, there is particular urgency in the call to arms. As the sense of oppression grows, the language becomes heightened. As Leroi Jones (Amiri Baraka) writes:

> The Revolutionary Theatre must Accuse and Attack anything that can be accused and attacked. It must Accuse and Attack because it is a theatre of Victims. It looks at the sky with the victims' eyes, and moves the victims to look at the strength in their minds and their bodies.[58]

Within the UK – and emerging from the protest culture of the late twentieth century – the Theatre of Black Women appeared to take a page from this manual, adopting a name that according to Bernardine Evaristo, one of its founders,

> did the job of spelling out our identity and our intentions. It was an uncompromising proclamation that was sometimes seen as an act of defiance. It was also an act of self-determination and self-affirmation: a naming of ourselves in a theatre culture that was predominantly white and male. Our remit was to counteract the notorious lack of representation of black women in all areas and levels of theatre through the project of being at the helm of our own creativity.[59]

The 'group mind' is therefore fermented in a very particular subculture of protest. In such an act of parboiling, politics and aesthetics become fused. As a result, such an activist model of performance will always attract criticism from the host culture. And it is usually the aesthetics that will be separated out and picked on, to mask the fact that the critics are hiding their own political persuasions. It's also quite likely that they may not understand such a model of performance either in its aesthetic or political aspects. This is hardly surprising if what the scholar Larry Neal says is true: 'The motive behind the Black aesthetic is the destruction of the white thing, the destruction of white ideas, and white ways of looking at the world.'[60]

Away from a protest model, practitioners within the UK have evolved other modes of production that de-individualize the performer and prioritize the ensemble. Jonathan Kay has developed a particular approach with his 'Fool Ensemble' that treats classic plays in a way that is intended to strip them of their association with the celebrity-focused 'Kenneth Branagh IS Macbeth' school of show business. It might be seen as a logical development from a practice that Brecht often insisted on; in rehearsal of his plays, players swapped characters to strengthen 'the all-decisive social standpoint from which to present [their] character[s]'.[61] This involves a practice in which 'everybody learns all the script'. All the actors learn all the parts and it's not decided until show time who plays Macbeth or indeed any other role. This tactic inhibits, Kay claims, the spectators from engaging 'egocentrically': 'They can't fix it in their minds – "Oh, this person is playing this role" – so it breaks that tradition of theatre with its egocentric thinking.'

In looking for companies that consciously fashion a group identity based on equality over a long period of time, I was referred by Lois Weaver to Platform: not a theatre company but an arts and campaigning organization with the scope of its activities embracing performance, protest, lobbying and campaigns. It was started in May 1983 and has two members from that early time along with several others of over twenty years' standing. I asked James Marriott, who was there at the start of it all, how the organization subordinated personal identity to that of the group.

> We are a very committedly horizontal organization. I think this infects not just the ways in which we deal with the basic organizational functioning, but also the way in which we try to make a group sensibility. I think Platform is strengthened by not being dominated by one person in terms of one set of aesthetic proclivities. But there's reasons for that; we had a furious debate about whether or not Platform could or should exist without certain people involved in it. In the arts, the question as to whether a particular artist's work – be that Joseph Chaikin or Joseph Beuys – would continue after that artist is gone, is simply not asked. But in politics and campaigning, that's not the question. We moved on from that debate by deciding, no, this is bigger than any one individual.[62]

It's clear that over time the organization has developed a successful modus operandi: this particular combination of talents and passions evidently generates more tactical acumen and collective clout than might be achieved by those individuals alone. Certainly Platform's success in drawing attention to issues such as the Tate's funding from oil sources – attention that led to the Tate finally declining its BP sponsorship – has achieved national prominence.

So I came back to the key question: did he, James, not feel cheated that the name James Marriott was not as prominent as that of Platform? How did he feel about that? His answer was simple: 'Proud as fuck.'

Looking back through history, there is a long tradition of anonymity within protest movements. Captain Swing was the collective name given to an unacknowledged group of labourers who protested over the loss of jobs caused by the introduction of machines to Britain in 1830. Anyone could take up the moniker of Captain Swing and call themselves by it. And by sharing a fictional identity in this way, the protest moment allowed anyone who wanted to, to join. 'I'm Spartacus!' The shared nomenclature hides the identity of the individual who otherwise might be subject to persecution. A hundred and eighty years after Captain Swing and on a different continent, Nadya Tolokonnikova posted on social media the following statement:

> Anyone can become a member of Pussy Riot. Including any one of you. The only thing you have to do is be passionate about politics, make up a song, record that song, find a place, put on a mask and perform.[63]

Anonymity and the sharing of a single identity allows some degree of safeguarding for a defiant performance intent. And underpinning this approach is of course the principle of equality, of all looking out for each other, almost a sine qua non for a company using art for social change.

5. Equality

Definition in this context: The sharing of power to influence key areas of creative output and management

Equality underpins the exercise of collective working. Yet it's a value that needs continual reinforcement, for its expression runs against the primary momentum of the entertainment industry.

Its most complete expression is the ensemble in which power and responsibilities are shared equally. Unsurprisingly therefore, for an individual to make a commitment to an ensemble usually means sacrifice – not just once but repeatedly. It means side-stepping orthodox career moves in favour of sharing 'decisions on essential principles' about both art and life, argues John Britton. Not only that but it involves 'commitment to an ethic, perhaps from the beginning'. And the implications go further than simply choosing to work with a limited number of other performers. It's about 'finding other ways to be with each other', very likely over a long period of time.[64]

Scholars argue that the ensemble tradition started with Stanislavski and Copeau: 'In Moscow and Paris at the end of the nineteenth century, theatre was dominated by a "star system", where contemporary "celebrities" slotted into productions and delivered to audiences exactly what those audiences expected.'[65] It sounds spookily like the present day. Stanislavski and his colleagues took against 'the old manner of acting, against theatricality, against false pathos, declamation, against overacting, against the bad conventions of production and design, against the star system which spoils the ensemble'.[66]

Such protests continue today in the work of many companies: Breach, Dumbshow, Forced Entertainment, Kiln Theatre, Fluxx, One Zero One, Improbable, Showstoppers and further back Monstrous Regiment, CAST, 7:84, Impact Theatre Co-operative, Red Ladder, Beryl and the Perils, Hormone Imbalance and many others. The core idea of collectivism, of one identity encompassing others to the betterment of all, runs through political and artistic manifestos of the last two hundred years like the rebel Troglodistes run through sewers in the film *Delicatessen*. But what can legitimately be described as 'ensemble working'? Is it a group of actors working on a short project or another that's worked together for twenty years? And how does working in this way impact on productivity? Here in the UK, ensemble working is outside the norm, while in other European countries it is closer to being the norm. The Berliner Ensemble director Hermann Wundrich asserts that in Germany, for example, 'every theatre in every city in Germany' works with an ensemble.[67]

The actor Richard Katz has worked with many UK ensembles including Improbable, Complicite, Told By An Idiot and the RSC, to name just a few. In the Argument Room in 2013 he talked about the differences. In short-term ensembles, 'if you've only got eight weeks to make and put on a show, there's an imperative to learn the lines, do the blocking ... I'll see you on press night – and then the Director disappears'. The approach is by and large driven by pragmatism. In contrast to this, a company working together over decades has developed a mutual familiarity that allows quite different possibilities. This despite knowing what all ensemble performers know – that often 'the process is tedious, it is boring, it is hard work', as Julian Beck, founder of the Living Theatre wrote in his inspirational *The Life of the Theatre*.[68] Yet at the moment when a long-term ensemble does recompose itself, 'You go, "Yes, this is us – here we go again" – and it's fantastic. And it's like I've not been away'.[69]

Katz points out that the differences between short- and long-term ensembles are often to be found most evidently in the relationship to simple, creative play. In short-term companies (he cites an imaginary rep production of *Merry Wives* in Ipswich):

> on Day One there might be a stage manager there with a ball. [A name game would be played] and then after fifteen minutes the director will go, 'Right, shall we put the ball away? And it's Act One Scene One.. And that doesn't happen in a lot of the rooms I've been lucky to spend time in. In Complicite, for example, the ball never gets put away.[70]

However, Katz does acknowledge that despite the camaraderie and freedom to 'muck about' or 'pursue blind alleys', 'I don't have any ownership – Complicite is just this machine that carries on'.[71]

fetishising of equality

So what are the underlying hypotheses beneath the ensemble tradition? Here's an attempt at outlining them. First, there is the belief that the application of equality within the rehearsal room makes more effective theatre. It's the crucible philosophy. Everyone's individual contributions get melted down in a rough alchemy. Tim Etchells says that for him 'and the others [in Forced Entertainment] the collective dynamics of the six of us mean there's a kind of strength and a set of possibilities that none of us could get to alone'. The theatrical vocabulary is enriched by this collusion.

Second, there is the idea of prefiguration, contributing to social change by modelling it today. If equality is sought tomorrow, the argument goes, you should create it today in the rehearsal room. It's summarized in the declaration: 'Be the change you want to see'. It's the Robin Hood principle. It's Sophiatown in South Africa, bastion of jazz and mixed-race socializing at the time of apartheid. It's actors in Pristina during the Serbian war, rehearsing for the peace while the war raged outside.

Third, there is the belief that unequal apportioning of creative capacity actively disempowers group members to the disadvantage of everyone; whereas by giving everyone roughly equal creative status, the quality of everyone's input will increase. This is the mutual education principle. Ideas from the edge improve the centre; it's the message of Woody Allen's film *Bullets Over Broadway* in which the contributions of a junior mobster – sat in the back of the stalls during rehearsals – save the dyspeptic show otherwise heading for disaster.

Fourth, it's only in a democratic, same-status environment that criticism, an essential requirement of the creative success, can be exercised usefully without fear of retribution. This is the principle of the sweatroom culture where everyone takes hits on their contributions until something stronger emerges. Some creative teams even put rules in place to safeguard the legitimacy of criticism. The Monty Python team rule was: 'If one person doesn't like the sketch, it's not in the show'.

But of course it's one thing to have such principles and another to execute them: a truism worth rescuing in this context. The history of contemporary performance is decorated with the broken dreams of would-be ensembles who couldn't reconcile economics with psychology or psychology with ideology. Part of the battle lies in resisting the siren-like calls that can be heard through the window: 'If we had an artistic director with authority, we wouldn't be having these problems'. Such calls floated through the window of the company Monstrous Regiment in 1989. They were coming from the Arts Council – and this despite the company's considerable success as a woman-led, democratic ensemble. The voice said: 'If you want to continue to receive regular funding, you have to take on an artistic director'.[72] And the company agreed – 'foolishly', says Gillian Hanna, one of its central players. Two years later the company had ceased working. At time of writing in 2016 the argument continues. Topher Campbell, for instance, has argued for the complete elimination of artistic directors:

> Even though I have been an artistic director myself, we should see the end of artistic directors. The idea that one person has the knowledge, vision and know-how to create all the necessary work that a building needs in terms of output is a bit old-fashioned. The idea of a collective, of a more fluid decision making, a non-hierarchical way of working, is something theatre perhaps needs to see in the future.[73]

The story of Monstrous Regiment illustrates how an external insistence on orthodox management structures can impact negatively on a company's ability to determine its own evolution. A parallel story took place with the company Lumiere & Son, where external demands to increase the scale and range of the work contributed to the company's dislocation from its core practice. Several decades previously, similar compromises were demanded of Joan Littlewood's Theatre Workshop – again made in spite of the company's evident success. The company failed to be properly supported by the Arts Council because of its perceived 'management failings' – as in the previous cases, a euphemism for 'having a working practice that didn't reflect the prevailing hierarchical system'. However there was a further reason given by Council officers: the company generated work that insufficiently conformed to the prevailing idea of what theatre deserving of subsidy looked like. 'The Arts Council approved of only those methods of training that produced actors and artists willing to adhere to and reproduce the conventions of the field, including the emphasis on the text, the "star" system and fixed performances.'[74]

How is equality best implemented in an ensemble context? Traducers of the ensemble idea allege it involves individuals abandoning their expertise, somewhat in the fashion of Chinese intellectuals sent to the paddy fields. The reality is the reverse; equality can only work as an active principle if individuals are contributing according to their talents rather than what their position in the hierarchy determines. A further charge made by critics is that ensemble forces creative practice to be held subject to political viewpoints. Creativity is placed in hock to politics, in other words. This might have been true in former times; such an approach was characteristic of the radical UK theatre movement of the 1970s when politics did constantly threaten to strangle everything. I remember going to SCYPT (Standing Conference of Young People's Theatre) in the 1980s hungry to experiment with theatre games, only to be led deeper and deeper into discussions about miners' strikes, to which few of us could meaningfully contribute. Nor was I alone in feeling angry. David Hare has written that, at that time, 'playwrights were regarded as stubborn and unhelpful when they failed to produce the required works which would endorse those (angry) positions.'[75] But such allegations don't hold up today; theatre makers of any experience know that, as argued below in the chapter on Resonance, creativity starts with the personal, the autobiographical, the observational. They have learned that fashioning a show around a political viewpoint only compromises their reach into the general public. Some theatre shows used to be rallying cries, but the failure of agit prop forced a reassessment.

So what of the ways and means to implement equality? Here's to boldly suggest some strategies.

Individual talents can work in a complementary way. You see this in songwriters: Lennon–McCartney, Williamson–Heron, Bacharach–David, Andersson–Ulvaeus, Goffin–King. It's the same in business: Jobs–Ive, Hewlett–Packard. And comedy writing partnerships: Gervais–Merchant, Galton–Simpson, French–Saunders. By accident or good fortune, individuals function better when their talents are drawn out by others with whom they click. In a group context, when Performer A realizes that she can bring to the stage what other actors present don't have in their DNA, it strengthens her set of creative muscles.

Humility may get you further than self-belief. It calls for a certain humility to recognize there are some things you're just not good at. The person who does possess that skill you lack may annoy you almost to death. But possibly you should grind your teeth in silence, as the company will benefit from the exercise of the skill you simply don't possess.

Nothing erodes authoritarianism like transparency. We know that in mainstream theatre the custom is to keep much from the actors: design, costumes, touring and other production decisions. An alternative approach is to create a culture of transparency where it's permitted to wander into others' specialisms. As the actor Willem Dafoe writes of his former company, 'One thing that is special about the Wooster Group is that everybody's in the room at the same time: technicians, actors, designer, director … all in that room when we start making the piece.'[76]

The avoidance of personal attribution in any public way heightens a sense of collective ownership. Strong, creative ideas emerge via osmosis – they are rarely the product of one person. Credits should reflect this and acknowledge that it's the relationships that count, not the individuals. When the film *Monty Python's Life of Brian* was attacked by the religious right, a sharing of writer credits ensured that anyone in the team was equally able to defend it, as John Cleese and Michael Palin did on TV against Malcolm Muggeridge and the Bishop of Southwark.

There's merit in ceding authority to your own limitations. Improbable has a set of maxims to help with this, borrowed from Open Space Technology: Those Who Come Are The Right People, Wherever It Happens Is The Right Place, and Whatever Happens Is The Only Thing That Could Have. The weakness of such homilies is the implied invitation to operate in a way that lacks self-criticism. But as an antidote to becoming over-anxious about mistakes, these are useful. After all, theatre ultimately is rarely more than a small-scale, local event.

Recognition of personal expertise is not a bar to collective working. If a particular individual has a director's skill, it's not clever to keep that person from the director's chair, for the skill in question is likely to be about facilitating shared creativity. Chris Goode's notion of this role, as he wrote in his blog, is 'about authoring the negotiable aspects of the room in which the work happens ... to set the tone ... to create the right conditions for the making of the work'.[77] Emma Rice of Kneehigh argues similarly that one of her principles is 'to run a room that is free of fear'.[78]

It isn't reasonable to expect awkwardness to be excised. The group may be tempted to push its shared awkwardness and insecurity onto one person, hoping that good-natured soul will carry it away like the original scapegoat. But handing a sack of blame to someone can be a mistake. It may be time to switch to a different process, a different system, a different show. Notwithstanding that, a voluntary exit can also lift the mood.

Democracy doesn't mean an absence of leadership. It's not the case that simply because one individual founds an ensemble project, it has to be forever steered by that person. What's required from the founder is a facilitative function. Such individuals have, as Warren Bennis says, 'original minds. They see things differently. They can spot the gaps in what we know. They have a knack for discovering interesting, important problems as well as skill in solving them'.[79]

Seeing yourselves as the underdogs may work in your favour. Being underdogs binds people together in a shared cause: to upset the status quo. The England cricket team were never so strong as in 2012–13 when they struggled to overcome the Australians. Once they were the world's leading team, they went into decline; there was no one to beat. Apple computers also benefited initially from being the little guy: 'In marketing the Macintosh, which Steve Jobs did so brilliantly, he always contrasted his spunky little band of Mac makers with the staid industry giant, IBM.'[80]

Consensus is not preferable to management of difference. The problem with consensus is it can suppress what's vital in opposing points of view.

Better to manage those differences and stay together. How else did the The Who or Led Zeppelin survive? It's also possible to channel group disagreements into the work itself. The group Theatre of the Emerging American Moment (TEAM) did just this. They made the company's 'failure to live up to a utopian ideal a central theme of [their show] *Mission Drift*.[81] They turned their perceived company failure into material with wider resonance than they initially expected.

If there are unmanageable conflicts within the group, don't go touring. The experience can test the group to breaking point. The prospect of foreign touring is intoxicating; the reality can be hell – irrespective of the scale of the tour. These are the actor David Weston's comments on touring with the RSC:

> When we get back to the hotel, one of the younger members tells Dora [David Weston's wife] this is the most dysfunctional company he has ever been in. Certain members of the company have completely gone off Trevor [Nunn], others now question his production. What on earth is going on?[82]

For those companies that do manage to operate a policy of equality, the greatest challenge is not necessarily the internal balancing acts (of egos, budgets and time) but something else. It's how to manage the relationship with the general public, and doing this in such a way that allows a profile to be maintained, yet doesn't cheat on what the ensemble stands for. In 2015 the company Showstoppers, while lacking what might be seen as any platform of social change, achieved something remarkable: presenting a long-form improvisation show in the West End continuously over several months. In spring 2016 the company was rewarded with an Olivier Award for its efforts. It did this without any individual members having any kind of celebrity or professional profile in the world at large. One of the leading lights, Dylan Emery, had a background as a financial journalist. The achievement had nothing to do with showbusiness technique – although the company's technical skills were considerable – but a lot to do with intense hard work, practice and company development over the previous few years.

Such an achievement kicks the ass of any assumption that ensemble practice cannot feature within mainstream entertainment traditions. Ensembles like Showstoppers may be doing even more than this; they may just be chalking out tomorrow's social blueprints.

6. Prefiguration

Definition in this context: Living out in the present ideals we want to see replicated by society in the future

I have a notion that what attracts people to the theatre is a kind of discomfort with the limitations of life as it is lived, so we try to alter it through a model form. We present what we think is possible in society according to what is possible in the imagination.

Joseph Chaikin, *The Presence of the Actor*

Democratic and feminist campaigners through history have taken to the roads to spread their message. While on the tramp, rallying for the cause, they enact the changes they hope to see: more equality, more freedom, more tolerance. They model the desired-for change in how they are with each other. Hippies, yippies, punks, communitarians, libertarians, socialists and anarchists try to realize their vision for the future using camps, buses, alternative family structures, alternative economic models, bartering, communes or quite simply parties. The future is prefigured in the present. Social pioneers such as Edward Carpenter went about precisely this, albeit in the cramped front room of his Yorkshire cottage. He advocated a gay, libertarian philosophy despite almost universal homophobic social censure. It's no wonder Gay Sweatshop took the life of Carpenter as a focus for their play *Comrades* in the 1980s. But then Gay Sweatshop was a company that itself, in its performances, set out blueprints for sexual toleration. As Joan Littlewood argued to her biographer, Peter Rankin, Theatre Workshop wasn't just a theatre company, it was a 'design for living'.

Prefiguration in theatre happens in many ways, but perhaps primarily two: either a) by creating imaginariums – visions of the future onstage; or b) by using drama privately with people, enabling them as individuals to create better futures for themselves.

a) Onstage

In the first way, theatre operates prefiguratively through performances (or outdoor marches or demonstrations) that challenge audiences to accept what's in front of their eyes – to acknowledge the rightness of what is proposed or envisioned. Artists from Julian Beck to Nic Green and Milo Rau have offered images of human impulsiveness and freedom onstage that have triggered audiences to respond positively to these presentations. Tim Crouch put the argument to me like this:

As an activist in art we are allowed to create our utopias. We cannot suddenly create a perfect Syria. And then show Syria a perfect model of itself. That's just not possible. But in art, if you're working passionately, you can make models of how to interact and how to be. How to live together and how to think together. And how to tell stories to each other. You are capable of doing that in a utopian sense.[83]

Milo Rau makes an offer to audiences by way of political enquiry that the political establishment is incapable or unwilling to mount. His works *The Moscow Trials, The Zurich Trials* and *The Congo Trials* give opportunities for a questioning of the causes of particular scandals or atrocities within a dramatic framework, albeit one that models a civic tribunal of enquiry. In *The Congo Trials*, for example, there are no actors. Rather, soldiers, traders, officials and UN staff are interrogated in an exercise to better understand why the war in Congo continues to see so many slaughtered. It is not an enquiry that political structures can deliver; but with support, a group of artists can. And in this way, perhaps, art can nudge politics. As Rau asserts, 'for me that's what political art is; you show what seems impossible in reality and then it becomes possible'.[84]

The artist Oreet Ashery was angry and disillusioned with the scope for public protest following the termination of Occupy London. Her purpose was less enquiry and truth-finding than protest. 'There are so many debilitating state controls that stop people from protesting now', she said to me.[85] She felt opportunities for free artistic expression were diminishing. Her own practice was also cribbed by a fearful, controlling government. In response she created a touring show in 2012, *Party for Freedom*, which offered a different idea. The show makes 'freedom now' or as close as we can get to it. A maximum of ten people could attend. The show might happen in a gallery, a lecture hall or a private home. Looking at the photos, you can see the connection to the Happenings of the 1960s and 70s or to Living Theatre's *Paradise Now*, a classic invocation of anarchist-libertarian values. Most of the performers are naked, there are opportunities for spectators to join in; there is paint, improvisation, direct physical contact between the performers and also between performers and audience. It's an act of prefiguration, a be-the-future-you-want-to-see pageant, one that looks like an act of disobedience but is so only because of the controlling, authoritarian nature of the host culture.

Taking a different direction, some companies offer spectators a set of challenges through structured interactivity. These come in the form of puzzles presented to the audience, the solving of which helps to design and simulate better social structures than we have now. Much of this practice draws from or is influenced by Augusto Boal's notion of 'rehearsing for life', which has been written about extensively both by Boal and his admirers. The company Coney are leaders in this particular kind of exercise. For their show *A Small Town Anywhere*, Coney invited the audience to consider themselves citizens of a small town. The spectators' task is to respond to a bullying neighbouring country. There are no company members driving the decision making; the decisions are made by the audience. The model is reminiscent of a Theatre in Education show where children are encouraged to become familiar with decision making in a civic context and so flex their dialectical consciousnesses. The audience is 'inside' the fiction from the beginning, argues Annette Mees, one of the company members. It's a fictional world, albeit one that is a mirror to the real, that facilitates this engagement:

> There's a postal system, physical posts, there's radio news and there are messages from the big country. The small town is put under more and more pressure by the big country which is outside the theatre space. So the audience have to start making decisions about how they are going to stand up to oppression. And each night is different because each audience makes different choices.[86]

Fluxx has something similar; the audience is invited to consider themselves members of a (fictional) neighbourhood not unlike the neighbourhood they are actually in. The piece is always tailor-made for particular towns or communities. First, spectators (neighbours) watch a series of scenes that both bring the fictional neighbourhood alive and also introduce the conflict that is dividing local people. Then the audience is encouraged to move freely in the space. This way they can interact with those characters who they've already observed in the introductory scenes and who have vested interests in the dispute. They can hear more intimately about their stories, motives, fears and aspirations. They can interrogate these characters; they can ally with them if they wish. And they can bring – and usually do – their own personal experiences to bear in these private encounters which often turn into free-ranging conversations. In the third stage, usually following an interval, the spectators move to a public forum – a residents' meeting where the conflict is openly debated. The spectators/neighbours are encouraged to speak, express opinions and finally take a vote on the motion put forward: to take action or prevent action within the dramatic world – for example, whether a community centre should be occupied, whether an antisocial tenant should have their accommodation taken away, or perhaps whether decaying flats should make way for a park. Finally there is a series of enacted improvisations, involving the performers, that explore how events might flow from such a vote being taken. Claire Marshall, producer at Midlands Arts Centre, wrote about the process thus:

> The creation and devising process allows for people to genuinely influence what the live theatre will be and then their attendance at the events helps to shape what happens next. This allows people to talk about something important and have that dramatised to see what the impact of decision making – or not making decisions – can have on a situation.[87]

So in both the Coney and Fluxx models, a space is created to examine issues of social and political relationships, allowing the audience to be influential in decision making. Perhaps this a legitimate expression of some of the ideas that Chris Goode has outlined in his book *The Forest and Field*, where

> we can, perhaps through our art, make a kind of shelter, in which the terrible grindings logics of capitalism can be temporarily suspended through the wilful and consensual application of the technologies of subjunctivity and metaphor and the other theatrical apparatus that permits us to examine and reimagine our social relations.[88]

Outside the closed theatre event, there are more public manifestations of prefigurative challenge. In demonstrations and marches such as Pride and Slut Walks, the public is challenged to accept the righteousness of what is staged, enacted or demonstrated. Placards, dress and behaviour project imagery of what is so often frowned on – or worse, actively forbidden. The solidarity of the marchers acts as a necessary guarantee of safety for those who in other contexts may well be the recipient of violence from bigots, homophobes or the deranged. In Slut Walks, women march through a town or city in dress that makes no concessions to social norms. The women protest against 'victim-blaming, survivor-shaming and rape culture'. Their defiance challenges passers-by to accept their proposition, a challenge made stronger by the numbers involved. The prefigurative assertion is that

> one's humanity and intrinsic worth is not determined by clothing, age, race, immigration status, gender, sexual orientation, occupation, or class. We support all survivors and push back against the stigmas and myths surrounding sexual violence. We challenge others to have to confront their prejudices and the myths behind them that continue to let perpetrators get away with their crimes.[89]

b) Offstage

Prefiguration in drama also works by giving individuals a chance to imagine and create their own personal futures. They can articulate and enact these in private before attempting them in the real world. It's a fundamental hypothesis behind much of Augusto Boal's Image Theatre work. Because drama has this unique capacity to enable individuals to learn social and behavioural skills that will engender different life choices, business organizations try to borrow the magic to contribute to the implementation of their corporate ideals. But this isn't a great match. It's a bit like trying to steal the spirit of carnival and using it for commercial purposes on the wrong side of the world. This kind of drama work succeeds when mission is allied to craft; when the beneficiaries are those who deserve the magic.

Drama works with the dispossessed because of the demands which it makes on those who submit to its tasks. Just as the construction of a table requires the ability to measure, cut and piece together wood, to create a collaborative dramatic scene requires listening, appreciating, responding, empathizing, negotiating, acting on understanding, communicating and teamwork. They are what I would call skills. Faced with the challenge of drama, it's these skills that are brought into being. Equally important are what I would define as aptitudes. These are nurtured more often as by-products of the work. I would define these as conviviality, humility, generosity, patience, tolerance, broad-mindedness, civility, willingness to risk and a capacity for spontaneity – all attitudes, I would suggest, essential to any imagined 'better future' for civic society.

Going one step further, the business of making a show calls on both aptitudes and skills in a more intense way. The deadline of an imminent performance spurs adrenaline, increases focus and galvanizes cooperation (usually …). So with all these benefits kicking in, it's a wonder improvisers aren't invited into government. Well, the fact is, you can find Facebook groups dedicated to that very idea.

This co-option of theatre making to teach life skills has a certain irony. Historically the acting profession has been seen as being full of miscreants, prostitutes and no-goods. In Roman times, actors were even legally denied positions of responsibility. Now they're invited to the White House. It's therefore worth looking in more detail at just what drama's affordances are that have been so reappraised and re-evaluated. They might include the following:

Exteriorization – the capacity of drama to liberate forgotten or repressed selves. Via acting out, the individual can become more self-integrated and less repressed. Behaviour that is frowned on in the world can be licensed and brought forward. What has been suppressed can be released. This way the world gets taught to be a little more accepting. Doing this in the bathroom doesn't work; what makes the work efficacious is the act of it being witnessed. Then the line between 'oddness' and 'normality' starts to dissolve. The pioneering work of Gay Sweatshop showed how gay relationships were as deserving of equivalent value, status and expression as straight ones. The company took behaviour previously hidden and private, elaborated it in workshops and made it public on the stage. This transformative work subsequently helped shift social prejudice.

It's been a similar story for companies of learning-disabled actors and Down's Syndrome performers, often the victims of prejudice and bigotry. This account of a workshop improvisation comes from the UK-based company Them Wifies, as written up by their supporter, lecturer Ali Campbell. The participants – members of the Lawnmowers Theatre Company – are taking the opportunity to get their own back on religious bullying they've experienced in their lives.

Take One: Billy on floor. Enter nuns.

June and Sharon have dispensed with dialogue. Each has managed to fashion a wimple from the dressing-up box and crucifixes have been improvised from something culinary close to hand. The nuns gaily skip around Andy as he shrinks into an ever-smaller ball. They are singing: 'How do you solve a problem like Maria?' and hitting him with home-made crucifixes. 'YOU WANA KNOW WHY WE'RE DOING THIS, EH? WELL, JESUS IS DEAD, AND IT'S ALL [*thwack*] YOUR [*thwack*] FAULT!' A pause. Some of us are literally on the floor.[90]

Identity formation – the drama space is one where latent talents can be practised and new identities formed. It may be that internal propensities have been inhibited during growth to adulthood. The case of so-called offenders is a case in point. An 'offender' may well have been nurtured in a criminal subculture where displays of weakness or generosity are discouraged. When this individual gets to prison, which often happens, these attitudes can be further reinforced by other inmates. However, this can all change when that individual walks into a prison arts workshop. Here there's an encounter with a radically different mode of thinking. A willingness to apologize is encouraged, creativity is valued for its own sake and prejudice is challenged as a matter of routine. Perhaps most importantly, there is an encouragement to recognize and give vent to emotions that are usually regarded as 'weak'. In this way, the individual's sense of identity is altered. The individual starts to feel different, realizing she has permission to be spontaneous, generous and emotional. In this way drama becomes a nest for hatching new selves in.

As one participant commented not untypically after a production of Barrie Keeffe's *Sus* in HMP Dovegate: 'Well, I could have spent the last six weeks working next door in the pallet workshop earning £40 a week, which is a lot of money by prison standards. But instead I did this because, well, it made me feel like a human again.'[91]

Articulacy – theatre making is a vocabulary-extending exercise. So it's valuable for those with low literacy or limited vocabulary. But by comparison with a reading class, for example, where reading and writing are the primary outputs, in theatre making, articulacy is a by-product. So there are no 'tests'. There's no pressure to be articulate but there is pressure to get the show on. Feelings and ideas therefore need to be expressed and understood. So the work continuously calls for the putting of thoughts and feelings into words. But because articulacy has a clear function in the present rather than it being something useful in the future, learning happens more laterally. This makes the exercise more appealing to those who are classroom-averse.

Teamwork – it's axiomatic that the generation of drama, performance or improvisation requires teamwork. As suggested before, this is one reason why corporate organizations engage impro troupes. Managers and administrators are drawn reluctantly away from their computers into team-building exercises where they have to sing, be funny and agree to play ducks opening a restaurant. But the same rewards are available for social or voluntary sector organizations too. The work has more resonance and impact here; one reason for that is that hierarchies may be less prominent and a sense of a shared cause more evident. The issue of social change is always on the agenda and directly connected to the workings of teamwork.

Leading workshops for those disadvantaged can be, and usually is, rewarding for the theatre artist at many levels. It's my experience that many improvisers find this just as rewarding as struggling to be funny in front of beer-fuelled audiences. Yet this engagement with the dispossessed or the disenfranchised has traditionally brought some questions in its wake. Or as Peter Bürger writes it:

> In bourgeois society, the arts has a contradictory role: it projects the image of a better order and to that extent protests against the bad order that prevails. But by realizing the image of a better order in fiction, which is semblance [*Schein*] only, it relieves the existing society of the pressure of those forces that make for change.[92]

The same point is made by the scholar E. Patrick Johnson in respect of black liberation. He writes that 'black performance has the potential of simultaneously forestalling and enabling social change'. In other words, by taking the sting out of the situation, by helping the disempowered release their energies via an exercise with therapeutic outcomes, revolutionary change becomes less likely. This ethical puzzle was wrestled over constantly in the radical arts conferences of the 1970s and 1980s. The argument was often made that art should be in service of the political struggle, a stance which led many creative souls to find things to do with their time other than go to conferences. In such bruising and long conversations, the question of how to actually craft or make theatre often took second place. Aesthetics was separated out from politics and stood in the corner of the room until some good use could be found for it. Often, none was.

In less confrontational times, it is almost uniformly accepted that for those groups who are subject to discrimination, the 'relieving of pressure' is justified by the immediate benefits to those so marginalized. It's a perfectly valid argument. Furthermore, it's one supported by the recognition that such lines of struggle can happen in parallel; the political, activist struggle for change can just as well happen alongside the work of addressing the immediate concerns of the dispossessed. Fulfilling the second priority in no way limits, circumvents or negates fulfilment of the first.

The case of disabled actors is a case in point. While there have been disabled actors since the dawn of the profession, disability has in modern times been seen as a bar to access. In 2015 a study revealed that only around 0.3 per cent of actors were visibly disabled. It has taken the efforts of twentieth-century pioneers like Nabil Shaban, who founded Graeae, to change public perceptions to get even this far. Shaban has no doubts about the value of such work because of the way it offers a means to counteract social bias – and get disabled actors to conspire in making a better future for all, both able-bodied and less so:

> If I die tomorrow, I wouldn't mind. I consider my greatest achievement, with Richard Tomlinson, was the founding of Graeae. Because of the opportunities that Graeae has given to disabled people, to become performers. The most important thing that's happened is that disabled people have had an opportunity to see themselves onstage. And on TV, film. It's given thousands of disabled people the chance to believe that they can be actors. Before that, opportunities were very, very rare. So the achievement is to put disability arts on the map.[93]

2. Tactics

These chapters are concerned more with tactics that allow an imagined disobedient theatre to fulfil a role in community or public contexts.

1. Animation

Definition in this context: Engaging the general public in activities enabling creativity, productivity and collaboration

We are the ridiculous people who insist, to universal scepticism, that not only must our fictions means something: they must achieve something as well.

David Hare, Obedience, Struggle and Revolt

The work of imagining better futures is linked with the tradition of community arts. A crucial period for the development of this body of practice was in the 1960s, 1970s and 1980s when the great dream of community artists was the dream of animating the people. With projects like ED Berman's Fun Art Bus setting out through the streets of Camden inviting audiences to jump on board, with the Instant Theatre of R. G. Gregory acting out stories from the words of audiences and with Welfare State taking pageant participation to levels unheard of since the Middle Ages, anything seemed possible. It was a dream that proceeded from a key idea: that citizen Jo or Joe would become more alive, more connected and more 'in tune' with the world and ultimately with their fellow citizens by participating in creative invention. In turn this would lead us to a 'creativization' of society to the benefit of all. This burgeoning tradition has flowered since into many different iterations, both into mixed media work – carnivals, festivals, processions – and into more purely theatre-based work by companies such as Rimini Protokoll, Chris Goode & Company and Ontroerend Goed, hallmarked by the prominence of non-professionals onstage. This in what has been referred to as 'Theatre of Real People', a contemporary tradition the roots of which can be seen in the early work of pioneers such as the People Show, whose performers, while clearly demonstrating extraordinary stage charisma, lacked any orthodox training or experience.

In recent years, however, much criticism has been javelined into the fields of community arts and participatory performance, not least by commentators such as Claire Bishop. In her book *Artificial Hells*, mentioned earlier, Bishop drives a large pen through the misfiring that sometimes characterizes this work. The accusations from her and others have ranged from the charge that art is being reduced to instrumentalism, to the claim that poor project management has led fatally to the misuse of activist enthusiasm. So perhaps it's time to return to some of the core concepts that were first sketched out in that early period to evaluate whether or not they still have traction. One way to do this is to look at a figure central to the movement: the animateur or facilitator. It's this role that embodies so much of the strategic ambition. Does this role have a place in theatre for social change? And if so, what is its scope?

Arguably the role emerged from post-1960s drama in education. Dorothy Heathcote was an early and significant influence, someone who wanted to collapse distinctions between leaders and the led in order to nudge the latter into expressivity. Her influence and singularity makes her an obvious point of focus. Crucially it was her focus on relationships that mattered:

> If I am to aspire to excellence as a teacher, I must be able to see my pupils as they really are. I mustn't discourage them – I must accept them. This means adjusting myself to my pupils, and seeing things from another standpoint. As an excellent teacher, I must not be afraid to move out of my centre and meet the children where they are. If I do this, I shall not be afraid to try unfamiliar things.[1]

Heathcote's aim was always to challenge the notion that the world was divided into artists and non-artists, a position now widely respected, associated particularly with the German artist Joseph Beuys, who wrote: 'Every human being is an artist, a freedom being, called to participate in transforming and reshaping the conditions, thinking and structures that shape and inform our lives.'[2]

More than anyone else Heathcote provides us with a role model for the facilitator who championed this idea. Her conception is anchored in a notion she described as 'mantle of the expert'. Her 'expert' was crucially not the teacher but the child. In this way she reverse-engineered orthodox teaching practice. 'Oh good', she is credited as saying at the beginning of a particular lesson with a grumbly group of kids, 'I'm glad you've still got your coats on – because today we're going somewhere very cold.'[3] Without abandoning leadership she's created an expedition from the children's resistance – and joined it. In her terminology she's found a 'fellowship' between what the kids are already doing and what another group of people did or might have done in another time. Now within the activity of this 'expedition', she can lead the pupils into discovery and learning. She's created an imaginative bubble, an alternative world, and to enter it no professional qualification is required.

Explicit in this vision of the teacher's role is the necessity to adapt and by so doing, devolve a measure of authority to the children. But this is not to abandon pedagogical structure. It's rather to create a different kind of structure, one that aligns with the children's imaginative momentum and which dissolves the artist/non-artist distinction. In this way Heathcote sidesteps the orthodoxy in which pupils are kept at a distance by the use of a reasoning voice outside the bubble, as in: 'What should this character do now?' 'Why do you think this character acted in the way she did?' These questions, to which the answer is already known, keep the teacher safe in a zone of expertise. As a result, any characters in the drama tend to be objectified and any paradoxical or contradictory psychologies flattened out. Once the facilitator moves inside the dramatic frame, however, the questions become different: 'What should I do now?' 'How can we get out of this mess?' The facilitator role becomes partially collapsed into that of the performer, ending the subject–object split.

This approach to collaboratively constructing a realm of imagination in which expertise dissolves was simultaneously being explored in a range of community arts contexts, most successfully by R. G. Gregory's Word and Action (Dorset), whose short plays acted as provocations to the audience to leave their seats and join the imaginative world created by the actors. Or the company might simply start without pre-scenes altogether, posing questions to the audience, the answers to which created a world and a narrative. No answers were censored or refused; contradictions were fed back for resolution. To imagine an example:

Questioner Where does our hero live?
Spectator One In an attic.
Spectator Two In a shoe.
Questioner So how is it possible for our hero to live in both an attic *and* in a shoe?
Spectator Three The shoe was left by mistake in an attic and that's the shoe the hero lives in.

Spectators then animated this world by joining it and acting out the story, a process facilitated by the company. Paradox, contradiction and ambiguity were inevitably the prevailing keynotes of this play-world in which, it should be noted, all elements both human and non-human were played by people. Animation of the story was always shared; the actors would never act out the story on behalf of the audience.

To some extent this principle of the facilitator/performer straddling the worlds of both the actors and the audience to animate the audience echoes the Joker role as conceptualized by Augusto Boal. The Joker is one who interrogates the actors, if necessary jumping in to play a minor role, yet is also close to the audience, representing their questions. Yet the different conceptions were developed quite separately on two different continents: Heathcote's and Gregory's in the UK and Boal's in Latin America. They also have different purposes: the latter more clearly rooted in an activist/political sensibility, the former in learning, imaginative play and the extension of the child mind.

Since these times, the role of facilitator has been significantly developed and extended. It's become a sophisticated blend of leader, teacher, entertainer, ally, clown and, in some cases, therapist. It is employed in a wide range of contexts: not just schools but hospitals, prisons, clubs, arts centres, community centres, even theatres. In the course of this evolution and in the work of successful animation, it's also become evident that the role is inseparable from a number of ethical questions – in particular, the extent to which the facilitator should reflect the racial, gender or age aspect of the group. For it's undeniable that nudging the constituency into animation requires trust – and trust in turn depends partly on how the facilitator is 'seen'. Perceptions are important, especially in a context where the group might be distrustful of authority, for example in a youth club, a pupil referral unit or a prison. This is why in my own practice I've always advocated that facilitation should be a team game. As a white, middle-class male often working with groups of quite different orientations, I want to be working with colleagues who are closer to the participant group in terms of identity markers. It doesn't matter if these concern 'experience of prison' or 'experience of a black minority culture', the same applies: we need to bridge the visual gap.

Of course it's not guaranteed that my female, black, ex-prisoner colleague will make a more intimate connection with the group than I will – although it's very probable – but her presence in the room makes an acknowledgement of the significance of race and gender. There's a potential for connectedness straight away. As the lesbian artist and performer Mojisola Adebayo said in an interview:

> All of us, me included, feel immense pleasure at being in the space with other people who know what it is to feel in a minority within a minority. To be different because of race and sexuality – those things are so enormous in terms of how they impact on your sense of yourself. It feels really good when you're in a space with other people who get it and you don't have to explain those details, you can express yourself creatively without feeling judged or laughed at.[4]

This is what a bubble enables: the dissolution of the expert/non-expert divide and the sharing of creative ideas away from judgement.

The techniques that Heathcote and others developed, therefore, continue to be used, modified and extended. They also get adapted as they become employed within different art forms. Community dance, for example, with its long history and abstract language, has this advantage; it can bypass the need for consensus around the value of the project. It is often enough simply to build consensus around 'Let's dance!' So the art form offers great scope for animative practice. Nic Green, Fergus Early, Rosemary Lee, Gaby Agis, Royston Maldoom and Dave McKenna are just some of the significant artists in the UK who have been working over years to engage people of all ages from all sections of the community in fully professional dance or movement projects. Watching their shows, audiences may find it hard to pick out the professionals from the rest; in part this is because the choreography has emerged out of conversations between the parties rather than being imposed externally. The 'experts', instead of creating the vocabulary, have created the bubble and it's filled by a conversation in movement.

In this way such projects serve as a reminder of a pre-capitalist, perhaps even pre-agricultural time, when the function of dance was precisely to break down social distinctions and unify the tribe. As the cultural historian Barbara Ehrenreich puts it, the purpose of dance was to unite everyone in the space. She sees dance as

> the great leveller and binder of human communities. To submit bodily through the music through dance is to be incorporated into the community in a way far deeper than shared myth or common custom can achieve. In synchronous movement to music or chanting voices, the petty rivalries and factional differences that might divide a group could be transmuted into harmless competition over one's prowess as a dancer, or forgotten.[5]

Today, the invitation to participate in a community arts programme often needs more underpinning than such aspirations indicate. 'Let's dance!' simply may not be sufficient. Certainly 'Let's act!' is very unlikely to form queues as an injunction in and of itself. While the benefits of dramatic performance – personal creative development, sharing of experiences, the chance to influence social policy or make a public statement – may be clear to organizers, they may not be quite so clear to potential but wavering volunteers. What's the structure? The process? Can we trust it? Do we get a job out of it? A certificate? It's possible there's already complicity through the construction of a mixed-race, mixed-gender team, but there may still be questions to be answered, especially in a theatre project where the vocabulary of theatre is so much less abstract than dance. So a holding form is required: a scripted play, a devising process or a course of improvisation perhaps? One way or another, potential recruits want a game plan and one that doesn't involve the unmediated acceptance of others' words, ideas or thoughts (the obedient theatre model).

In the Heathcote and Gregory traditions cited earlier, the imaginative world of performance draws on archetypal stories of journey, identity, loss, family or revenge – the classic narratives. The incentive to participation arises from understandings about the benefits of play, story and shared creative product. The facilitator's role in this case is not far from that of the enchanter who beguiles and entices participants into a work that has some mystery about it, some magic. Such a model operates in part mythologically, weaving new stories and making new sense for a modern, confused world.

But there is another strand of animative work which lies closer to the business of addressing specific issues of social injustice. Here, there is the opportunity to use art and performance to open up social conflicts and themes by improvising, as it were, within them. In Fluxx's Citizen's Theatre model, for example, or Coney's participatory performance work, it's the placing of the attendees into quite specific roles within the drama that enables this kind of exploration. Participants might be members of an imaginary street or town; they may even hold positions as councillor, mayor, postman, homeless bum, angry woman, etc. Within these roles there are opportunities to engage with the knotty problems of social prejudice, disparities of wealth, drug addiction or neighbourhood conflicts. When Fluxx performed in the town of Wirksworth as part of the company's 2012 UK tour, the actual mayor played the role of a fictional councillor in order to put forward proposals that he was hesitant of proposing in the real world. As a result, he found more support than he anticipated and the Wirksworth Neighbourhood Plan, the one belonging to the real world, was changed as a result.

The larger the scale of such animative work, the greater the challenge. For it to operate at the level set by Welfare State, where almost the whole town of Ulverston was part of or linked to the community arts event, a network of support and partnerships is required. Out in the relatively open contexts of the street or town centre, the role of a dynamic facilitator with charisma and drive shouldn't be undervalued. It may even be crucial. Someone like an Orson Welles perhaps, who in Utah in 1947 pulled off 'the greatest thing that ever happened to Utah', according to its governor, quoted in Welles's biography.[6] Welles's ability 'to galvanise a group of people, his sense of showmanship and his instinctive response to a particular space and to the specific individuals at his disposal resulted in a semi-improvised piece of spectacular theatre, here given special excitement because he was working with the community'.[7] But no amount of charisma can overcome the need for a set of rules and/or conventions that enable what will inevitably be a looser kind of assembly. How far can the bubble be extended? Inevitably, the larger it is, the less intense the engagement. However, the selection of public places for such work doesn't necessarily involve any abandonment of activist intent. Here's an example from the heart of London, where the Carnival Against Capital was organized – and joined – by a considerable number of volunteers:

> On 18 June 1999, in the financial district of London, 10,000 people gathered in the street … and to add flair to the event, organizers distributed colour-coded masks to participants: a note inside the masks suggested that the wearers follow the flags that matched their masks when the time came. Sure enough, at one moment, colourful flags went up and soon streams of masked revellers were running, following the flag-bearers through the narrow streets of the financial sector of London.[8]

In his chapter 'Carnivals Against Capital: Radical Clowning and the Global Justice Movement', the activist and writer L. M. Bogad gives these events the description of 'tactical performance' – assemblies that aim to influence minds over a local or national issue. He proposes that the aims of such tactical carnival initiatives are to 'to declare and occupy a joyous, partici-patory and semi-anonymous safe place for power inversions/subversions'.[9] It's no less a restatement of the bubble principle. Albeit they represent a short-term intervention, such tactical performances may well have lasting impact. Besides, they can be hugely effective in animating those who have little interest in the arts but a keen interest in protest. Witness the growth of CIRCA, the Clandestine Insurgent Rebel Clown Army; 'with its horizontalist organizing model, CIRCA practices a form of nonviolent direct action that joins collective buffoonery with satirical performance'.[10] The company grew from a handful of activists to a group of 150 clowning at the 2005 G8 Summit in Edinburgh and subsequently to informing the 10,000-strong Carnival Against Capital.

Here, the game plan for volunteers is evidently different; the parameters of the planned activity are publicized by a leadership and offered out to all-comers to realize in their own way. The incentive for participation in the carnival, for example, is clearly rooted in the chance to protest. There may well be intensive training or rehearsal – as sometimes happens in the Clown Army – or the rules of the game may simply be posted for volunteer participants to follow as best they can. The bubble of participation then becomes as large as the number who choose to enter it. In the UK in 2011, women in Brighton organized a breastfeeding flashmob. The trigger had been the experience of Claire Hughes-Jones who, fed up with being harassed

and complained about, 'decided it was time to make a statement to show
that mothers will no longer tolerate being harassed for feeding our babies
in public.'[11] She deliberately copied a previous initiative in central London
where people had lain down, covered with flags, to protest against Syrian
government brutality. Her rules were simple: mums should show up with
their babies, find a place around the Jubilee Clock Tower in central Brighton
and publicly breastfeed their babies. The event was blessed with that most
prized of rewards: national media attention.

However, it may be that the organizing principle is less about protest than
about simple play and subversion.

Improv Everywhere has no special activist intent; it describes itself as
a 'prank collective' which aims to 'cause scenes of chaos and joy in public
places.'[12] In No Pants Subway Ride, 'the idea is simple: random passengers
board a subway car at separate stops in the middle of winter without pants
[trousers]. The participants behave as if they do not know each other, and
they all wear winter coats, hats, scarves, and gloves. The only unusual thing
is their lack of pants.'[13] Since the initiative was started in 2002 the event has
been repeated each year in different locations across the USA and around
the world. There's a cumulative effect, so each year more join, more pants
are discarded, more strange looks are achieved. In 2014, it is claimed, tens of
thousands participated.

In referencing Improv Everywhere and a breastfeeding flashmob, we've
clearly moved a long way from Dorothy Heathcote's group of grumbly kids.
The facilitator role is operating on quite a different scale. Yet arguably many
of the same principles are still in evidence. There is still the cultivation of
impulsiveness within an aesthetically drawn bubble of defiance. There is
still the legitimation of protest inside this zone of safety. Facilitation still
involves leadership from an individual or a team and it's still geared to the
establishment and maintenance of a set of rules or conventions that permits
and gives safety to some unorthodox, freewheeling, subversive, impatient or
'disobedient' behaviours. There is still an ambition to create an impact on
the world at large.

There is clearly a sufficient case to argue, then, that the dream of
animating the people lives on. The shape of the bubble may change, its
manifestations clearly vary and its powering mechanisms are now many and
various, but to reactionaries' dismay, those early principles would appear to
still have much life in them.

'I'm glad you've got your coats on'.

2. Adaptation

Definition in this context: Changing plans and strategy in order to create a relationship with the chosen constituency that makes responsiveness possible

Any disobedient theatre practice worth the name needs to be able to engage the disobedient. It can't just rely on those who will respond to a Facebook invitation to meet in the park. To achieve that, disobedient, creative practice needs to be adaptive. It needs to change direction, art form or strategy in response to the chosen constituency. This is the case whether it's a classroom, theatre or workshop context. But how much adaptation is justified? Abandonment of political principles can hardly be an acceptable trade.

In this chapter therefore we're looking at workshop or classroom contexts. These are locations where the disobedient can usually be found: prisons, young offender centres, youth clubs. We're looking at a specific aspect of facilitation: how to animate the difficult group. It may appear a sign of weakness, both to the orthodox pedagogue and to the doctrinaire activist, to take this route. Yet experience suggests that without adaptation, creative work doesn't progress. Failing to adapt means ultimately you either throw the offenders out of the room or you go home yourself. Yes, it's true you can turn yourself into a sergeant-major to enforce the delivery of the programme according to the letter – but any spirit of play is likely to be lost. The legacy of Heathcote, Gregory and others has indicated clearly that communication through creativity can't be achieved by imposing truths on an unwilling body, however nobly conceived those truths may be. Having bravely said all that, it's never wise to completely rule out throwing the persistent offender out on his ear ...

Artists working in these institutional contexts often find themselves in far-from-ideal circumstances. The relationship between the artist and the group may not have been engineered well. Possibly the staff member responsible is not even present on Day One when the project is due to begin. The communications haven't been great, objectives are cloudy, and the drama room is entirely filled by massage chairs (this really happened). There are issues, in other words. It is quite likely in many such contexts that the group of participants may not even be expecting the artists. Rideout was once sent to work with a group of prisoners waiting to start a maths class. Absence of Maths Teacher + Availability of artists = New Maths/Art Experience. Some adaptation required then.

The value of an adaptive approach is that it minimizes conflict. It lets the participants into an executive level of power – and gives them authority in the process. But this is not to imply that an adaptive approach doesn't have principles, values or boundaries. Key values such as equality and free speech are still upheld. Instead, it's about knowing where you adapt and where you hold fast. If we want to build a castle in a particular project, there may be useful compromise over the shape, style and colour of the castle – but it still should be a castle at the end of the day.

There are two primary areas where shifting ground is tactically useful:

a) Dealing with behaviour.

b) Handling problematic content or material generated by the group members.

a) I spoke with Sara Lee from Music In Prisons about behavioural issues: when it was diplomatic to adapt and when to hold firm. She was clear that working successfully with this challenging constituency is not about following a rule book: 'It's more intuitive than that.'[14] She argues that what young people in a prison context want is 'a response' – 'and quite often it's very funny, what they're doing – and you want to be with them on the joke.'[15] It's the Heathcote approach again; 'joining them' rather than 'have them join you'. 'They want a response – but what they don't expect is someone to use that in a creative way.'[16] Lee's tactic, familiar from points made previously, is to bring the disruptive behaviour from the edge of the group into the centre. This is achieved by endowing it as having creative potential. For example, if there's a young person just thumping an instrument or randomly banging away at one end of the keyboard, that might be taken as the start of the piece. If that person is just hitting a radiator with a drumstick, this is *The Radiator Piece*; it's not as if in musique concrète there isn't a historical precedent. So instead of 'those sounds don't belong in our vocabulary', it's 'let's construct the vocabulary around those sounds'.

This approach may look like we're abandoning pedagogical orthodoxy, but it's not as if formal music education is working very well in itself. As Sarah Derbyshire, Managing Director of the Children's Orchestras, has written:

> The established music education sector remains fixated on formal learning, and in doing so fails to reflect the diversity of young people, the ways in which they engage with music and the achievements of those who learn away from the exam system.[17]

In a prison context, pragmatic adaptation is far more likely to succeed. But for an artist sent to lead workshops who is unfamiliar with these contexts, adapting can be tough. Sometimes the struggle is about status. Some artists find it difficult to let go of their authority, to let go of the notion that 'the artist knows best'. The ego insists on holding sway. What makes this wrestle particularly galling is that such groups often have it in their DNA to resist whatever is offered, even if what is offered is precisely what they requested. Resistance is a powerful weapon – sometimes the only weapon available to those who are relatively powerless or traumatized. And they know it. Here's a parallel:

One approach to training a wild mustang is to break its spirit. It can be beaten into submission by yoking it to a post and then violently yanking on its bit and bridle until the animal is bent to the trainer's will. This does work, in a way, but the horse becomes sullen and suspicious. A gentler approach is that epitomized by Monty Roberts – a 'horse whisperer' who trains wild animals by becoming attuned to their language. He trained a wild mustang colt on the great plains of America; he allowed the colt to run and run while he followed behind on his own horse. He let the mustang go wherever it wished. The colt eventually slowed and acknowledged his presence. At that point, Monty stopped his pursuit and went in the opposite direction. The wild horse then began to follow out of curiosity. Within two days, Monty had earned the horse's trust and just hours later a rider was on its back.[18]

But of course not even an adept and adaptive strategy is guaranteed to be successful. Too often I've read books on community arts where the sheer gut-wrenching frustration of facilitators is insufficiently acknowledged. But speak privately to those who work in these fields of combat and you hear different stories: 'They'd been winding me up for a while … and I just totally lost my rag in the middle of a session and I just started screaming and swearing – and we were in the church.'[19] But Sara Lee found that the response to her outburst was surprising. 'The whole project vibe changed at that point – for the better. Although I wouldn't advocate that behaviour!'[20] The choreographer Rosemary Lee reached a similar break point with teenagers in Bedford. She admits to finding this constituency tough to work with: 'They can push my buttons.' She was creating a show and 'nothing in my toolkit seemed to work. So I went backwards and started doing 5-6-7-8 [a dance count]. And my team were going, "I didn't know you did anything to a count!" – and I felt so awful. But it worked! And it surprised me that it was OK to do that.'[21] Sometimes the application of a very intense exercise that uses a very disciplined structure is exactly what pulls the wavering, fragmented group together. But as Rosemary Lee also comments, 'If I work too much like that, I will lose the artistry'.[22]

The examples above have come from music and dance contexts. But the adaptive approach has value in a drama context just as powerfully. For example, a group of prisoners 'saying no' can easily be taken as the start of a scene. I remember one case where several prisoners, instead of participating in the session, decided to lounge instead. The remainder were keen. But to get everyone sitting in a circle was out of the question. I and my colleague tried to coax the reluctant to sit down, but it didn't work. So I did some reverse-engineering. I asked the willing pioneers not to act but instead to be the spectators. So now they were sitting looking at the resistant prisoners, lounging against the wall, who were then miraculously 'onstage'. Luckily they accepted this. I then asked the loungers to imagine themselves as a criminal gang holed up in a foreign country. They'd done a bank job and they were waiting to be picked up by helicopter. I was reasonably confident this would appeal to their collective vanity. It would also bond them together. Possibly this was an equivalent of *The Radiator Piece*: 'The Lounging Piece'? The lounging, previously a nuisance, now had a purpose and a dramatic function. We were entering the prisoners' world rather than demanding they enter ours. One or two of the prisoners even started to elaborate: 'Yo, we should never have employed that muppet. What if he never gets here?' 'I guess we're stuck here.' 'That'd be your fault.'

Such a sleight of hand is fine but begs the question 'What next?' Well, hopefully Scene One will be sufficiently enjoyable to make Scene Two a possibility. It happened here.

b) As for the second of the two concerns – for example, the proposing of bad or offensive language that's impossible to work with – Music In Prisons have a system of dealing with this situation. There are restrictions placed on them too, because 'so much is guided by the prison'.[23] Sara Lee continues:

> But we try not to censor if at all possible. If someone does bring really inappropriate lyrics in, we'll go, 'I don't think this is going to work' and they'll go, 'Why not? You don't expect me to talk about flowers and trees and shit, do you?' And this was an actual line someone said. And I'll go, 'No.' And I'll try and urge that writer into taking a more observational position. That way you don't talk directly about what you want to do to people – slit their throats or stab them. 'Maybe you could be a fly on the wall or another character?' If this doesn't work, another tactic might be to remind the writer of family considerations: 'If you do write and it goes out on a CD and your Grandma hears it, what's she going to think?'[24]

In a drama context, it's unsurprising if young offenders bring forward tales of bank robberies (successful), armed attacks (unpunished) or drug deals (successful enough to lead to retirement in Spain), and for these to be performed in the appropriate vernacular. The correct task of facilitation is not to dismiss or alter these storylines but to elaborate them. Perhaps going back in time to explore the trigger for the bank robbery. Or by setting up exercises around relationships that are implied by the story but not mentioned by the proposer, such as with a mother, a straight friend or a next-door neighbour. Such improvisations may in turn lead us to a situation where there is sickness or poverty in the family, to which other characters are reacting differently to our bank robber hero. Another approach might be to elaborate into the future. What happened to the individual consumer of the dope? Or the bank teller traumatized by the raid? (An actual bank robber told me that it took him decades before he started to think of his victims' experiences.) What's life really going to be like in Spain for our escapers – without any family present? Scenes can be constructed around these questions. Once they are up and running, it's down to some sidecoaching to nudge the performers into weaving a narrative that does more than simply celebrate the thrill of the criminal escapade. A more multilayered, more psychologically complex story can then be constructed from the initial fantasy. We need these other stories both for contrast and to extend the scope and ethical range of the narrative. It's important to retain the fantasy element – that's how the young people bought into the exercise in the first place – but now these fantasies have absorbed contradiction, paradox and conflict. They have hopefully become a little more grounded in the real world.

The participant is always more likely to be cooperative if he or she sees the facilitator is open to negotiation. This will help achieve a more level playing field where status gaps are minimized. In this way the participants start to achieve a measure of agency in the room. Perhaps the skill to make this adaptation involves what the Greeks call 'metis': 'A person with metis possesses a mental map of her particular reality ... has acquired a set of practical skills that enable her to anticipate change ... knows when to apply the standard operating procedure but also when to break the rules.'[25]

There's an example of this willingness to 'break the rules' in a project led by the artist Deborah Jones, who was working in a women's secure institution. All the women wanted to do was make cards. 'This would drive me nuts because I got so fed up sticking bits of paper onto card.'[26] Jones was initially adamant that such an activity was too prosaic, inartistic and without resonance. It lacked any visible aesthetic. However, the women were keen and Jones was reluctant to override them. It finally came to her that something else was going on she didn't initially understand. She came to realize that 'they were making cards specifically for people in their lives – friends, children or members of staff – and using these to consolidate, repair or even make relationships. So the transitional object became a carrier of a whole set of relational things. And they were doing this with great intelligence and sophistication.'[27] Once Jones had understood the cultural currency of card making had more resonance than she had initially credited, it became the centre of the project.

Tim Harford wrote a book about adaptation in which he covers a range of studies where individuals have adapted to circumstances across military, business and social science fields. He ranges far beyond the world of the young offender institution or the women's secure institution. And what's remarkable is how the lessons being applied by artists in the young offender institutions are found reflected here also, albeit in very different cultural contexts. For example, Harford writes about how the choreographer Twyla Tharp created a show, *Movin' Out*, with music by Billy Joel, that previewed in Chicago with disastrous results. She had clearly imposed the choreography on the dancers. 'She was the one who had persuaded Billy Joel to hand over his life's work. The New York press were waiting for the theatrical car crash to arrive on Broadway.'[28] At its first run-out, it bombed. But rather than keep insisting on the show's brilliance, she adapted. She made a fundamental turnaround by deciding to rehearse an entirely new show during the day while the cast performed the old, failing show in the evening. It might have been another disaster – but that didn't happen. Instead, 'it was widely acknowledged to be the most rapid and total transformation of a Broadway show in many years'.[29] What's interesting is less the issue of success/failure but how it was managed: by ditching the ego and changing tactics to suit the situation, just as musicians and artists have to do with difficult groups in prison. Tharp's comment was: 'It [the situation] required you to challenge a status quo of your own making.' With this achieved, the task of adaptation became easier. 'How could I, such a 5* award-winning choreographer, possibly make rookie errors?'[30] Well, it happened.

Harford suggests that when the person fails to adapt, in the classroom, the prison or the rehearsal room, it's because of cognitive dissonance – a failure to reconcile conflicting truths. I know this to be true: I'm there extolling the virtues of an exercise but it's failing in front of my eyes. Clearly the group is in a different dream space altogether and needs, for its creative momentum to be realized, something very different. In such a situation, becoming increasingly assertive simply fails. What's required is close obser-vation of what vehicle might propel the group into its own future. But to make this shift requires some humility.

Leon Festinger wrote about a radical group called the Seekers who predicted the apocalypse: then it didn't arrive. The group is suddenly confronted by a gap between former belief ('The end of the world is nigh!') and current information ('We still seem to be alive!') – a cognitive disso-nance therefore. Some kind of shift is necessary, otherwise you might have to buy some dynamite and blow yourselves up. ('We were right – it's the end of the world!') It's a dissonance that is something similar to the gap between 'I'm a great artist and everything I do is wonderful!' and 'It appears everyone hates my show!' Or even between 'This is the kind of music we're making today' and 'Who's banging the radiator, I can't hear myself think!' Collapse the status gap between these two statements and you can start to have a real conversation.

3. Responsiveness

Definition in this context: Interaction based on both parties making an equal impact on each other

I personally don't believe in The Theatre. I don't believe in the proscenium arch, I don't believe in the stalls. I want to take a baseball bat and smash them all up – I'm not interested in them, I'd set fire to them.

Simon Casson, *Programme Notes*

In trying to pin down what might be a relationship between an artist and a community, I'm reminded of an exercise of Boal's. I use it a lot and have referenced it in other books; it can serve as an analogy for this relationship. The exercise is called Pushing. It's about the simple physical business of one person pushing against another. You don't even have to stand; you can do this in a wheelchair. You don't even have to do it physically, it can be done vocally. I imagine it can be done telepathically but I've never tried it.

'Pushing' involves one party pushing against the other, hands on hands, with only as much force as will 'help him (i.e. the other player) to apply all his strength'.[31] Each player is therefore adapting to the other, moderating physical strength and energy to ensure a play mode rather than a fight mode of interaction. Boal writes:

> This is a very important exercise, above all because it shows physically what the actor's maieutic action should be during a Forum Theatre session. The exercise is about using all one's strength and still not win![32]

The exercise works as a metaphor for a dynamic relationship, one constantly in flux. It's not about the artist imposing on the community by way of cultural enforcement. Or indeed vice versa, in which the artist simply delivers back to the community what the community wants to hear. It's about a mutual exchange. The artist facilitates the community and – crucially – vice versa. So what happens in Pushing when one player is physically stronger than another, when one is a dominant force? Or one has particular expertise in games such as this one? The answer is not unlike what happens down the road from me on a Sunday morning. A group of adults take on a group of five- to seven-year-olds at football; they could easily win and sometimes they do, but generally they don't. They become facilitators in the role as opposition, using enough resistance to prompt the kids to extend their skills against this superior force. That's the responsibility of strength. For the artist therefore it's not about cowing the community with a dazzling display of pyrotechnics, fireworks or acrobatics (inviting admiration) – it's about prompting the community to exercise its own capacity for creativity.

But to create real-world blueprints for such a model of responsiveness – between theatre artists and communities – is something of a design challenge. There are models available in the mainstream, but 'what mainstream theatre doesn't offer is any way to think about how you design and create for any audience who has agency and is active – it's a completely different discipline', explains Matt Adams of Blast Theory.[33] It's not enough just to throw audiences and actors at each other or encourage Q&A across the footlights. For 'once you enable someone to interact, how do you allow them to have an intellectually and emotionally rich and subtle experience? You need to know what you're supposed to be doing', argues Adams.[34]

It's the laying waste of our folk culture over previous centuries that has led to our current cultural poverty. In the period following the Middle Ages, what did exist by way of carnival and folk enactment was driven out by the twin forces of Christianity and Victorianism. So what might have been available to create a twenty-first-century participative folk culture was legislated out of existence:

> In the long-term history from the 17th to the 20th century, there were literally thousands of acts of legislation introduced which attempted to eliminate carnival and popular festivity from European life. Everywhere, against the periodic revival of local festivity and occasional reversals, a fundamental ritual order of western culture came under attack – its feasting, violence, processions, fairs, wakes, rowdy spectacle and outrageous clamour were subject to surveillance and repressive control.[35]

This sanitizing, authoritarian culture coerced people away from rowdy, ill-disciplined, pagan-influenced rituals and towards passive enjoyment of 'the spectacle for its own sake'. We left behind notions of 'people sharing together' and adopted instead entertainments that 'people made a journey to witness'. The village festival was replaced by the V Festival, the Guild by the glitterball. As for theatre-going, this became associated with gaining access to a higher culture rather than sharing an inebriated frolic in which authority was lampooned. And what replaced this 'popular festivity'? The promotion of cinema, ticketed theatre, television and the rise and rise of mass entertainment – a more consumer-oriented culture under the control of a middle class.

However, despite this decimation of our folk legacy, Adams argues that new blueprints of responsiveness are now ready to be unrolled:

> I think we're in the middle of a revolution now in terms of how art and culture is created. We're transitioning away from an industrial model – large entities mass-producing something to be consumed by a mass of people. We're now moving into an era where participation and interaction is back again central in culture as it was in the previous few millennia.[36]

This argument is underpinned by the wide range of recent micro-projects such as B Arts' Baking Bread project, which 'brought a diverse group of aspiring bakers from a range of cultural backgrounds (Botswanan, Zimbabwean, Afghan, English, Polish, Iraqi and Slovakian Roma) to share skills, recipes and experiences around baking, and to put these skills into action by catering at public events'.[37] There is also Ladder to the Moon's work with people in care, Green Candle's intergenerational work and the work of many others, only a small proportion of which are captured in the nets of this book.

Of these many micro-projects, what is always the more challenging to nurture is the kind of responsive, interactive event in which local concerns rise to the surface and become the subject matter of performance. There is immediacy in the social and political content, in other words. Prickly, awkward and potentially transformative, this is a kind of cultural alchemy less understood.

Phelim McDermott of Improbable argues that what is required should borrow from the model of conversation:

> A real conversation can change the world and as we know, the conversations that started in coffee houses led to revolutions. It could be a difficult conversation. It might be a conversation which will involve you feeling vulnerable. It might be challenging because you don't know what the outcome will be. It might involve saying something that isn't easy to say. It might involve hearing something that isn't easy to hear.[38]

Such a conversation would prompt questioning of values on both sides. It would rest on a notion of partnership yet not shirk from the problematic, contentious issues. There's no value in painting pretty fields with sheep chewing grass when the actual landscape is full of drug needles in alleyways. Such a conversation, as McDermott points out, draws from vulnerability.

It requires a certain willingness to be confessional without dissolving into blame attribution. Yet all this needs to happen within an aesthetic frame, otherwise it's pure politics. To take a simple, perhaps even simplistic, example, there might be a blueprint such as this:

- One, the audience gives its attention to the performers.
- Two, the performers engage the audience in the language of performance, creating an imagined world.
- Three, the spectators enter the world of performance.
- Four, conversation takes place within this world, allowing confession, storytelling or revelation on current concerns.
- Dramatic action flows from this sharing.
- Five, action takes place within the world outside.

The first two of these stages represent the orthodoxy. This model is found across the world from Shaftesbury Avenue to Ealing Broadway. And in the civic square also. The third and fourth stages are the less orthodox, more 'disobedient' enactments. But in models explored by Fluxx, Cardboard Citizens (Forum Theatre) and Coney, this is where experimentation is being carried out. Other companies too are setting down markers. Chris Goode's work in inviting all-comers to attend and perhaps join in devising rehearsals should be cited (Open House at West Yorkshire Playhouse 2011); much of Oreet Ashery's work – discussed elsewhere – is relevant and so is that of Nic Green.

In starting to make a list of experimental artists, I'm rapidly becoming aware of just how inadequate any such list is going to be. So let's return to the idea of the conversation and, in particular, what might be the implications of adopting such a model. What Chris Goode suggests in his book, *The Forest and The Field*, is the importance of an emphasis on same-status relations and on a vernacular within the performance work itself that is not so strange it alienates audiences.

> Most often these days, particularly if I'm performing in a show, it starts with a kind of direct address … it starts with me saying 'Hello. Thank you for being here. My name's Chris'… For me, 'hello' is simply how we begin a conversation on the 'outside', and to use it as a marker for starting (or, some might think, for being about to start) is partly a sign of wanting to show how the social patterns of our everyday interactions need not be suspended within the 'special' domain of theatre.[39]

This may appear banal or self-evident, yet it is remarkable how powerful such modesty can be as a means to connect with an audience. Audiences need to trust the relationship if they are to enter actively into this arrangement.

Yet where should such conversations take place? Can they happen within our current architectural legacy? Most theatre buildings tend to confine audiences to passivity within a fixed seating arrangement. Yet our model calls for spectators to be influential, active, vocal and responsive. They need to be able to move from their seats. Topher Campbell, director of the Red Room, said at a Theatre 2016 Conference that the people he had worked with felt theatre buildings and institutions 'need to be revised, revamped or taken down'.[40] Jake Orr, director of A Younger Theatre, goes further, making the crucial point that current architecture combines with still-present archaic routines to actually hold back the audience:

> Nowadays young people have a problem in stepping over the threshold of the theatre and following the rules of the theatre: buying a ticket, sitting quietly, not responding ... The rules of theatre are very laid out and we're looking for a way to break those rules. There's an appetite for something different, making work that is about the active involvement of the audience, whether that's setting up the scenario or being able to alter the situation. It's really about giving control over to the audience.[41]

The implication is clear: if same-status, active relationships are to be triggered, then many existing theatres need to come down, be adapted or just avoided altogether. Jake Orr's arguments on behalf of younger audiences is also supported by scholars: 'Theatre architecture not only forms and manipulates audiences' perspectives on events but also upholds social hierarchies and ideologically laden visions of the world.'[42] The point is crucial: new models based on equality and activism will inevitably be compromised if the architecture is simultaneously projecting the merits of social hierarchy.

Perhaps the first step is wider consultation – with the community, with theatre makers and with community workers – when a theatre building is designed. Such consultation needs to be an integral part of the process. But this often doesn't happen; when Rideout consulted prisoners over prison architecture issues, the response was amazement – surely architecture is a discipline with its own gold standard? One that is ruled entirely by architects? However, there are exceptions: Battersea Arts Centre's partnership with architects Haworth Tompkins has involved consultation at all stages. Such collaboration inevitably leads to better understanding of what exactly a responsive theatre model requires, just as the architect Will Alsop came to understand schooling when he was commissioned to design school buildings for Southwark Council in 2011:

> When it opened recently, some parents wept with amazed gratitude. As for the students, they queued to use the lavatories because, having been

asked by the architects what they wanted most in their new school, they demanded 'beautiful loos', according to the head teacher, Karen Fowler.[43]

So besides new architecture and new toilets, what else is necessary? Here are some pointers culled from personal experience:

- Audiences vary tremendously. A younger audience familiar with theatre practice will be more self-motivated than an elderly audience or one unfamiliar with active performance modes.
- If the model can't progress without audience input, it's always going to carry some vulnerability. Yet audiences in this model will have more power.
- The more the spirit of game-ness pervades the exercise, the easier audiences will find it to engage.
- Because our cultural context is one in which the audience expects to be passive, to become proactive the spectator needs to find the volition to do so.

The point about the Pushing exercise, mentioned above, is that it takes a mode of combativeness to make it playful. It's not about people being nice to each other within some anodyne stereotype of community theatre reassurance. In the Pushing exercise, each player has to 'listen' and 'feel' what's happening for the other person, and only then calibrate what degree of energy or force is appropriate. Once calibrated, the energy can become explosive. The listening comes prior to the responding. When the exercise works well, its dynamic is robust, energetic and powerful. Cannot this principle of a dynamic responsiveness be on the table when theatres are imagined and designed?

4. Immediacy

Definition in this context: Action that emerges unplanned and unanticipated within a given aesthetic field

Theatre companies over the world boast that liveness and immediacy are their trump cards. Going to the theatre can't be beaten, their slogans read. But more often than not the message is propaganda. The construct of the drama, the immutable text and the constraining architecture box in the actors so that 'liveness' is achieved only in a very limited sense. The impression of immediacy is fashioned in rehearsal and replicated onstage. The moves are blocked, the intonations practised; there is a compact between the actors that the show will be presented just this way. After all, the critics are coming.

There is the familiar argument, offered by Erika Fischer-Lichte and Peter Brook among others, that structures set up in rehearsal are activated by the spectator in performance so no performance is ever the same – which is undeniably true. However, the repetition of the same lines and moves every night inevitably takes its toll, diminishing the performer's degree of engagement. Actors who are in the same play over a long period will tend to fix their performances unless consciously encouraged not to do so by the director. Mike Alfreds has written about how 'a long-running production, un-nurtured, can easily become a slick and empty display. Actors, having a deep instinct for survival, rapidly develop an effective muscle memory that can easily take over without their even realising they've gone onto auto-pilot.'[44]

The efforts expended in the illusion of immediacy extend beyond the actors' lines and moves. There is a tradition here that embraces productions from the small-scale to the large. In 2005 the RSC went to the lengths of engaging 200 extras to heighten the illusion that the show was really happening in Roman times before our eyes; 'yet the effect of such a crowd onstage was to serve as a reminder that however many extras there are, and however authentically stereotyped the postures and the get-up, they can never be enough to turn the theatrical fiction into something other than a theatrical fiction', the scholar Joe Kelleher observed.[45] The tradition is a fragile one, too. When Carey Mulligan performed in *Skylight* on Broadway in 2015 she had to cook spaghetti bolognese from scratch – onstage. The show usually went well and the audience were impressed by the veracity of the action. However, one night the cooker didn't work. As a result, she had to pretend to cook – only with dried pasta and raw meat – then serve it up as a cooked meal. It is in such moments that the veil of 'immediacy' is torn away.

Similarly deceptions are practised on the small scale where so-called 'immersive' shows can be as closed as an RSC or Broadway production. The illusion of immediacy is often profound, to be sure – until, that is, the conceit is unmasked:

> There is a scene in Punchdrunk's *Sleep No More* when the mad Lady Macbeth takes a bath to try and wash Duncan's blood from her hands. After the bath she stands up in the tub and raises her arms towards the audience gathered around her, inviting them to pass her a robe. One evening a few weeks ago, an audience member didn't understand the cue. When Lady M rose from the bath naked, wet and shivering, and stretched out her arms, the audience member, confused, returned the

gesture and moved to embrace her. The performer playing Lady M broke character, screamed and a group of black-masked crew materialized to escort the spectator from the show.[46]

Audiences have responded positively to the work of Punchdrunk and other companies who transform spaces to imaginative effect. Yet as this account indicates, the frisson of excitement generated by running between rooms belies the conventional dramaturgy underneath. It is true there are directors such as Phelim McDermott and Mike Alfreds who give freedom to actors to move spontaneously and be altered by audience reaction – and McDermott's directorial innovations are rightly lauded for this – but in most mainstream work what is fixed is far more embedded than what is free.

To truly explore immediacy, the improvisatory element is required to go beyond shifts of movement and intonation. For actual immediacy carries the mark of uncontrollability. It's closer to vagrant behaviour on the street. It's unpredictable, foolish and contrary. Its essence is spontaneity, a response to the moment – whatever that moment comprises. It's awkward, casual, often unfulfilled. Immediacy is the active component of a theatre that values shared vulnerability and a proposed dissolution of some absolute distinctions: between me and you, us and them, private and public, actor and spectator. A live, immediate connection fully realized between actor and spectator means not only the avoidance of prepared moves but an exploration of the impact of both sides on each other. To make this step, however, means leaving behind much of theatre's prevailing orthodoxy.

The practice of theatrical immediacy has provenance; it was seized on by artists in the USA during the 1960s and 1970s as part of a lexicon of protest. These artists collided event and art, smashing them together like molecules in the Hadron Collider. It was art, yes, but it was also life. It was sometimes even allowed to appear pointless. But there was political purpose under the surface. As Allan Kaprow wrote, these 'Happenings … invite us for a moment to cast aside these proper manners and participate in the real nature of art and (one hopes) life – [we] grow a little in such circumstances.'[47]

Such events refused traditional spectatorship. In smashing everything up Dada-style, it was hoped a force would emerge from the debris to surprise everyone. It would be a force to contribute to the swirling political currents of freedom: 'In this way theatre broke free of the auditorium, art tore itself from the gallery and the museum. Even audiences were transformed, no longer limited to those who knew they were an audience', as Andy Field described it.[48] The spirit of such activity emboldened not just artists but political activists, those with an expressed interest in unsettling the status quo – and this was very much the purpose. The stunts of Jerry Rubin anticipated Pussy Riot and the Clown Army by decades with adventures like this trip to the New York Stock Exchange:

> The Stock Exchange official looks worried. He says to us, 'You can't see the Stock Exchange.' We're aghast. 'Why not?' we ask. 'Because you're hippies and you've come to demonstrate.' 'Hippies?' Abbie [Hoffman] shouted, outraged at the very suggestion. 'We're Jews and we've come to see the stock market.' We've thrown the official a karate punch. He relents. The Stock Market comes to a complete standstill at our entrance at the top of the balcony. The thousands of brokers stop playing Monopoly and applaud us. What a crazy sight for them – longhaired hippies staring down at them. We throw dollar bills over the ledge. Floating currency fills the air. Like wild animals, the stockbrokers climb all over each other to grab the money. 'This is what it's all about – real live money!!! Real dollar bills! People are starving in Biafra!' we shout. The cops grab us and throw us off the ledge and into the elevators. The stockbrokers below loudly boo the pigs.[49]

Artists who are politically driven today find it more difficult to operate in this carefree, Hoffman-ish way. Careful subterfuge is increasingly necessary. Training and preparation are necessary – paradoxically – to ensure immediacy. The contemporary 'happening' is sometimes a far more discreet affair. It carries a more calibrated and sophisticated ethic of performance. Oreet Ashery's work, for example, is crucially informed by her awareness of how social and ideological oppressions have impacted on her and her colleagues. Ashery told me how back in Israel she'd taken considerable risk at one time to join a large congregation of Jewish orthodox men in order to dance with them. She'd aimed to mingle. 'I wasn't supposed to be there. It was at my own risk. If I had been spotted, it would have been serious.'[50] In a later project she took the idea further: she dressed as a Jewish elder and invited visitors to sit and talk with her in a hotel room or the curator's bedroom: 'I was myself, but in costume. It was a simulacrum. The closest most people can get to meeting someone like this.'[51] In portraying this Jewish elder, she noted how the exercise became confessional: 'People made confessions to me – about Judaism. They wanted to touch various parts of me.'[52] Ashery also provided a camera so visitors could take pictures of them together but with the spectator 'doing something they weren't supposed to do'.[53] The work allowed visitors to vent at the mask, to be angry, transgressive and disobedient. They used the permission granted by the artist to hit back at an oppressive culture, employing an anger doubtless held back over years.

Wafaa Bilal's project *Domestic Tension* took a similar idea into a more dangerous iteration. Again, audiences were invited to reveal themselves through their actions – a crucial litmus test for immediacy. Bilal, an Iraqi-American artist, created a space for the disobedient, transgressive energies of the spectators to be directed back at him. His childhood had coincided with Saddam's rise to power. He had fled to the USA to establish himself as an artist, but when his brother was killed in Iraq during an American bombing mission, he realized he 'had to produce work to address this chasm between the comfort [his present world] and conflict zones [where his brother died], both to examine the duality in which I (Bilal) exist and to push the limits of understanding of those ensconced purely in the comfort zone'.[54] So he set himself up in a gallery and allowed himself to be shot at. As a professor within the School of the Arts Institute of Chicago, he had access to a range of technological expertise and settled on a paintball gun driven by open-source technology. He built a machine that allowed viewers connected through the internet to attack him remotely. 'I had been aware for some time of the ways in which the U.S. military uses video games to recruit youth and glorify war, and that was deeply disturbing to me'.[55] The aim was to call the sting into the open, to bring prejudice into the art space. And to explore its impact on him within an aesthetic sphere.

Bilal stayed in the space, a target, for a month, hardly ever leaving it. For long periods, the gun, control of which was fought for by anonymous individuals throughout America, fired almost non-stop. 'The cesspool of yellow paint disgusts me, but it is impossible to clean it up with new shots being fired so rapidly'.[56] The word spread rapidly through the shoot-em-up communities of the USA. As Bilal wrote after three weeks of being fired at:

> I'm increasingly concerned about the health problems I've developed. Insomnia, nightmares, paranoia and other post-traumatic stress symptoms; shortness of breath, chest and abdominal pain, strange freckles on my skin, rashes from the fish oil, exhaustion. When I face the video camera my eyes are watery and swollen, and I jerk spasmodically as I speak.[57]

Then something happened. There was a crack in the wall of hate. An Art Institute graduate developed a strategy to defend Bilal by constantly clicking the gun left – away from him – and organized others to join her. A defence posse had suddenly formed, unprompted. Bilal came to see this as 'a form of cyber-political resistance'.[58] Finally the month came to an end. As it did so, 'I count 39 people continuously turning the gun left, protecting me. They're battling about 200 more who want to shoot me though, causing the gun to jerk spastically back and forth. "Hope is alive!" I proclaim melodramatically'.[59]

The savage yearning of so many male Americans to use the internet to channel their aggressive views had found in Bilal a 'real' target. They were seemingly unconcerned they could be identified via their IP addresses. They simply took the opportunity to fire at the stranger with a dark skin and a beard. But they didn't get it all their own way; the emergence of an online counter-army was an unanticipated and very positive outcome. It was a consequence that could only come about by Bilal leaving the door open to a multitude of possible outcomes. In this way the artist, in making himself vulnerable, drew into the open not simply hostility but also comradeliness, a progressive force that took a stand against the aggression displayed.

By refusing to manipulate the audience response, unanticipated outcomes become possible. The audience takes the initiative. And through taking it, a greater sense of 'ownership' of the project is achieved.

But the element of risk is evident. The artist is putting himself or herself at the mercy of strangers. Perhaps there's no more tantalizing expression of this kind of artistic risk than two projects by Yoko Ono and Marina Abramovic respectively. In the first, Ono's *Cut Piece* (1964), she invited spectators to use the pair of scissors to cut away her clothing, as much or as little as they liked. The action of cutting away therefore makes the cutter complicit in the revelation of the female body that has been the object of so much art history.

In her project *Rhythm 0*, Abramovic stands for six hours at a table which has seventy-two objects on it. These are available to any spectator to use against her. They include a loaded gun.

> It began tamely. Someone turned her around. Someone thrust her arms into the air. Someone touched her somewhat intimately. The Neapolitan night began to heat up. In the third hour all her clothes were cut from her with razor blades. In the fourth hour the same blades began to explore her skin. Her throat was slashed so someone could suck her blood. Various minor sexual assaults were carried out on her body. She was so committed to the piece that she would not have resisted rape or murder. Faced with her abdication of will, with its implied collapse of human psychology, a protective group began to define itself in the audience. When a loaded gun was thrust to Marina's head and her own finger was being worked around the trigger, a fight broke out between the audience factions.[60]

Again, as in the Bilal piece, we see a group of spectators band together to protect the artist. Again, as in the Bilal piece, such an outcome was not foreseen. Yet arguably it is the one outcome that emerges precisely because of trust expressed by the artist in the audience. Abramovic said afterwards that she'd learned that the audience 'can kill you'. Yet she also learned that they can choose not to. They can even act to defend you.

5. Un-timing

Definition in this context: Breaking down conventions around how time is organized

If a disobedient theatre values experimentation, then how it locates itself in time must be also subject to examination. We know that theatre conflates time, jumps time, extends time and compresses time. It's a characteristic of the genre. Yet most of this activity takes place in a precisely organized time slot between Curtain Up and Curtain Down. This is ENTERTAINMENT and it fits right in when you're tired from the working day. Work done, kick back, here's your reward.

In previous days, prior to the sixteenth century particularly, these time frames would have appeared unnecessarily schematic – for in the Middle Ages, time itself flowed differently. 'Rural time was always vague', argues the historian Emmanuel Le Roy Ladurie.[61] There was back-breaking work, of course, which framed social interaction, but 'the working day was punctuated with long irregular pauses' involving spontaneous conversations, drinking, eating or idleness.[62] The calendar was ordered by the seasons and the light of the sun. Work patterns were dictated by necessity rather than contract.

There was less pressure to be at a certain place at a certain time for a certain event. Minstrels would roll through the town and spectators would choose their own relationship to them, turning up or not. The *pantomimi*, for example,

> in little companies of two or three, padded the hoof along the roads, travelling from gathering to gathering making their own welcome in castle or tavern, or, if need were, sleeping on some grange or beneath a wayside hedge in the white moonlight. They were, in fact, absorbed into that vast body of nomad entertainers on whom so much of the gaiety of the Middle Ages depended.[63]

Such itinerancy was complemented by the equally anti-Christian traditions of localized folk events within villages that honoured the passing of the seasons or the promotion of fertility.

But when industrialization became the driving force of social and economic change across Europe, everything changed. New contractual relationships were introduced in which work, time and recreation came to be scheduled into certain time slots. There started to be something called 'the working day'. Uprooted from a culture that allowed some control over work patterns, workers were compelled to leave the country for the city to set up entirely new ways of organizing time. For 'the factory system demands a transformation of human nature, the "working paroxysms" of the artisan or outworker must be methodized until the main is adapted to the discipline of the machine'.[64] So wrote E. P. Thompson, who for good measure quoted D. H. Lawrence: 'They believe that they must alter themselves to fit the pits and the place, rather than alter the pits and the place to fit themselves. It is easier'.[65]

But several hundred years later, artists are correcting the balance again. Their argument is that performance should encourage a different sensibility wherein the pits and the place are adapted precisely to suit the people. So a claim is rightly being made for a reordering of performance time. Current artistic developments therefore give us durational performances or time-based art that open out into many different configurations of time-orderedness. To defend such re-gearing the philosopher Henri Bergson is cited, for whom 'the deterministic scientific conception of time, of which "clock time" is an exemplary form, does not reflect and can only distort what he perceived as the inner experience of time'.[66] The importance of this is that within this contemplative experience, the spectator can attribute value as he or she wishes, to whatever he or she wishes – an opportunity denied by the kind of theatre event that coerces or manipulates the spectator into attributing value as the event organizers wish. One tactic within the re-gearing exercise is to use surprise – for example, catching people unawares and putting them into the role of spectators when they aren't expecting it. The activist L. M. Bogad argues it thus:

> Surprise is important at a tactical level. Surprise is also important for cultural work because it is the opposite of cliché. Cliché dulls the senses and bores the mind. Surprise activates us. Our synaptic network is momentarily disrupted when we are truly surprised, as our brain scrambles to figure out what is going on. This is not a sinister experience; it is a moment of openness and freshness, in which new perspectives, response and reflections are possible.[67]

While the absence of a continuing folk tradition within the UK has already been commented on, nevertheless there are vestiges of village folk traditions still remaining, linked to the promotion of fertility or the celebration of local identity, which treat the notion of time very differently. They offer anti-orthodox models of communion and festivity that can be learned from. Communal events such as the Padstow 'Obby 'Oss, the Atherstone Ball Game and the Haxey Hood usually last all day and attract hundreds, who enter and leave the event at will. This is how the Haxey Hood runs. Having begun at sunset:

> On Plough Monday itself, the Lord and the Boggins make one more

round of the village pubs, settling down in one of them to paint the
Fool's face, mostly in black and red. They then process towards the
church but on the way the Fool tries to escape but is caught and carried
back, shoulder high by the other Boggins, and is placed on the mounting
stone; from this vantage point he makes a speech of welcome but the
Boggins light a fire of straw to 'smoke' him.[68]

The crowd then follows the Fool up to Haxey Hill where the game takes
place, up to 300 or so competing for possession of the leather hood. In the
'sway' it does almost feel that time stands still, so intense is the packing of
human bodies. The game is only concluded when one of the teams manages
to defeat the sway sufficiently to bring the coveted prize to that team's pub.
The Atherstone Ball Game is a similar disrespecter of spatial and temporal
boundaries. It roams right through the town from early light. There's a
delirium that takes over, becoming more intense the closer you are to the
centre of the pack. Ambulances stand by in the side streets. The police
generally stay away. Anyone and everyone can play; several hundred attend.
The person who is holding the giant ball at the end of the day is the winner.

Such events were in their heyday consciously defiant, and still are. As
nineteenth-century records show, they were 'firmly in the hands of the lower
or working classes of the area', as the historian Steve Roud writes, 'with active
opposition coming from the middle and upper-class residents'.[69] Even the
game of football 'could provide an excuse for assembling and a cover for
violence'. For example, 'in 1740, "a Mash of Futtball was Cried at Ketring
of five Hundred Men of a side, but the design was to Pull Down Lady Beey
Jesmaines' Mills"', writes Barbara Ehrenreich.[70] Such activities operated on a
spectrum; partly they were about protest, and partly they were a chance for
communal intoxication. One way or another, they always smashed the clock
in the interests of a party.

As for contemporary initiatives to rekindle the time-free carnival spirit,
Welfare State International, perhaps more than any other company, managed
to draw from and reignite the folk tradition in the UK. They picked up and
reinvigorated the celebratory pageant, not simply in terms of form – carnival,
procession and spectacle – but in social purpose. For as John Fox said to me,
their performances always represented 'both an allegory and a celebration'.[71]
It was in the allegorical dimension in which the politics were carried, as in
their anti-Thatcher piece, *The Raising of the Titanic*. Their events carried the
joy of subversion while at the same time engaging thousands of local people
in activities that clearly turned a nose up to time-orderedness, as is evident
from this description of an event in Barrow, so clearly evocative of events
like the Haxey Hood:

In the event, the tribal performers had a kind of surreal, non-specific nursery-rhyme quality, with faces and costumes in very unrealistic primary colour. At 11.45, pubs mustered for the admirals' wheelbarrow race up Hoad Hill to raise funds for a heart defibrillator for Ulverston Health Centre in which very fat men had to be wheeled uphill as fast as possible. At the stroke of twelve and a half bells, the whole cavalcade of eventually five thousand people, led by the mayor ... all assembled in a mass picnic on the crown of the hill at the feet of the monument.[72]

Such collapse of temporal frames in the durational event provokes a shift of emphasis from a more consumerist viewpoint – 'I've bought this show and I'm going to enjoy it' – to a more open or ambiguous one – 'This event is happening and it's up to me to define my relationship to it'. The spectator's attention is held not because of expectation – 'The show runs two hours, apparently' – but by what catches attention. By such means as these, the clawing embrace of consumerism with its attendant sets of relations is (partly) thrown off.

> This should be a theatre of World Spirit. Where the spirit can be shown to be the most competent force in the world. Force. Spirit. Feeling. The language will be anybody's, but tightened by the poet's backbone.[73]

And as the durational performance event rolls on into the night, we're invited to ignore our usual civic, social responsibilities. There's neither Curtain Up nor Curtain Down. The sense of 'time passing' in any orthodox way becomes eroded. The improviser Jonathan Kay argues that this is a central and special responsibility of performance work – to 'stop time', as it were, and to open up a perception and experience of this inner space:

> There's the inner world and the outer world. The theatre is an inner world. The audience attain permission by means of their ticket, to look at the inner world. The inner world is nothing like how it's preached about by people in the outer world. The outer world has time and the inner world has no time at all. None of our thoughts and feelings and history have any time in them.[74]

Kay's view links with that of Henri Bergson, referenced earlier: 'Pure duration is the form taken by the succession of our inner states of consciousness when our self lets itself live.'[75] It's possible therefore to see durational work not only as an act of defiance against over-routinization, but also the promotion of a bid to understand better the inner, psychic realm that the 'outer world' so refuses to acknowledge.

> There are things known and there are things unknown, and in between
> are the doors of perception.
>
> Aldous Huxley

Such durational work, it is hoped therefore, changes the spectator, but
also by default changes the performer. Marina Abramovic, champion of
durational practice, writes:

> I have had my share of long durational performances, and I know that
> when you are working in this way, psychological and physical change
> takes place. You are affected by duration: your perception and your
> reality become different.[76]

It's no less true in the world of long-form improvisation. After years and
years of short-form and then long-form developments, 'impro' has now
embraced very, very long form. In New York, Amsterdam, London and
Montreal, troupes perform unstopping over three days or more. Often no
one sleeps, neither performers nor spectators, who often bring camp beds.
Here too, there is a clear purpose to the psyche-altering of the performers
in order to inform the nature of the evolving drama. Dylan Emery wrote to
me of how this works:

> You become too tired to censor yourself. You stop worrying as much
> about getting onstage, whether you are being funny or not, whether
> what you say is appropriate or not, whether you should be there or not.
> Your inner judge gets very sleepy and drifts off, while your limbic system
> is still firing on all cylinders, so emotions run high, energy is released,
> and being silly seems fine. Giggling is common.[77]

But such projects run only a few days. The performer/artist Tehching Hsieh
ran his projects for a year or more at a time: 'While many were sprinting, he
did marathons'.[78] Between 1970 and 2000 Hsieh created a series of extraordinary artwork/performances. One of his year-long projects, *Time Clock
Piece*, operated, according to Adrian Heathfield, as 'a systematic critique of
the temporal logic upon which the social and cultural organisation of late-
capitalism is founded'.[79] Every hour for a year Hsieh punched a time clock,
the same time clock in the same room in the same building. 'He could not
stray far from his studio-loft, nor could he sleep continuously for more than
fifty or so minutes.'[80] Hsieh was simultaneously rebuking the clock world
for its inhumanity while using its rhythms to enter an altered state. While
Hsieh himself is relatively casual in talking about his experience, Adrian
Heathfield, his chronicler, is clear about the impact on his body and mind:

> This is a body, wracked by time, locked in a faltering flux: an agitated

spasm of differentiation. This is a body lacking temporal continuity and physical integrity, a body whose borders oscillate and twitch; yet a body whose still point, whose gaze in the ruins of visibility, holds its observer remorselessly in its grip.[81]

The same description could be applied to a shaman.

> To enter into contact with the spirits or to obtain guardian spirits, the aspirant (shaman) withdraws into solitude and subjects himself to a strict regime of self-torture.[82]

In the way it erases personality, such work anonymizes the doer. It prioritizes the ideas behind the work through an emphasis on repetition, personal discipline and attention-avoidance, existing as it does on the edges of public visibility. In another of Hsieh's projects, *I Shall Stay Outdoors for One Year, Never Go Inside*, he walked New York, without legal status, never going inside any building – except when the cops dragged him briefly, resisting, into a police station. He was the outsider, a status bestowed on him by his migrant status, acknowledged by Hsieh, and given substance within the project. The migrant, always travelling, never still. It's probably the case that such projects are more appreciated following their conclusion than during their enactment; but still, the reverberations exist to prompt reflections on this saintly self-discipline.

By contrast, every year on the second Friday in August in South Queensferry, Scotland, a local man is covered in burrs, small sticky growths plucked from a hedge, until there is no visible trace of his personal identity beyond his eyes. He goes on foot, 'encased as if he were in armour in his suit of close-sticking burrs, grasping staves adorned with flowers'.[83] He sets off on his rambling, irregular twenty-mile journey. He is periodically greeted with shouts and gifts of alcohol that he is compelled to drink through a straw. He continues in this way for the length of a day, without rest. It is thought locally that the figure represents a scapegoat, one who must be given up to be ruined, in order to appease the sea-gods and save the community.

Unlike Hsieh, who as outsider nominates himself to undergo a trial, here the figure is nominated by the community. Both are scapegoats, nomadic, peripatetic, on the edge of society, both seeking some reconciliation of outsid-erness – the Burryman representationally and Hsieh with a greater degree of actuality. Both to different degrees echo the role of medicine men who, in Joseph Campbell's view, 'are simply making both visible and public the systems of symbolic fantasy that are present in the psyche of every adult member of their society'.[84] Campbell argues further, quoting Geza Roheim: 'They fight the demons so that others can hunt the prey and in general fight reality'.[85]

The untying of performance from traditional routines of theatre-going allows artists to reframe the performance experience to serve new purposes. While not overtly activist, such durational work is clearly anti-capitalist and usefully repositions theatre in such a way that allows it to become more embedded within the life of the community, perhaps echoing the role that folk performance took in times past. Continued experimentation feels therefore not just desirable but essential. In the Argument Room in 2011 the Director Chris Goode proposed a 'rolling, 24-hour' theatre experience that would allow spectators to drop in at any time. It's a model of practice with considerable potential, holding out the notion that such a theatre might even replace the role of the Church:

> A fantasy for me for a long time has been a 24-hour rolling theatre, both a civic and a dissident space. One that you could walk into at any time. It would be about sitting in relation with something that is unfolding, and you could be with it for five minutes or all night, if you want. For the visitor it would be about going into a space where it's possible to do things that we don't value enough otherwise, like simply paying attention, which can have a therapeutic aspect to it. You're not seeing character driven stuff, instead you're seeing people meeting each other and figuring stuff out together. It would be interesting also, if you rocked up there on the way to the gym or coming back from work, to see how much you could shape what was happening there. In this way theatre can be part of a transition culture. Theatre is uniquely suited for this because we can model how else things might be. We can allow the audience to shape its own experience. But one thing this model wouldn't do is offer closure. So we're talking about something that never ends.[86]

3. Transmission

This section deals with issues of communication. How does the artist find a voice in the world, and from where does this voice come? From consensus, from dissent, or from out of the air?

for whom?

1. Voice

Definition in this context: Voice is as close as we can get to the unadulterated sense of truth that emerges as fiction

One characteristic of the resonant image, scene or motif within performance is the extent to which it is both new and yet somehow already known.

How – or indeed whether – the artist, playwright or theatre maker arrives at resonant material is often informed by the artist's attitude towards the creative process itself. Is there a sustained attempt to develop a uniqueness of approach or is the hope simply to replicate what is already admired? The latter approach, associated with making career a priority, may be the safer route. Hopefully, thinks the aspirant, there is still room on the dance floor where everyone is gathered. The former approach is much more challenging yet represents a more rewarding option if the artist aims for distinctiveness. Taking this route may mean having to withstand critical contempt or peer disregard along the way. It may mean building a whole new ballroom. In a visual arts context, those such as Lucien Freud and Gilbert and George respectively developed their own unique voices through positively disregarding the favoured moves of their contemporaries. The lesson should perhaps be noted by theatre makers. Certainly writers like Samuel Beckett and Arnold Wesker made similar decisions, arriving at their distinctiveness with such impact that they bred many imitators in their wakes.

Within a disobedient theatre model, the issue of voice-finding takes a further twist; this is because of the additional element of political conviction. To operate outside the mainstream cultural consensus makes the struggle for attention and critical approval only more problematic.

It appears that a process of individuation – coming into a sense of creative autonomy – starts paradoxically in copying. Arguably this is the case irrespective of politics. As Stephen Pinker has forcibly argued, no child comes into the world a blank slate; the creativity and encouragement of those in a parental role can only be influential. And it's evident that children copy adults while groping to achieve this autonomy. Likewise artists copy their heroes to discover their *own* voices. Tim Etchells of Forced Entertainment talked to me of watching Impact Theatre Co-operative in the 1980s: 'We thought, we want to do something a bit like that.'[1] For their part, Impact had been influenced by the People Show; the People Show's early work was influenced by the jazz of Chet Baker. In music, there are similar patterns: Bob Dylan's early songs are barely distinguishable from those of Woody Guthrie in terms of rhythm, tempo and tone. As Ken Robinson wrote of Dylan, 'By discovering the journey of Woody Guthrie, he began to imagine his own.'[2]

The writer Daniel Coyle offers a theory of how this process happens: through immersion in copying the artistic outputs of others, the novice begins to engage in 'deep practice'. Here, neurons are fired by signals that become wrapped over time in what is called myelin. 'The insulation that wraps these nerve fibres increases signal strength, speed and accuracy. The more we fire a particular circuit, the more myelin optimizes that circuit, and the stronger, faster and more fluent our movements and thoughts become.'[3] So the practice generates pathways along which thoughts or creative ideas can more easily travel. The banality of the aphorism 'practice makes perfect' holds good and is underscored by the now-familiar argument of Malcolm Gladwell that you need 10,000 hours of practice before you get mastery of craft, an argument that traditionally cites examples of the Beatles, Mozart and Roger Federer.

The moment of the artist's shift into an individual voice – or its splinter into several voices for a playwright – can appear like a radical departure in art form terms but it usually reflects the hard work that preceded it. It is therefore both an outcome of that former process as well as a consequence of it. The Rolling Stones performed exclusively R'n'B standards, which they grew to know extremely well until the moment when, as Richards alleges and Jagger disputes, they were locked in a room by their manager and told to write original material. Tim Crouch, when he started writing shows for himself, veered off in what seemed like an entirely new direction, using as 'lead characters' props donated by the audience. Yet this was anticipated in the private context of workshops he'd run for the National Theatre. Augusto Boal threw away his agitational playscript when challenged by his audience to be as flexible and responsive as his playscript indicated they should be. Yet Forum Theatre was a turn in the road already anticipated by Simultaneous Dramaturgy.

For many, then, copying, practice, experimentation and emulation leads to the discovery of an individual creative voice. But this is not to negate the role of expediency: there is simultaneously a pragmatic dimension. Why did Leonard Cohen start writing songs? In part because his novels weren't selling. Why did Keith Johnstone start Theatresports? Because he wanted to give more opportunities to so many actors keen to improvise in public. Even Boal's decision to allow a spectator onto the stage was a pragmatic response to a difficult audience member. It's rarely a 'moment of inspiration' that comes from nowhere. It's partly coming up against an obstacle that nudges or forces a practitioner to adapt, alter course and swerve off-road uncertain of the terrain. But will the new direction be sustained? When the answer is yes, it may be because the new direction is justified by a personal commitment to a political viewpoint.

In the later chapter on Resonance, the case is argued that 'starting at home' is one way to creatively release the resonant image or narrative. The same lesson often applies to finding your own voice. 'Talk about what you know' is the truistic, oft-cited advice. Yet this should not be taken to imply reportage or documentation. Instead it's about being informed, perhaps moved, by circumstances from early life, allowing these experiences to as it were 'take the controls'. Paradoxically, finding one's own voice is often accompanied by a release of control, almost by a kind of channelling. The artist as it were 'hands over authorship' of the material. Jez Butterworth alleges that 'I know from an absolute fact it [the material] doesn't come from you [the playwright]'.[4] David Hare goes further: 'Every line of dialogue, every exit and entry, every development of the story, every deliberate change of mood on the page pleases or displeases the author for reasons they would be at a loss to explain.'[5] Many artists and writers see this act of generating material – irrespective of political position – as 'finding ways to be spoken to'. It involves the writer 'getting themselves out of the way' in order to let through what needs to be heard – as if, perhaps, there are messages emanating from the unconscious, or the world beyond.

Despite Mike Kenny's success as a children's playwright and elevation into a middle-class world, he still recognizes how he is spoken to by 'the place I grew up, the people I grew up with. Ironically I thought, this place has no value, but into my 60s I still use those voices all the time.'[6] He talks of how distinct characters like his grandmother would surface in different plays, in different manifestations and quite without his prompting. Arthur Miller acknowledged similar roots specifically in respect of *Death of a Salesman*: 'The origin of the play was an uncle of mine, although he'd never recognize himself in this play.'[7]

How did voice-finding work for the playwright Andrea Dunbar? She wrote her first play *The Arbor* when she was just fifteen years old. Her story suggests a different kind of journey from those cited already. It's almost as

if the material spoke to her without any preceding immersion in the plays
or texts of others. The play 'was written in green biro in an exercise book. It
was an extraordinary piece of observation about life on a brutalised council
estate outside Bradford. I thought it was outstanding', said Max Stafford-
Clark, to whom the writing was sent.[8] In this interview, made some time
after Dunbar had passed away, Stafford-Clark continued:

> This was a voice I'd never heard in the theatre before and the youth of
> the writer and the fact that she was writing about own childhood on
> the fringes of Mrs Thatcher's Britain made it a particularly important
> voice.[9]

In interview, Dunbar had been, for someone who spoke through plays
more than speech, appropriately inarticulate. When asked, 'What gave you
the idea for this [her second play, *Rita, Sue and Bob Too*], was it what you
saw on the estate?' she answered: 'You see things happening on an estate. If
you live there, you see things.'[10] And, by implication, you hear things; you
listen. There had been no 10,000 hours, no guiding hero, no mentor. Just
the television and the estate. A maverick? Or simply a contrary spirit able
to channel what was going on in her immediate surroundings? Her story is
not dissimilar to that of the earlier playwright Shelagh Delaney, who sent her
script *A Taste of Honey* to Joan Littlewood. According to Kenneth Tynan, she
too brought 'real people on to her stage, joking and flaring and scuffling, and
eventually, out of the zest for life she gives them, surviving. She is nineteen
years old and a portent.'[11]

For Delaney, Dunbar, and doubtless others, it appears there's a different
kind of gestation. A jump straight into the art form, lifted by bravery and
talent, laced with naivety; the written play giving voice to the world in
which the writer finds herself, made possible by what musicians and writers
always come back to: the listening. The watching. The paying attention to
what's around you. Improvisers can't function without it: it's the sine qua
non in this practice where writing and performing are collapsed into one
function: 'If you are not listening to what the other person is saying you
are not going to build anything together', says Andy Smart, a Comedy Store
Players regular.[12]

This notion of 'hearing voices' was in early society associated with the
possession of special gifts. It was seen as an indication of a possible call to
shamanism. The individual was 'called' to a unique role within the group
which required being metaphorically 'torn apart' then 'reassembled' into a
new person, someone equipped to be the eyes and ears of the spirit world.
Something of that still persists in the personal experience of an individual
being 'called' to be a performer. This can feel a profound and dislocating

experience. The individual decides, 'I'm so shook up, I need to channel this, I need to perform.' Certainly my drama school had a reputation for 'breaking you down' and 'building you up again' in an image of an actor who had the capacity to feel things in a unique way. This feeling of being 'called' is also often associated with the lot of the outsider, the one who doesn't fit. Outsiders of this ilk often find themselves, as they grow up, using clowning and wit to find accommodation with others. So it is that a so-called 'gift' is developed which is all about verbal articulacy and quickness of mind. In earlier cultures an equivalent might be the facility for what is called 'speaking in tongues'. Stand-up comics likewise talk of being steered by the audience in ways they don't understand.

When it comes to achieving a uniqueness of voice, therefore, nothing here is straightforward. While copying, experimenting and the hard graft all seem essential, it's observable also that some artists are able to jump these hurdles. Such outsiders appear to make their own luck. They are driven, it appears, by the necessity to challenge authority and defy convention simply as survival tactics, so horrified are they by the way the world is organized.

2. Contrariness

Definition in this context: Inverting what is held to be true in order to expose the possible falseness of a so-called truth

These are the artists and writers who have contrariness coursing in the blood from an early age. For them there's no clear evidence of following in anyone else's footsteps. Disobedience comes naturally. Quentin Crisp begins his autobiography thus:

> From the dawn of my history I was so disfigured by the characteristics of a certain kind of homosexual person that, when I grew up, I realized I could not ignore my predicament.[13]

He set about reversing society's expectations from the get-go. It was the only way to save himself from the repressive and stereotypical orthodoxies that clustered every street of his world. Each of these banal conformities he disobediently reversed in order to survive. It was his contrariness that saved him. Crisp and those like him are strong-headed individuals who trust their instincts and resist easy absorption into the cultural milieu. They are probably our saviours. They are certainly our role models. Another is Alfred Jarry, who wrote *Les Polonais* when he was fifteen years old. His *succès de scandale*, *Ubu Roi*, presented when he was still only twenty-three, was largely *Les Polonais* rewritten. Keith Johnstone is cut from the same cloth:

> He observed the world in a different way, figuratively and literally, and right around the age of nine, he adopted a contrarian attitude to everything: 'I decided never to believe anything because it was convenient. I began reversing every statement to see if the opposite was also true.'[14]

This approach of Crisp and Johnstone is very much in the spirit of a disobedient theatre, questioning authority through impish play. It's about saying, let's not accept what feels false. Let's resist what may be simply manipulation. OK, some great truths are being presented to us as evident morality, but do they really stand up? If we examine them closely, it may be their proposers emerge from the examination with their pants down.

This approach echoes the stance of the fool in literature where the fool is a function, not a character. Inasmuch as he is within society, he is, like Crisp, an outsider, asking impolite questions. The writer Tim Prentki quotes Jan Kott in his book *The Fool in European Theatre* to nail this function, arguing that the fool is one who 'while moving in high society, is not part of it, and tells unpleasant things to everybody in it, who disputes everything regarded as evident. He would not be able to do all this, if he were part of that society himself.'[15] And the primary function of the fool, therefore, is to be locating the drawstrings of pants.

To be a foolish outsider, however, doesn't mean fearing the open road. Quentin Crisp himself, after being arraigned on the street by bullies for his make-up, his dress and his deportment, was known, after he had been assaulted, to thank those who had assaulted him – as a result of which the bullies roared with laughter. Touché.

Prentki tracks the evolution of the theatrical fool in literature from the Bible to early Greek theatre through carnival, on to Shakespeare and up to the present day, as a barometer of how our society is moving. He notes the key shifts as social progress advances and the fool begins to be shunted further and further offstage. The fool function, then, has no obvious place in a 'well-regulated' society – except possibly in a psychiatric ward. In *King Lear*, once the king ceases to be king and goes mad, the fool disappears entirely from the text. Such a moment might be seen almost as an indicator of the fool's departure from English literature itself, banished as it were by the new literalness. But this is very much fool as idea. Contrarians in life are inevitably more compromised and complex.

By the time he was invited to be William Gaskill's assistant at the Royal Court Theatre Writers Group and Actors Studio in 1958, Johnstone had evolved something of a methodology to support the spirit of his contrarian philosophy. His first move, as Irving Wardle described it,

> was to banish aimless discussion and transform the meetings to enactment sessions; it was what happened that mattered, not what anybody said about it. Keith started to teach his own particular style of improvisation, much of it based on fairy stories, word associations, free associations, intuitive responses.[16]

I'd heard about Johnstone's work and was led via his book *Impro* to a week's workshop with him in Dorset. Also present were Jonathan Kay, Phelim McDermott and others. Like them I was beguiled by the adoption of reverse-engineering to arrive at truthfulness, emerging through theatre games but resonant of life. Johnstone did this by 'teaching the skills that my teachers had ignored. I encourage negative people to be positive, and clever people to be obvious, and anxious people not to do their best.'[17] And all done through an appreciation of the value of laughter. Johnstone was the great popularizer of theatre games. But did his contrarian approach mean that he was without principle? Is all his approach simply about being mischievous? Not at all. Johnstone became quite annoyed when he discovered what happened to Theatresports as it travelled around the world. He resented the fact that his game/sports format had become over-commercialized and over-competitive. In becoming accommodated within mainstream culture, he felt its original spirit had been lost. He regretted not having set out clearer rules in his book *Impro*. It's clear, then; his foolishness has a principled fence around it.

Dario Fo is another contrarian who makes clear the principled nature of foolishness, but additionally argues its political function:

> I'm interested in discovering the basic contradictions in a situation through the use of paradox, absurdity and inversion. This enables me to transform one reality into another reality, not as a trick, but so people will understand that reality is not flat, but full of contradictions and reversals, and that often absurdity is a reality that is closer to the truth than those things which seem to be sacred and absolute, but are almost always false.[18]

Johnstone teaches and writes about the attitude required for foolish, disobedient play, one that reduces self-censorship and welcomes this Fo-ian absurdity. He teaches about taking delight in the contradictions of the world. This is one reason why so many non-professionals come to his and other teachers' impro workshops. They feel stuck in their own lives; they're looking for a way to get unstuck. Impro unsticks them. It teaches them fluidity and allows them to be passionate, to invest foolishly. As a participant, you learn how to be laughed at. Disobedience in this contrarian context becomes obedience, albeit to a code of play in which so many social rules are reversed. The guidance is: allow mistakes and elaborate them, provoke tragedy, make wrong assumptions about other characters, and look to 'get yourself into trouble'. Players are additionally encouraged not to take success or failure too seriously. And once learned in the room, this attitude-set can be a coping mechanism outside, encouraging participants to remain sanguine about the grandiosity of politicians, remembering that however engirdled with achievement a person is, he can always be brought to earth with a banana skin.

Jonathan Kay is a performer who has explored the role of the fool over many years, teaching and performing thousands of improvised solo shows. He never builds a naturalistic world on the stage because if he did, he'd have to leave it – because the foolish function has no place within 'realism'. Instead he creates a world of imagination without set or props. This exercises the spectators' propensity for imagining, while it allows him as performer/ facilitator to bring them into this world of fooling. Spectators can discover themselves in this world as different to who/what they thought they were. The comedy performer Eric Davis, who plays the character Red Bastard – 'a dangerous, seductive comedy monster' – does something similar; he sees the performer's task as being 'to bring your audience into your world, transform them, and bring them back with a new awareness'.[19] Both Kay and Davis want the audience to travel with them on a journey. As a result, the audience is changed by the experience of being fooled with – transformed for the duration. Both Davis and Kay are in the habit, for example, of getting the audience to change seats, move around the space and, in Kay's case, set off into the world outside the building. It's not that the foolish world is out there; rather it's the world looks and feels different with a fool's hat on. Arguably such tactics keep alive – or hark back to – the carnival tradition in which there would be activities 'aimed at dissolving the normal social boundaries of class and gender'. The parallels are clear: 'There would very likely be ribald humour enacted by a man dressed up as a "king of fools" or "lord of misrule" and aimed at mocking real kings and other authorities'.[20]

Ali G, as played by Sacha Baron Cohen, has lured many into his upside-down, topsy-turvy world with a very specific intent of 'mocking real kings and other authorities'. By appearing more foolish than he actually is and by deliberately suspending traditional respect for his interviewees, he points up the essentially fabricated, socially constructed attitudes prevailing in such interviews. Bishops and rabbis alike are lured in to his net by such lines as:

Can God do better stuff than David Blaine?

So let's talk about this man, the main man, the McDaddy of the Christian thing – what was his name again? – Yo, that's the geezer with the tash and the sandals and everything? Ain't that a coincidence that he was born on Christmas Day?

Why do some of you lot chop one of your nuts off?

Ain't it hypocriticalist that so many nuns also work part-time as strippers? I was at my mate Rikki C's 21st and there was this nun that came in and twenty minutes later she had her babylons out and she was whipping shaving cream off his thighs.[21]

In a world where 'striking the correct attitude' has become the necessary obligation of every citizen, Ali G reverse-engineers what is 'correct' and 'respectful'. His targets are left, if not with pants down, then at least with pants visible, often with a silk lining. Cohen, Fo, Kay and others adopt similar approaches; by engineering a sequence of inversions, truths are revealed in the spirit of carnival or saturnalia. The policeman is exposed, the profiteer disarmed, the priest debunked. As Dario Fo puts it, by implication inviting others to follow:

I am the jongleur. I leap and pirouette, and make you laugh. I make fun of those in power, and I show you how puffed up and conceited are the big shots who go around making wars in which we are the ones who get slaughtered. I reveal them for what they are. I pull out the plug, and ... pssss ... they deflate.[22]

3. Resonance

Definition in this context: A moment or series of moments in performance that catch the minds of the audience

Whatever else creative practice aims for, it aims for resonance. Devising, improvisation, 'socially engaged practice', live art – all search to identify the significations that grant meaning to the work. It's the same with comedy. Comedy doesn't work unless the jokes reverberate in the audience.

If we as spectators do see something that brings us up short, surprises us or engages us in a new way, it's an indicator of something we need to pay attention to. But it's hard to define resonance, for it exists as a consequence of something else. It's the radiation that impacts and is welcomed, not the radiation-generator itself. Yet the recognition of its value legitimately belongs in this part of the book, and some effort to identify the radiators and how they are constructed is arguably necessary. After all, a disobedient theatre has as much need of mysterious alchemy as any grand opera. And it's often the contrary spirits who are delivering those statements we need to hear.

Playwrights and theatre makers know the value of searching out this elemental gold. When it's discovered, chances are it arrives after a lot of material has been abandoned. The painter Frank Auerbach says he throws 95 per cent of what he's painted into the bin: 'I think I'm trying to find a new way to express something. So I rehearse all the other ways until I surprise myself with something I haven't previously considered.'[23]

Such are eureka moments; something glints in the room and everyone goes, 'That's it!!' like starved gold-diggers. It matters not where precisely it came from, only that it arrived. It won't necessarily be possible to say why this material moved everyone in that moment. Partly this is because the impact of the resonant image or sound usually precedes its justification. Partly this is because this material may operate at a symbolic level with its potency partly hidden. As Jung said: 'A word or an image is symbolic when it implies something more than its obvious and immediate meaning. It has a wider "unconscious" aspect that is never precisely defined or fully explained.'[24]

There's much of this resonance in folk tales and mythic stories. These are the tales that never die and are returned to by producers time and again to feed audiences over the world. They deal with life, death, identity and growing up; the perennial questions that recur in the *Odyssey, Antigone, Hamlet, Beauty and the Beast, Waiting For Godot, Little Red Riding Hood, Dracula, Faust* and *Tristan and Isolde*. These stories signal an eternal correspondence with a collective unconscious where vital questions are never definitively answered but still need to be returned to.

There is another kind of resonance also – a more local or temporary one that exists for particular communities. This might come about when a community shares a predicament or moment in time, a sense of grievance or a mission. In Lockerbie, there are images that will resonate for decades locally as a result of the air crash in 1988. Where a community is defined instead by a particular trade or industry, there the imagery of that common weald always defining the locality. It's seen as the natural subject for local theatre makers. Its resonance is apparent. Or it might be that a community defined by migration finds via performance a connection back to their culture of origin. When the Muldoons' Hackney Empire in London started programming Caribbean comedy troupes, 'the audience loved the play, and howled with laughter all night long ... the shows serving to remind the Caribbean-rooted audience of the manners of the Islands, and how they have adapted to life in London.'[25] Or it may be that a local concern is agitating people right across the locality: the building of a motorway or a railway, the siting of a mosque, the closure of a hospital. These concerns can be quite geographically specific. When the theatre company Fluxx toured to Lincoln in 2012, research led us to identify a widespread concern over payday loans; there was a glut of salespeople going door-to-door enlisting the elderly in high-charging schemes. The interactive show was constructed around this issue. Yet when the show was repeated sixty miles away in Burton-on-Trent (because of lack of time to research in Burton), the issue simply didn't grip the audience in the same way. Why take that subject, they asked us?

People often assume that 'community theatre' is engaged solely in just this task: evoking local resonance. Yet the greater challenge is linking the local and the universal. When there is no resonance beyond the local, there is a weaker argument for tackling those themes. Theatre directors drawing up programmes of work often get approached to take on such purely local stories. Nick Kent, when director of the Tricycle in London, was frequently approached with requests to take up a local cause held passionately by a few. His response to them pointed to the limitations of such work:

> People would say, 'Why don't you do this play about my brother who's been unjustly incarcerated?', and I'd say, 'I could do that BUT it would be about your brother and wouldn't have wider ramifications'. And they'd say, 'But you did a play about Stephen Lawrence', and I'd say, 'But that was about police attitudes towards black people in this country and that goes much wider'.[26]

As Kent intimates, the strongest projects are those which link the universal and the local, irrespective of geography. However, it's a mistake to assume that what has resonance locally won't by definition have meaning beyond that relatively small group. Many local stories do carry: witness the success of *London Road* about the murder of prostitutes in Ipswich. Those stories spoke for a wider constituency than just East Anglia. In fact to arrive at a more global resonance, which is so often the goal of theatre makers, it may be that this journey is achieved only as a result of an engagement initially with a small particular. This is Robert Lepage arguing the point:

> *The Far Side of the Moon* for example took 'reconciliation'. It's a huge theme. At a universal level. The Americans and the Russians [were engaged] at the time [of the play]. The Western world and the values of the East also in conflict. You cannot have the pretension to say you have the answer to the Jews and Arabs and the other conflicts. The only thing you can be sure of is your own experience, your small history. For

example you and your brother when you were eight years old and you
shared the same room and there was a bookshelf between you. And you
got into conflict over the most trivial things. That is a story you can tell,
that you know intimately. So instead of saying this is about the conflict
between Israel and Palestine, don't start there, get there at the end. If you
have some kind of universal consciousness, the rest will come out. The
best way to be universal is to talk about what goes on in your bedroom
and your kitchen and your little community.[27]

Ewan MacColl summarized the point by saying: 'Politics moves from
the general to the particular, but art is different – art must move from
the particular to the general.'[28] Peter Brook said to Suba Das: 'Before
something can be about everything, it has to be about one thing totally.'[29]
It seems the point is almost universally recognized. The route to big picture
is via small detail. Travelling in the opposite direction, moving from big
theme to big narrative via nothing more than a rickety rope bridge of
deeply held beliefs, may feel adventurous but could pitch the travellers into
a deep chasm.

An accompanying sin is being a little too focused on trying to define
how the show is going to be received. There's a notion here that the
relationship between stage action and audience response is an instrumental
one. Agit-prop made the same mistake, driven by a sense of righteousness
and a horror of capitalism. But there isn't such a relationship between means
and ends. Spectators are no Pavlovian dogs waiting to salivate at a whistle.
Keith Johnstone has admitted to this delusion:

> I started my work on narrative by trying to make the improvisers
> conscious of the implications of the scenes they played. I felt that an
> artist ought to be 'committed', and that he should be held responsible
> for the effects of his work – it seemed only common sense. I got my
> students to analyse the content of *Red Riding Hood* and *The Sleeping
> Beauty* and *Moby Dick* and *The Birthday Party*, but this made them even
> more inhibited. I didn't realise that if the people who thought up *Red
> Riding Hood* had been aware of the implications, then they might never
> have written the story.[30]

Moving to the art of playwrighting, I asked the director Colin Ellwood
how a playwright moves towards resonance. He acknowledged the virtue
of starting at home. Playwrights, he said, even when politically motivated,
should 'head for the sound of their own gunfire. For what disturbs them. You
have to ask yourself, "What can I write about – the outcome of which will
lead me to be slightly embarrassed?"'.[31] The approach is supported by Arthur

Miller, who argued in an interview that 'The stage shows you stuff that you didn't dare want to look at before'.[32] Ellwood continues:

> In choosing that, in unpacking that, a lot of things about the particular milieu [in which the playwright operates] can be drawn out. And in drawing these out, you discover things that help you to work out your own issues. And you hope that that particular set of individual issues will map on to – or match – those of your particular world.[33]

This would suggest again that the route to any kind of universality is via the personal. But Ellwood makes no guarantee – hence the phrase 'hope that'. To achieve this, he talks about 'putting what concerns you have inside a kind of "reaction chamber". You're talking about yourself under the guise of something else, under the guise of deniability. If you remove that deniability then you're talking too directly.'[34]

Harold Pinter famously said: 'I have nothing to say about myself, directly. I wouldn't know where to begin.'[35] In his case, it meant taking a grain of personal experience then transmuting it into something less recognizable, putting it inside his own nuclear container. But also what's important about handling this autobiographical material is that there's something in the mix that niggles, that is not fully understood. Pinter might have expressed sympathy with the playwright Mike Kenny's comment that he, Kenny, tries to 'build a piece around a question I don't know the answer to'.[36] Other playwrights concur in the way the key devising work takes place below the surface, resisting definition but arousing curiosity. Edward Albee, for example, argued against trying to analyse the playwriting process too closely. He cites the story of a centipede who is challenged about how it gets so many legs moving in the right way, to which it answers: '"Well, I take the left front leg and then I ..." And then the centipede thought about it for a while, and then of course he couldn't walk.'[37]

When resonance is achieved, the play ripples through the audience, but very likely in different ways, in part because of the degree of homogeneity within that audience. Each spectator has their own register of reception that vibrates differently; hence the show that has a mixed sound palette will tend to draw more in. This is Colin Ellwood on a play that in his view achieves universality of resonance through its use of not one but multiple themes, thereby drawing in different spectators, each with different concerns:

> *Death of a Salesman* works on so many levels: father and son, commercialization, different generations, history. Plays like that draw in what is the subconscious of that particular time. In this way, such plays can

Assumption

be returned to [by different generations] and different bits of them activated in a slightly different way each time.[38]

Each new generation can find something for themselves in it. And to prove the play's resonance across cultural boundaries, the show has even been extensively played in China.

A classic example of an audience finding 'different bits' to suit itself might be the performance of *Waiting For Godot* that took place in San Quentin prison in 1957. This is a play that nowadays comes with its resonances well recognized. The prisoners in 1957, however, came to the play with neither knowledge of its provenance nor even any prior interest in theatre. Yet they were held attentive throughout, relating to the existential act of waiting in a way only prisoners could. It wasn't written for them, but the multivalency and opacity of the piece allowed them to project themselves into the situation of Vladimir and Estragon as easily as if it were their own lives onstage. As was written subsequently in the prison magazine:

> We're still waiting for Godot and shall continue to wait. When the scenery gets too drab and the action too slow, we'll call each other names and swear to part forever – but then, there's no place to go![39]

This all suggests that it's a mistake to become too prosaically and mechanistically autobiographical in the fashioning of performance. The mundanity of one person's everyday life is rarely sufficient to achieve resonance. The exercise needs to be lifted into a vocabulary where the scope to achieve resonance-for-others becomes more likely.

Sarah Kane's *Blasted* clearly had one of the biggest impacts of any play in the late twentieth century. As often happens with plays that confound with their audacity, its tale of violence, rape, child abuse and death in a Leeds hotel room was 'read' in many different ways by different people – but its impact was almost always profound. While UK critics frothed in moral outrage, in Belgium the production followed the exposure of a child abuse ring and so was read as directly connecting with this.

Kane's account of the gestation of the play is interesting as to how this resonance was achieved via a widening of the play's canvas – the world of it, if you like – while the central point of focus was retained. It echoes the point made earlier by Nick Kent about how a widening of the scope gathers in a greater constituency. Kane had begun the piece, she says, 'writing about two people in a hotel room in which there was a complete imbalance, which resulted in the old man raping the younger woman'. Then, as she explained to the writer Aleks Sierz,

At some point during the first couple of weeks of writing I switched on the television. Srebrenica was under siege. And old woman was looking into the camera, crying. Suddenly, I was completely uninterested in the play I was writing. Slowly it occurred to me that the play I was writing was about this. It was about violence, about rape, and it was about these things happening between people who know each other and ostensibly love each other.[40]

So while it appears there is no Royal Road to achieving resonance, there are some roughly hewn pathways created by Miller, Lepage, Pinter and Kane that offer means of study for the theatre artist. Not that these are the only roads available; witness particularly the muscular success of verbatim theatre. This tradition, harking back to the 1970s when Charles Parker interviewed workers and put these spoken words on the stage as Banner Theatre, continues to strengthen with the verbatim work of Alecky Blythe, David Hare and others. This is especially the case when it delivers shows as powerful as *Queens of Syria*: women telling their stories of living life under siege, stories of survival that have resonance far beyond their homeland. Witness too artists such as Bryony Kimmings, Mark Thomas and Caroline Horton, who use personal and family experiences to launch revelatory, onstage storytelling that brings social critiques to life. And looking back further still for other routes, Bertolt Brecht could not easily be bracketed with such autobiographical playwrights, given how he worked less from personal experience than from his own literary readings, alongside his observations at the way a broiling society in 1930s Germany made so many victims of its people.

Somerset Maugham used to say about novel-writing: 'There are just three rules for writing a novel. Unfortunately, no one knows what they are.' It's a temptation to take a similar view here. But while Maugham's aphorism may be a sanguine corrective to pedagoguery, it's equally true that beneath the surface of resonant play texts are many powerful secrets of craft ready to be unearthed and learned from.

For too generic, assumptions about the audience - different practices, no unifying line

4. Survival

In this section there's a focus on how artists look to create relationships with constituencies in such a way that can assist the maintenance of a theatre tradition.

1. Affinity

Definition in this context: A sense of kinship or closeness between admirer/s and artist/s

What Twitter does is codify and give approval to a social relationship that's characteristic of the modern world: that between the individual and a follower. Such a relationship is dependent on neither familiarity nor intimacy. It needs no friendship. It is constructed largely out of the follower's admiration, curiosity, respect or affinity (with variable ratios). Without disrespecting its socially activist dimension, it serves celebrity culture particularly well. At time of writing, seven out of ten of the most followed individuals on Twitter are music celebrities. It often matters little what is actually written; Harry Styles recently tweeted 'All the love as always', which received 820,000 retweets and counting.

Of all the art forms, theatre lends itself least to the accruing of followers. While music culture feasts voraciously on the fashions of its idols, both material and spiritual, theatre's denizens generally go about their business more admired than idolized. While music's primary output is transferable to disc or digital code, granting fans possession of creative outputs, theatre's products evaporate. A great performance is no more nor less than a piece of time taken up in a certain kind of activity; this ephemerality is both its charm and its limitation. Theatre's outputs resist commodification, NT Live and Antony Sher's diaries notwithstanding.

Arguably affinity is the glue of fandom. It's a sense of empathic connection with the artist. So how do you engender this while working outside the mainstream? How does an activist using performance win affinity with strangers? It's not easy, given that the 'product' disappears at the point of its creation. An initial question has to concern what's actually achievable. Anne Torreggiani. who heads up the Audience Agency, points out that in respect of winning the loyalty of theatregoers it's a mistake to assume very much at all is possible: 'You actually get very small numbers of people displaying what we would call loyalty or frequent behaviour; people are coming back much less often than we think they are.'[1] However, she acknowledges that this may not be an indicator of lack of affinity between theatregoer and venue or artist/s but rather just a feature of theatre-going. After all, 'they may still feel attached even though they don't go'.[2] They may still feel attached, she says, to a venue like the Albany in South London, but only go maybe twice a year. When it comes to particular theatre companies, the pattern is similar; she believes there are 'artist followings' but they are only 'a tiny proportion of the actual audience'.[3]

One such company with a significant following is the Brighton-based clown company Spymonkey. Having been consistently building a fan base since 1998, the company in 2016 managed to fill the Brighton Theatre Royal (capacity 1,000) on seven consecutive nights, cheering in an entirely new and unseen show *The Complete Deaths*. So while acknowledging Torreggiani's point, it's equally true that presenting high-quality, funny, subversive and accessible work over eighteen years clearly isn't a bad way to create affinity with an audience.

The contrast with sport and music is stark. Music is a business which is built on a fan base worth $33bn, whereas in theatre, less than 10 per cent of theatregoers attend more than three things a year, generating a value of around £5.4bn. The challenge for theatre is that, unlike football or music, the potential spectator is less likely to be presented with 'a formula' that's already familiar, hence it's less easy to sell a visit to the show. Torreggiani asserts that 'it's important for us to recognise how crucial the familiar is for 90–95 per cent of our audiences'.[4] The familiar is 'their doorway'. People like to know what they're getting for the most part, it's a premise of consumerism. Here then lies the paradox, for 'avoiding the familiar is theatre's speciality'.[5] This is especially true in relation to the kind of work discussed and presented in this book. Difficult or disobedient theatre is most likely to be found in work that's away from the familiar, the predictable and the safe.

How to tackle this paradox of creating affinity with such work is inevitably the business of marketing, often the least favoured skill set for the dissenting artist. However, there's no reason why a radical tradition of culture and theatre making should be disadvantaged in creating affinity simply because it's outside the mainstream – rather the reverse. PR experts such as Mark Borkowski see the personal dedication and commitment of fringe performers to be precisely their strength when it comes to winning audiences. Borkowski rejects the argument that marketing experimental theatre is fundamentally different from marketing mainstream work. He says he does his job because in his view 'theatre is about changing people's lives' and marketing is simply 'communicating that passion' irrespective of the politics. He argues that it's about asking the fundamental questions: 'What is interesting about the work? What are the visual pictures that will sell it, that will distil its impact? Who are the people who are likely to be excited by it, outside the traditional arts ghettoes?'[6] So there's clearly a campaigning dimension to his approach. He talks of the importance of engineering a close connection between those responsible for marketing and the company marketed. He refers to spending two years communicating with David Jubb, director of Battersea Arts Centre, planning one particular project. 'What you've got to look at is still: is the show good, or is it going to be good? That's really the only consideration.'[7] His cheerful refusal to finesse what 'good' means is perhaps a welcome counter to those who link 'good' with 'impossibly niche'.

So, Borkowski's argument runs, building support for work on the alternative spectrum is more easily done, since this is about channelling the work of 'collectives of people with a vision. The commitment of these people is their power. So marketing becomes about channelling this single-mindedness.'[8] To counteract any inherent weakness in the pitch, Borkowski organizes publicity stunts; he's killed off a (fictional) tap-dancing dog, arranged motor bike jumps over traffic queues, staged a ballet of vacuum cleaners and gift-wrapped a house. For Borkowski and others, there's no hand-wringing over principles or left-wing angst over marketing practices; there's simply a determination to tap into the traditional UK welcoming of English eccentricity.

To take an example of the kind of piece Borkowski might be speaking about, the production *I Stand Corrected* came about when Mojisola Adebayo was working in South Africa and met a dance artist called Mamela Nyamza. What fuelled the subsequent creative process was clearly the affinity they each discovered between themselves:

> We were interested in each other, drawn to each other. I'm interested in attraction – it's something that we don't talk about very much in this field when we think about community. But what we have in common is that we're both lesbian women, we're both black women, and our work has a very real political commitment. We both got really excited by each other's work and identified an area, an issue, that we both wanted to address: so-called corrective rape – the incidence of lesbian women being raped and usually murdered and the perpetrators justifying it on the basis that those women need to be corrected.[9]

Amber Massie-Blomfield of the Albany and Camden People's Theatre has worked with Borkowski and agrees that it's essential not to abandon the core passions of the artists when it comes to marketing. Affinity, she argues, is achieved between artist and audience via 'an engagement that is totally about the core mission of your organisation'.[10] This in turn flows from the kind of personal commitments talked about by Adebayo, which are rarely a feature of mainstream theatre. Massie-Blomfield argues that there shouldn't necessarily be a difference between a company and a building in this respect; the challenges are not dissimilar. Her own experience is primarily with buildings – first the Albany in Deptford and then the Camden People's Theatre in North London. With the Albany, she argues that 'there's a real sense that the building is owned by the people of Deptford'.[11] She suggests one reason for this sense of ownership is that the building was originally a local resource centre and during this time acquired a reputation for utilitarian value within the local population. Only in the 1990s did it become dedicated to the arts, but the perception of the building as a community resource continued. There remained a sense of the building being 'for us', for the people of Deptford. To sustain and build on this legacy, arts programming is informed by how the building still houses an adult social care programme, among others. So there's a blending of functions: the creative and the social. And to better achieve the blend, artists are put in charge of the social care programme: 'So we've got artists coming in doing circus, spoken word.'[12] And for those local people who are not already sold on the idea of the building as an arts hub, there are imaginative strategies also for getting first-comers in.

> Every season we take our mobile box office out to the market and sell tickets for one pound to any show in the season – in the first year, 65 per cent of sales were first-time bookers and 70 per cent were local people.[13]

It's true also that the design and atmosphere of any community-focused venue has to reflect the core policy, and has to be viewed as part of the strategy to build affinity. When Gwenda Hughes took over the New Vic Theatre at Stoke-on-Trent, she felt 'there was a very masculine feel about the place'.[14] So the bar was redesigned – 'we made the bar more wine-focused' – and the foyer and other areas were made more woman-friendly. The issue of how the programme might appeal to women also became a key part of the conversation. Hughes

> wanted to programme shows that had something to say to the tribe but that didn't look frighteningly like art. I wanted to make it look like an evening in the theatre where you wouldn't feel foolish for 'not getting it' – in my head I was programming for my mum. But she wouldn't have had a good time at Complicite.'[15]

At the ARC in Stockton, director Annabel Turpin recognizes these priorities. As she puts it:

The way you communicate, the venue, the whole offer has to seem relevant. Otherwise, why would people come? However relevant the themes of the show are, if the leaflet makes it look too expensive, uses words not commonly used by your target audience, or talks about awards or other plaudits not known in your area, why would it feel relevant to local people?'[16]

The notion of holding true to a core mission, while simultaneously making the offer to audiences as unfrightening as possible, appears unassailable. To compromise a sense of mission by diluting the company's fundamental passions simply in order to get people in – putting out misrepresentative publicity, in other words – can only lead to audience disappointment. When Hughes presented *Top Girls* at the New Vic, some spectators found it out of key with what they'd been led to expect from the publicity – and there were letters telling her so. The lesson from this simply reiterates what David Hare has pointed out, that 'the thoughts and feelings with which the audience arrive are half the story'.[17]

As for sticking to your core passions, the music world again offers a point of comparison. Eventually the world did come around to Anvil and Seasick Steve following a period in the relative wilderness where those artists struggled on without abandoning what they understood as their mission. Even the Beatles, faced with a choice between almost guaranteed success with someone else's song they didn't like – 'How Do You Do It?' by Mitch Murray – and sticking with their own songs, chose the latter option. John Lennon said: 'We'd sooner have no contract than put that crap out.'[18]

For the director Chris Goode, the music industry also offers a useful comparison, but only if the theatre becomes less showbiz and less show-oriented:

One of the things I would love to do, if I were brave enough, is stop making pieces. Because I think that model takes us down the wrong kind of route. If you think about a band, you'll go and see that band, obviously it'll have something to do with their material, but it won't be about a particular piece, it'll be about seeing that band. We can then get away from that whole thing of 'this is the same show tomorrow as it was yesterday'.[19]

However, it would be fair to acknowledge some hesitancy in drawing too easy comparisons between the music and theatre industries. Arguably these two media operate in quite different political registers. Music fandom, especially in its most intense and adolescent forms, relies often on a particular kind of performer–fan relationship. This involves a degree of projection in which the performer is created as fantasy figure within the mind of the admirer – hence the extraordinary volume of fan stories on the web in which the music star just happens to end up living next door. Whereas theatre – of the kind discussed here – is largely dedicated to a reverse process: the digging beneath fantasy to uncover some dirty, but perhaps still beautiful, truths. So while the case needs to be made that we should be winning admiration for the performers, disobedient theatre artists are not necessarily trying to cultivate worship. They tend to be more concerned with the elaboration of theatre as a medium of revelation.

Arguably the best strategy of all is to create unique, distinctive, radically inclined work that grows audiences who love this stuff. Perhaps You Me Bum Bum Train and Secret Cinema have in part achieved this. Marina Abramovic certainly has, you might think – after all, she breaks rules and has queues round the block – but her success has prompted commentators to raise some ethical questions. This is particularly true in respect of achieving large-scale affinity between fans and artists when the artist is positioned as it were on the edge of cultural norms. Abramovic's body of work clearly indicates a degree of agency – hence the proposed Marina Abramovic Institute – and many acknowledge her work has altered forever perceptions of what art can be. But what for many brings up short any unreserved enthusiasm is the perception that her work conceals the fostering of a personality cult. These comments of Asimina Chremos summarize the fans' predicament:

> I don't see a problem with artists starting institutions for the further development and preservation of their excellent work, and to inspire, support and educate next generations as well. Meredith Monk, Robert Rauschenberg, go for it. What is disturbing about Abramovic is her self-fulness in all this. I suppose it is a natural outgrowth of 'The Artist is Present'. She's been insisting on her presence since the beginning. Her bold embodiments were at first quite radical, but now, in the environment of late-capitalist USA, 'presence', instead of being numinous and luminous, has been subverted into the solid and smooth airbrushed facade called 'celebrity' with all its attendant, devilishly dancing dollar-signs.[20]

While learning from the work of celebrity-artists, can we not be allowed to draw a line between those two hyphenated words? Arguably the real challenge lies not in building affinity with a personality but with a practice. This would be one that incorporates and provides an umbrella for a number of different artists in the way that the Live Art Development Agency does. If additionally the spectator's hopes, fears and dreams become in this way part of the conversation, there's the basis then for the spectator to become less of a worshipper and more of an equal. And more of an ally perhaps.

2. Allies

Artists need allies. And in the essential and ongoing business of creating them, there are some useful distinctions to be made between the different kinds of allies that can be made:

* Volunteers – those who sign up for a particular project, or sequence of projects, to participate or assist in that project's realization.
* Supporters – individuals who take initiatives on the artist's behalf (although it may or may not be their responsibility to do so).
* Partners – an organization or a body of people, independently managed and run, that may partner with the artist/s.

An artist may seek all of these at different times. In this chapter we're looking primarily at supporters and partnerships. The former category more usually consists of individuals; the latter category more usually consists of organizations in an arrangement where there is some shared risk and shared investment.

Matt Adams told me that his company Blast Theory relies strongly on a range of allies who support the company:

> We have a category in our mailing list called Allies. We've built that list over fifteen years. Our Kidnap Project – no one would fund that. [In this project the company advertised for individuals willing to be 'kidnapped' – and found a good few.] So we essentially lived on fresh air for about a year. Our allies were people who took raffle tickets and sold them for us.[21]

I asked a number of artists about their allies. Their answers varied widely. Some cited friends, curators, supporters, trusts and foundations. Others cited family members. There was little by way of a uniform pattern. Very few, however, failed to recognize the network of professional allies put there by national government to 'support the arts' using funds and person time centred in the Arts Council of England. But despite the prominence of the institution, when it came to actual support, many artists have experienced an intention/realization gap. They have found that what is actually delivered often doesn't reflect what's written in the policy documents. This is especially true outside London, within which funding is concentrated. Despite the slogan 'Great Art for Everyone', Chair of the Arts Council Peter Bazalgette acknowledged in 2013 that 'more should be done' to rectify the London funding bias. A year later, the Parliamentary Culture, Media and Sport Committee noted that this hadn't happened and that the balance should now be 'urgently rectified'.

Artists have also been impatient about the ways in which, as it appears to them, support has increasingly gone into infrastructure and away from artists themselves. Mike Bradwell described his experience of a mistaken shift in priorities, which he observed while director of the Bush Theatre in London, thus:

> Our move [into a new office] also marked the beginning of a subtle change in the culture. Deborah and I had run the office by simply talking to people and having conversations in the pub. Now there were schedules and memos and agendas and meetings and minutes and reports. The Administrator had mysteriously become the General Manager, and there were plans to recruit an Assistant General Manager. Suddenly there were Heads of Department and Line Managers and Targets and Staff Appraisals and Disciplinary Procedures, all of which seemed more appropriate for a multinational conglomerate rather than for a radical theatre company.[22]

The criticism will be familiar to many, though years have passed since Bradwell wrote his book. Other critics have pointed to a parallel trend: the triumph of civic over artistic values in policy making to the disadvantage of artists. It's a triumph also, they aver, of political correctness over artistic momentum. Bradwell goes on to talk about how the Arts Council in the latter part of the last century became obsessed with the idea that the arts could be

> transformed into a catalyst for social change. Theatres would now have to prioritise social and sexual inclusion, cultural diversity, education, disability, outreach and access. The ideals were exemplary; the problem was that most of the directives were ill-conceived, spurious, and often contradictory exercises in box-ticking.[23]

This new focus, bringing together both artistic and civic policy goals, is now a consistent feature of arts funding. Yet the good intentions/poor execution gap can – while attempting to energize both civic and artistic goals – jeopardize both, especially when the Arts Council, as it has been known to do, judges more civic-led initiatives by largely arts criteria and arts projects by civic ones. For applicants it can be a lose–lose situation.

Another reason for this partial failure in building artist–allies partnerships is that for these good intentions to be carried out, there need to be visionary and determined agents on the ground putting these policies into practice. But such allies are often hard to find. What's more, within the antiseptic civic offices perched on the streets where vagrants stroll, the concept of what 'being an ally' actually means varies widely. Often what the in-situ arts officer is working to achieve isn't at all what the artist dreams of. As a result, artists have sometimes to fictionalize their endeavours precipitately to make them qualify for funding. This may involve presenting one view of the work to the funding authority while maintaining another in the rehearsal room. This requires what Tim Etchells has described as 'the skill of holding the [rehearsal room] door closed with one hand and saying to the funders "We're going to do this or that" while acknowledging to this other lot here [in the room] "We don't know what the hell we're doing"'.[24]

Such arm's length detachment between would-be allies and artists can be found in touring theatre companies' day-to-day experiences. A particular incident illustrates both this detachment and the policy/realization gap. When Fluxx toured the Midlands in 2012, we approached an arts officer who worked for a city council to help us identify a venue. We needed allies: it was unfamiliar geography. She explained she wouldn't be able to support any part of this process until I had submitted a paper outlining our plans. She would then take this to the relevant committee and the committee would decide whether or not she could help me. I did this and the committee approved. Armed with her permissions, she then offered to drive me to the council-run venues so I could pick one for our show. First we'd visit the council-run leisure complex – the 'jewel in the crown', as she called it. After twenty minutes, I began to recognize landmarks through the car window that we had passed previously. Was this city one of endlessly duplicated versions of itself like a Minecraft world, or were we going round in circles? The question was answered when my guide pulled over and engaged a passer-by for directions. The 'jewel in the crown' venue-for-the-arts could not be found by its own arts officer driving from her own office. At that moment, indications of a future successful partnership were not much in evidence.

Nor indeed was this the end of the confusions. Sometime later, a venue having been located, the council committee decided to instruct the arts officer to withdraw support from the project; apparently it was now deemed 'unsuitable' because local 'planning issues' were particularly sensitive. The committee had been misled by the title of the show *Without Planning Permission*. Once it was explained that this referred to the improvisational element in the show, they insisted there was an additional reason they couldn't support the event because … it might be offensive to Muslims. It emerged that someone in the council had picked up something on our website about a show storyline – never used in performance – where we explored Muslim sensibilities towards graphic sex and violence in films. The ignorance and myopia demonstrated by the council was breath-taking. It could only conceal a fundamental antipathy towards any live arts that didn't come with a script, a song and a Shaftesbury Avenue gloss. So we did the only sensible thing – gave up trying to build an alliance with the council and turned instead to the local amateur theatre company. They welcomed a partnership and gave us six volunteers to perform. We additionally created a news story from the council's decisions; the BBC picked it up, gave it some prominence, and the hall was packed.

Such stories point to the failure of a poorly made civic policy towards the arts and a profound misunderstanding of what it is to be an ally. The failure led to a self-defeating series of supine initiatives that floundered from the first. Unfortunately this kind of approach – controlling yet detached – has become increasingly evident in the context of economic cuts. However, the good news is: True Friends and Allies do exist. It's just that sometimes they exist more frequently outside the state-defined organs of support:

> There's always been people in my life that support me – sometimes they appear like angels – even when I did my MA in St Martins and this guy literally appeared next to me on a bus and asked if I wanted any help – then he came to my studio for three days and painted it; at that time he was just a young person although later he became a curator.[25]

This is the artist Oreet Ashery talking who, while acknowledging institutional support, finds the personal commitment of individuals to be invaluable in both surviving as an artist and building networks. For her, what characterizes an ally is not necessarily the job description. Often those who've helped have had little or no responsibility to do so. Allies can emerge from anywhere, she's found, propelled by a connection with the work. Facebook and other social media can be vital in linking the artist and the ally – witness the campaigns that have kicked in to help save organizations from cuts or closure: Hackney Empire, Big Brum, Red Ladder and Out of Joint, to name just four. It's also possible that key allies can be found within the arts infrastructure. In the struggle to make the Hackney Empire work as a popular culture centre, Roland Muldoon found that 'Despite the odds, two sympathetic officers from Hackney Council's Leisure Department squeezed enough money from the increasingly philistine borough to underwrite and promote the qawwali music superstars, Nusrat Fateh Ali Khan and the Sabri Brothers'.[26] In another part of London, those who rallied to help Battersea Arts Centre after its fire in 2015 included professionals from across the arts spectrum as well as local people who made it possible for the BAC to resume its programme almost without delay. A total of 1,750 people gave

£52,000 in the weeks following the fire and Battersea Power Station stepped in with £100,000. The English way is, it seems, often to offer the greatest commitment only at the time of greatest threat.

Yet there is always competition to win allies. Mission statements compete with mission statements, adverts with adverts, and theatre itself has to compete with the enormous power of both subsidised (BBC) and non-subsidised (all the rest) television companies. ITV alone had an external revenue of £2,590 million in 2014. By comparison the Arts Council of England will have spent around £341 million in that year.

Perhaps the answer to the ally conundrum lies at home. If a company's spectators can begin to be viewed as potential allies – beyond the token 'tell your friends about us' post-show – then the notion of supporters gets reframed. Spectators who are responsive and enthusiastic can morph into friends and perhaps even powerful allies. But for this to happen, companies' work may need to be more porous. One strategy is to enable show structures to be more 'open' than 'closed', the former offering more scope for interactivity between performers and spectators within the actual show itself. Or there is the option to recruit supporters in innovative ways, as the company RashDash does:

> We don't spend the day dropping flyers on tables; we split off and have conversations. We speak with people on the street, sit with people in cafes and organize visits into schools, colleges and universities. The volunteers, in return for their time, they get a hot chocolate, mentorship with the company and a ticket to the show.[27]

The buildings that house such shows may also need to break the distinctions between volunteer, spectator and ally, as BAC are doing. Similarly, Manchester Royal Exchange is also offering a strategy of presenting some unorthodox invitations to the general public; as artistic director Sarah Frankcom reported in 2015:

> We invited 100 people aged 9 to 73 to a sleepover in the theatre. We asked them onstage to tell us their stories and make puppets of themselves; we read them a bedtime story and sang them a newly commissioned lullaby. We wanted to say: this really is your theatre, so why not sleep here?[28]

Then there can evolve the basis for a constituency that more effortlessly unites around that organization's practice. As David Micklem commented, even before the fire: 'Battersea Arts Centre would close tomorrow if we had to pay the 200 people who volunteer for us.'[29]

Much of this book has argued in favour of the slow dissolution of previously-held-to-be-firm distinctions: teacher/pupil, facilitator/group, actor/

audience, aesthetic space/public space. Affinity helps to close a further gap: that between audiences and performers.

When it comes to partnerships, here support for the company or artist becomes embedded more formally in an alliance with a supportive organization. This template offers potentially a more integrated, sophisticated and powerful network of support. It can form the bedrock for a community play or large-scale project. It can deliver a sequence of events over months or years. My own company's struggle to build such partnerships, as illustrated in the anecdote above, will not be unfamiliar to others working in the field. However, it's not that solid partnerships can't be created. It's just that some have more success than others. So I talked to John Fox, whose record of animative projects with Welfare State International was extraordinary. In the conversation, he made some key points. One resonated with me in particular: 'You can't do community art as a touring company.'[30] To achieve significant participation of local people, he said, takes a long time. Contacts and allies need to be nurtured. The American artist Pablo Helguera concurs: 'It may take many years ... to find a true method to the madness of intruding upon and affecting environments whose populations do not always expect us.'[31] Welfare State spent seven years in Cumbria and another twelve in Ulverston. When he spoke to me, Fox talked a lot about honesty and plain dealing in the business of making the residencies work. The company took great pains to avoid people feeling manipulated. Accommodation and food would be arranged for volunteers. He said he always 'worked from the principle that people are good and want something wonderful. And people get blocked by all kinds of circumstances. So you try to get through to them as individuals and don't patronize them or abuse them.'[32]

Fox talked of spending many hours sitting in Labour clubs to build allies. And the problem was, 'They don't speak the language. We were either Marxists trying to dumb down the art or weirdo extremists doing eccentric political carnival.'[33] Claire and Roland Muldoon had found something similar trying to win hearts and minds to the cause of the Hackney Empire. Muldoon wrote subsequently: 'From the Lottery's supremo to the lowliest Hackney councillor there was not one with the slightest grasp of the concept of popular theatre.'[34] But councillors in Ulverston did come round slowly, as they did in Hackney, especially once they saw the benefits of the work. Then the personal contacts books would be opened. But constant negotiation and renegotiation was always required. For example, when Welfare State presented their show *King Real and the Hoodlums*, 'it provoked people – it upset people a bit and we had to ingratiate ourselves after that with a show at the Town Hall about Queen Victoria.'[35] Persistence and diplomacy seemed key to this slow-burning process.

Claque Theatre, formerly Colway Theatre Trust, is in a not dissimilar position. It would struggle to gain access to its constituencies without strong, effective partnerships with civic, business and voluntary sector organizations. In 2015, just to prove it could be done, the company forged a partnership with the City of London Authority based, it would appear, partly on a symmetry of objectives. It's such symmetry that case studies suggest offers the most potent recipe for success. In this situation, the company needed volunteers to be part of the show while the City was currently recruiting volunteers to join a longer-term volunteer body to help them engage with social development locally. It was a natural fit. The partnership enabled the recruitment of volunteers and once in place, there was scope to create allies from the individual volunteers.

Such challenges in the UK are as nothing compared to those experienced by the Free Theatre of Belarus, where civic authorities haven't been just incompetently fearful or disingenuously obstructive, but actively hostile. Here a very different kind of tactics was required by the persecuted company. The authorities had pursued the company relentlessly from the moment of its formation, in particular threatening anyone who offered space that could be used for performance. The threats made to such potential allies ranged from destruction of an individual's business to eviction from an individual's own home. Even a School for the Blind was threatened with eviction when it offered a venue. Given this context, it's no surprise that any dividing line between show attendees and allies becomes blurred, for even attending a show brings a level of risk quite unfamiliar to those chomping sushi down Shaftesbury Avenue. Spectators, by simply attending, become allies, with many starting to share the same risks that the company took daily.

Given these pressures and the potential risk to local allies, the safeguarding tactic adopted seems like a natural consequence of this persecution: it was to reach out beyond the borders of Belarus. There, the risk to allies is less acute. Furthermore if such allies could command global attention, all the better. As Natalia Kaliada, director of the company, told me:

> The first appeals were done by Mick Jagger, Tom Stoppard and Vaclav Havel. The messages of such people are much stronger than any statement from us or European politicians. Artists don't have executive power but they have moral power to put pressure on their governments.[36]

However, such an arm's-length strategy comes with its own problems:

> After those messages we received a lot of trouble for the company. Next day our campsite was completely destroyed. People here in the UK don't

believe that someone's voice can make a difference back there but it
does, the effect is enormous, especially when it is done by prominent
people. When your website is hacked or you are attacked, it shows you
have done something right.[37]

This tactic of appealing for help outside the country over the heads of the
authorities was a tactic forced on the company rather than deliberately
chosen. Disobedience was, as it were, thrust upon them. The company
would have preferred to function as a regular theatre – its initial planned
programme was in fact built around a Chekhov play – but the authorities'
awareness of the individuals involved and their previous journalistic activities led them to the assumption that the company's purpose was socially
disruptive. It was these assumptions and the resulting persecution that led
ultimately and ironically to the creation of a sequence of shows that was
more evidently critical of the state: *Trash Cuisine*, *Operation Jeans* and *Red
Forest*, despite the fact that such a defiant programme had not initially been
scheduled. In a further irony – and testament to the pointlessness of trying
to squash theatre practice into the ground – this programme was seen by
a much wider audience than would have been the case had the Belarusian
authorities left the company alone. For since they were denied performance opportunities at home, the Free Theatre of Belarus decided to flee
the country altogether and took up an offer of refuge within the Young Vic
in London. Here the company created shows without censorship or inter-
ference, which were not only well attended but live streamed to supporters
and allies around the world.

3. Agency

*Definition in this context: The facility to influence and cause change
through the actions of an organization*

The action of agency is a game of influencing hearts and minds. Theatre is
one of those games. Perhaps more than any other idea, the notion of agency
distinguishes a particular kind of theatre practice. It carries the aspiration of
being catalytic. Performance that aims for agency is forged in different heats
from those created purely for entertainment.

The concept of 'agency' has for many activists supplanted the word
'mission', which with its colonial and religious overtones strikes as too
evocative of the evangelical. Agency embraces not just activist notions
of protest and provocation but those of passivity and non-cooperation
as well. In a society which relies on compliance with advertising and

consumerism for the maintenance of economic stability, simple, passive resistance to these forces can become as effective and necessary as street-angry opposition. The contemporary idea of agency can even therefore become an 'agency of inaction', as Adrian Heathfield puts it, 'for there are times when passivity speaks more powerfully than activity'.[38] However, tactical shifts are periodically necessary, because the opposition – be it the police, the civic authorities or the media – is likely to change its tactics in response to protests made.

For theatre to function as agency, therefore, it needs to be more than Joan Littlewood's 'design for living', quoted earlier. It has to influence hearts and minds while being flexible enough not to fall victim to an unadaptable politics itself. It needs to prove itself sufficiently spirited and mercurial to operate in any context where theatre has a role, while not imposing a uniform idea of what that role should be. It has to be adaptive and responsive to local culture, economics, geography and social climate. Theatre is after all always a local event. This implies that its practical application – the extent to which it is applied – may need to alter to suit local conditions. Yet this should not be taken to imply that its principles of democracy, human rights, equality and creativity will therefore change. There are contexts where to simply operate a model of defiance and provocation would be like organizing a rooftop protest in a prison that was burning down. When the Syrian revolution broke out, a call was sent to Forum Theatre practitioners around the globe to come and assist the struggle. But was this really the time and place? A disobedient theatre practice cannot rely on a single set of tactics applied irrespective of context.

These issues are most acutely relevant in times of war. When I talked to the academic and practitioner James Thompson about how a radical theatre should function in times of extreme conflict such as war, he spoke of how a traditionally defiant function needs to be altered. He referred to the need in such circumstances for art to be 'a bunker you can retreat to ... a lot of the work [in Sri Lanka and Lebanon] is about struggling to hold on to art forms, dance forms, song forms that are in danger of being lost'. He stresses that the function of art rightfully alters at times of conflict: 'Sometimes the arts are about saying no to power and sometimes the arts are about recuperation and something to keep you safe for a little while. It's important not to devalue either of those functions.'[39] It follows that a useful notion of agency is therefore not one of didactic inflexibility, but one of a careful and constant recalibration of role, its barometer always set to register local conditions. It may even be the case, as Thompson has said elsewhere, that 'there are times when your work is so compromised by the political environment that you should not be doing it'.[40]

In a UK context, lacking war on the streets but still exhibiting a multitude of restrictions on citizens' freedoms, the Live Art Development Agency presents an agency model based on an offer of recalibrated cultural priorities. Its methods are to some extent beholden to the artists with whom it has relationships, yet there is an over-arching idea. It models another kind of responsiveness to local conditions via a notion of agency. It manages this by encouraging live artists into a consumer-driven world to quietly and surreptitiously go about their business of gentle disruption, questioning aspects of the status quo. Lois Keidan, its director, is quick to stress how their notion of agency was about, yes, creating change, but more about presenting alternative cultural initiatives rather than simply campaigning. Agency, she said, is about making an invitation to the world to consistently re-question the relationship between art and life. Live art is, she argues, 'an approach, an attitude that's shared by artists from different fields'. The approach has something of a 'disruptive intention, not in the way of being wilfully bad but by asking questions about what form theatre can take ... what can be the relationship between an artist and audience'. She makes the point that agency in this context doesn't mean 'we're against anyone, we're just working in different ways'.[41]

Live art practice does tend to resist easy definitions and its practitioners are comfortable with that. Adrian Heathfield argues that to accept constraining definitions simply plays into a commodifying vernacular. This notion of agency has another characteristic also; it avoids what Heathfield refers to as the creation of 'identitarian' relationships, those founded on notions of the person as being 'solid, fixed, substantial'. In this way it has a natural fit with an approach that resists seeing people as consumers primarily. So the approach is less 'object-driven' and more about 'spiritedness, a certain quality of energy directed towards the world'.[42] Art is not for consumption. Heathfield cites the fluidity of Tino Sehgal's work, discussed later, which, by setting up particular relations between the different parties involved in the theatre event, avoids fixing any of them into narrow terms such as performer/audience or professional/volunteer. With this emphasis on relations and relationships, the invitation to the public moves from a notion of spectator as consumer and gets closer to that of spectator as citizen – a notion that allows the spectator/citizen to influence what occurs.

The determining of relationships and how people relate to each other through creative practice is a particular affordance of arts centres. This has been a prerogative claimed through recent history. Rightly they are seen – or should be – as hubs of experimentation, places where you can reasonably assume that routines of shopping, worshipping or getting fit will be avoided. Within the history of UK performance culture, there have been organizations like the Oval House and Battersea Arts Centre that have, through their promotion of certain types of work, functioned as just this kind of key agency for experimental practice. By bringing together art, protest and innovation, different ways of speaking about personal and collective experiences have been made possible. The Oval House has operated for years as a creative refuge for malcontents. I myself walked in there during the 1970s at a tender age, declaring presumptuously that I wanted to be a performer. A few minutes later I had a blindfold on and was part of a show. 'The Oval House hummed from 7am to midnight, some people lived there, there were happenings all over, in the car park. People would drop in, Dustin Hoffman for instance.'[43] The Oval had to some extent replaced the Arts Lab in Drury Lane, which occupied a similar role. There too the emphasis was on production, experiment and community. As Jim Haynes, founder of Arts Lab, recalled: 'I remember Steven Berkoff coming in one day, he was like a young boy, he said, "Can I produce a play that I've written in here?" And I said, "Yes, when do you want to do it – next week?"' Haynes recalls how people lived 'in various corners of the building; in the cinema, the projection booths ... we really felt we could do anything'.[44]

Such a libertarian, relatively unregulated vision of agency allowed Pink Floyd to cross with the People Show and Peter Cook with Pip Simmons. Such hubs were instrumental in the flowering of new work in the 1960s, 70s and 80s. But times have changed; the gates of a controlling civic regulation have come down sharply in the intervening period. Roland Muldoon's Hackney Empire was a great example of the adventuring spirit – 'we waved the flag of non-conformity'[45] – but had ultimately to knuckle down and become a great deal more businesslike in the 2000s. While artists presenting there could 'demonstrate that they were not part of the prevailing bourgeois ideology',[46] compromises were inevitable, a process that Muldoon referred to as an 'endless nightmare'.[47] Artists and their allies needed these buildings for their own survival, so if a compromise with the world of legislation and commerce was required, then so be it; those compromises were made.

However, the truth remains, as Peter Bürger puts it, that 'within the history of the avant-garde, the social effect of a work of art cannot simply be gauged by considering the work itself but that its effect is decisively determined by the institution within which the work "functions"'.[48] In other words, radical, questioning work might very likely lose its punch in a building disempowered by too many compromises. When the compromising finally became intolerable, the Muldoons handed over the Empire to others but arguably emerged with integrity intact: 'I believe what we achieved has had a lasting effect: to encourage, and present to a wider audience, comedy that brought into the public arena artists who challenged the conventional normality'.[49]

Managing arts hubs with a radical social or artistic agenda comes with
a variety of such challenges. It's also, quite simply, expensive – especially
in a case like the historic Empire – which means in turn forever reaching
out to identify new audiences and new allies. And with so many potential
new audiences locked into the familiarity paradigm discussed earlier by
Torreggiani, it takes lateral thinking to write a game plan that balances
these forces. The ARC in Stockton and Slung Low in Leeds have tackled this
challenge by asking audiences to book tickets for shows in advance but pay
no money. Afterwards, spectators are asked to pay what they thought the
show was worth. Annabel Turpin, director of ARC, wrote subsequently of
this initiative:

> I'm pleased to say it has been a huge success, with some startling results.
> Audience numbers are up by 58 per cent on the same period last year
> and income is up by 82 per cent, increasing our average ticket yield by
> 15 per cent – all way beyond our expectations. Even more satisfying
> is the 15.6 per cent of audiences attending theatre at ARC for the first
> time, compared with 10.8 per cent last year. Ten per cent of ARC's
> theatre audiences had never booked tickets for our shows, compared
> to 5.9 per cent in the previous period. ARC is located in one of the 0.1
> per cent most deprived wards in England, so we are also pleased to have
> increased the number of customers from our surrounding postcode
> area.[50]

It's a tactic that others might emulate. The Forest Fringe initiative has won
the admiration of audiences and artists alike by running similar 'pay what
you can afford' policies. But running an arts hub while championing alternative values both performative and economic will always require some
daring. And there is no guarantee that venues are always in a position to
programme those 'unfamiliar' shows. Both Nick Kent from the Tricycle and
Gwenda Hughes from the New Vic acknowledged to me the core priority of
creating a balanced programme that is shaped by finding what as a priority
has resonance for that local audience. The reality is that in such buildings
where there is a clear civic function, the more radical, experimental or
provocative work will only be programmed if it can find its place within
this more holistic, generalist programming. It's not surprising then that the
more adventurous, provocative or mischievous productions can get left out
in the cold, leaving the difficult/disobedient show-makers to seek their own,
left-field solutions. Students leaving Rose Bruford College in 2015 to set up
their own companies expressed willingness to do just that: to seek out as yet
undefined opportunities using whatever means appropriate. If necessary,
said student Aidan Ross, 'I would perform in my own front room'.[51] The

comment reflects a historic predilection of the avant-garde: to make work at the small scale where the context can be controlled and managed without sacrificing political priorities.

4. Scale

Definition in this context: The relative size of any theatre event

Alternative and radical theatre makers traditionally head for the small-scale. That's certainly how it was in radical theatre's most adventurous period: the 1960s, 1970s and 1980s. As time has moved on and larger-scale experiments have been made possible – usually due to funding – it's been possible to observe how scale impacts significantly on intimacy, immediacy, responsiveness and those other aspects of practice that a disobedient theatre prizes.

When Hilary Westlake met David Gale, it was theatre at first sight. In 1972 Gale was already in an experimental company called the Phantom Captain and Westlake was looking for a way to become creatively more proactive. She had already worked as a performer with London La MaMa and seen a range of shows that inspired her – by Ariane Mnouchkine and Joe Chaikin's Open Theatre, to name two. He wanted to write; she, direct. They formed Lumiere & Son. They decided they wanted to deal with 'the dark insides of people, their appetites, desires and dreams', drawing from the language of film.[52] But in 1972 it wasn't easy to find funding. David Gale came from Cambridge and knew members of Pink Floyd, so he asked Roger Waters and came away with £1,500 – a fair sum in those days. With this they created *Tip Top Condition* which they presented at Oval House, one of the few venues open to entirely new work. The show 'established a grotesque humour and physicality that would become signature elements of the company's output for some time'.[53] Lumiere & Son then created a sequence of highly visual shows over the next twenty years, which despite Gale's recollection of their being 'trivialised, infantilised and mocked'[54] by the critics were by a core of enthusiasts highly regarded. These included *Jack! The Flames!* which featured Julian Hough, a charismatic and unique performer who fell victim to mental illness and died in 1989.

Lumiere & Son toured small venues around the country and were commissioned by organizations like the Bush. But in the early 1990s, according to Lois Keidan,

> The Arts Council put them under completely inappropriate pressure to change their work. They said you need to be upping your game, working on a bigger scale. They did a big show at the Riverside. It got critically slammed and it basically did for Lumiere.[55]

This shift from playing to 30–35 – a 'small cult', as Gale described it – to playing for 350-plus didn't, in Keidan's opinion, work out. Hilary Westlake agrees that the Arts Council's approach was unhelpful, but more because as the scale of the work increased, the more they were placed under scrutiny and watched for any sign of faltering. The Arts Council's approach was purely 'mathematical', as Westlake put it. It was as if the paternalistic authority had its own vision of how the company should develop. When faltering occurred, the company was cut. The story is familiar; the small show in a back room is admired in principle but regarded as lacking in cultural significance. There is a value placed on the larger event in the mainstream theatre which, it is felt, all should aspire to. If you're good, you should be good on a big scale – why not? But what is unrecognized in this argument is the relative benefits that apply in the different contexts. The small bestows certain possibilities, the large bestows others. They don't sit on a continuum from aspirant to successful.

This chapter is therefore an argument for the awarding of value to the small encounter, the great reckoning in a little room. And not least for a reclamation of the Schumacher-ian motto, 'Small is Beautiful'.

The argument is this: it's only in the relative freedom of unmonitored, low-focus encounters that artists and spectators can really meet each other in a way that allows true responsiveness. The smallness of the scale makes this kind of intimacy possible. On the larger scale, the emphasis inevitably moves towards spectacle and people management. It's the same in comedy. As Stewart Lee argued on Channel 4 News:

> Comedy has become such big business now. A lot of the promotion of particular sorts of people tends to be about the sales figures they turned over and the size of venues they did. But we know as comedians that's a bit of a fluke. We know that the best things happen in the smallest rooms.[56]

Many of the more experimental directors working in theatre argue the same. Chris Goode made the point in an Argument Room that 'the work that I'm interested in making – and watching – may have a glass ceiling on it in terms of the number of people who can be in the room at once and what kind of connection they can hope to have with the work they are seeing'.[57] Another pioneer, the late Adrian Howells, made an art form of the intimate meeting; he 'would offer to wash an audience member's hair while gently encouraging them to open up and talk. He always took his cue from the participant: it was just as likely that the performance might simply involve the two of them sitting companionably in silence or spooned against each other in bed'.[58]

But as indicated, there are pressures that shift artists away from developing this kind of work. They flow in part from the funding authorities' consistent emphasis on involving greater numbers and on 'the proof of benefit' to these numbers. Many artists would be happy to involve more people in a theatre process, but they know that in any move to a larger scale, something will be lost – which is why artists are often ambivalent about the requirement to 'demonstrate that the arts can involve a lot of people', as John Kieffer has put it.[59] The criticism offered by Bill Aitchison is similar: 'There's an idea that the more people you have, the more significant it is.'[60] The demonstration of such value is expected to be evidenced in plans and reports. What's important is the numbers and a rather concrete set of indicators that 'measure' participation. The result of this emphasis is that theatre comes to be seen as a service, not as a medium. It's certainly easy to monitor numbers – but capturing quality of experience is like counting clouds.

For those radical or experimental theatre artists who are happy to work on a large scale, there are different challenges – such as balancing the books. A large scale means more performers. In 2012 the project *Babel* created by WildWorks involved around 800 volunteers. As David Micklem, a WildWorks director, has acknowledged, the project wouldn't have been possible without them. It simply wasn't economic to pay them. Yet using volunteers instead of professionals brings its own issues. Are there any ethical issues arising from pay disparities? Are volunteers simply unpaid spear-carriers of others' visions? Exploited in other words? Many volunteer opportunities are sold on the basis of creative involvement. But as John Kieffer suggests, it's the case that in such projects, 'we do have to ask questions about the depth and range of that involvement'.[61] Frances Rifkin argues that in such projects, 'there are ethics of participation that need to be very carefully defined'.[62]

These questions lead us to You Me Bum Bum Train, which in order to operate at its desired scale means involving large numbers of volunteers. The company takes over a large building and spectators make a journey through a number of different scenes, each involving between two and twenty performers. None of the volunteers are paid but there's an understanding here as elsewhere that the experience will be creatively rewarding. But there are restrictions placed on volunteers' creative freedom. As spectators/partici-pants pass through and experience different encounters (the show is largely a giant version of 'What's My Role?' played by spectators), those meetings must necessarily be brief, otherwise the train ride gets held up. Kelda Holmes found that, working as a volunteer,

> there is a repetition to it and a frustration that you can't get very far with someone [the spectator] in three minutes – and people fall into traps as improvisers because they're not experienced working with an audience – so it's frustrating, you're kind of banging your head against a brick wall for three hours a night and you think, 'Why am I doing this?'[63]

The success of YMBBT and Secret Cinema nevertheless indicate there is a huge appetite for such large-scale interactive theatre adventures. For many spectators, these mechanics serve them well. One strategy that addresses the issue of payment for volunteers has been taken up by Claque Theatre, who engage 150–200 per show. When working in London they utilized a process of time credits: 'one hour of volunteering brings a time credit – and there are various places around the City you can spend them', as Jon Oram explained.[64] These can then be redeemed for classes or entertainment. Welfare State International never paid volunteers but accommodation and food were always provided. However, challenges remain, particularly to work out a set of organizing principles that safeguard the integrity of the interactive encounter. Adrian Heathfield put the challenge thus: 'the dilemma of any participatory, relational practice is "How can it stay in the moment of relationality in a meaningful way?" and "What aesthetic principles will sustain meaningful relations?"'[65] Heathfield references Tino Sehgal, whose work has some points of similarity with YMBBT: 'He's quite brilliant at understanding the nature of the new economies. He installs a set of relations in a place that are the keepers of the knowledge of that world.'[66]

In certain of Sehgal's shows, such as *This Situation*, it's largely through the direct intervention of spectators that activity is triggered. In Sehgal's *This Objective of That Object* 'his actors are instructed to look out for approaching visitors to the space as their cue to begin, amplifying the encounter in radiating convulsions of explicit recognition.'[67] As spectators arrive, performers respond choreographically. If the spectators contribute verbally, conversation begins. If they don't, the performers sink slowly to the floor. Just as in *These Associations* in 2014 at the Tate, 'there are no objects: we are the subject. It is about communality and intimacy, the self as social being, the group and the individual, belonging and separation. We're in the middle of things.'[68]

It's a little hard however to reconcile this rather abstracted definition with my own experience of the show. This was initially rewarding and I appreciated the personal encounter with a performer, during which she told me stories and raised philosophical questions. But not unlike a call centre worker, she seemed disarmed by my subsequent questions in reply, for which she apparently had neither answer nor response. So she retreated from me. Perhaps – ironically – it was the scale of the event, taking place in the Turbine Hall at Tate Modern, involving dozens of performers, which had meant a certain sacrifice of detail in the preparation.

Away from the Tate or the Southbank, it's in workshops or small perfor-mance contexts where it's most possible to redesign how people might relate to each other. Spectators do want the different, the non-passive, the surprising and the unexpected. They want the chance to be influential in the unanticipated moment. Slyly artists can make this happen, knowing perhaps it's actually what many people have come to the theatre or drama experience for (although they may not easily admit it). As Jake Orr puts it, for younger people especially, 'there's an appetite for changing the event'. Being entertained is not always the main priority. To be influential may be more important, more desired. In such contexts therefore, being a spectator may feel more and more like being a volunteer. This surely encourages a greater sense of ownership of the event, and in turn can lead to artists offering more unorthodox time frames within which the spectator can engage. It may even lead to artists abandoning theatre buildings altogether and looking to occupy others.

5. Occupation

Definition in this context: The act of illegally (often but not always) occupying a non-theatre building for the sake of presenting theatre

A dissenting minority makes its protest most evident in acts of occupation. Whether it's Fathers Inside on the roof of Parliament, the IRA smearing excrement on prison cell walls, Abbie Hoffman invading the New York Stock Exchange, Occupy London camping outside the Stock Exchange or Pussy Riot dancing in the Cathedral of Christ the Saviour, the usurpation of property ownership has long been an activist weapon. If we take creativity to be the act of making 'new connections between old ideas',[69] then such actions, linking broadcasts about the injustices of property ownership with the assertiveness of performativity, are clearly creative.

Almost all theatre in the Western world takes place where permission has been given. But when it happens without permission, there's risk, danger, and the possibility of arrest and close-down. But there's also unprecedented attention that flows from these acts of evident, publicized disobedience. In our contemporary period one of the first occupations that sent signals round the world took place in Paris involving artist-activists from different parts of the world. The Théâtre de l'Odéon was occupied in May 1968 and a notice was put on the door that read L'IMAGINATION PREND LE POUVOIR – Imagination Takes Power. A 'committee of revolutionary action at the scene of bourgeois culture' was founded. The building was occupied for around a month and the whole world paid attention, but interestingly there was little actual performance, perhaps because the act of occupation was seen as itself a performance.

Taking hold of such a space, redesigning its spatial properties and creating action with allegorical intent maximizes the potential of occupation. There may be nudity, burnings, dancing, shouting, leaping, ceremony, masks, processions, slow motion, fast motion, wax, feathers, music, drumming, invocations, exhortations, depositing, pleading, castigating, desperation, meditation or laughter. Much of this is not fundamentally different to what happens in a theatre space, albeit not one probably in Shaftesbury Avenue. Yet within temporary occupation there is scope for more impact, more force, more surprise, more levity. This is partly why site-specific work – even of the legally permitted kind – gets the attention it does; the space is wrenched away from its usual function and has a signpost erected that points to the transformation.

When Theatre Delicatessen took over a former BBC building and later a former *Guardian* one, it was as if to say, 'we're making a correction to this failure of property ownership'. It was a bold move negotiated in this case to ensure permissions were granted and to give theatre companies and artists an opportunity to develop, rehearse and perform their work at low cost. In London rehearsal space is expensive. It is surely also a crying shame that buildings such as these lie unused for months or years, not least since by their occupation – with permission – more theatre is made possible. Through such initiatives audiences are offered the almost libidinous excitement of participating in these acts of creative occupation. I used the space myself for rehearsal and auditions, and also visited a show there, so I was keen to find out more about the terms of engagement – how the permissions had been realized. Unfortunately, during the research for this book, I was unable to arrange a meeting with either of the company directors who could have enlightened me further. However, I still believe that the Delicatessen project is estimable and has the future written all over it. In such a space are established different relations: anti-capitalist, anti-profit, anti-mundanity.

When such an act of occupation goes further, when it takes place somewhere that has resonance of itself as a building, the impact is greater still. In 2015 the organization Platform ran a three-day unlicensed arts festival inside Tate Modern in London. They did this to draw attention to issues of fossil fuels and colonialism – and crucially the Tate's economic relationship with BP. It climaxed in the drawing of a giant hourglass on the floor of the Turbine Hall. The staff tried to resist this gentle invasion but failed; caretakers and cleaning staff, on the other hand, proved themselves more sympathetic and it was down to them that the installation stayed as long as it did. What was significant was the choosing of the site; anywhere else the impact would not have been as great.

On another side of the world and a few years prior, Pussy Riot didn't pick the Cathedral of Christ the Saviour by accident but because it was 'to the patriarch what the Kremlin was to Putin ... it represented the Putin era even better than the luxury boutiques did. It was a symbol of post-Soviet piety, superficial and generously gilded.' And so the girls sang: 'Virgin Mary, Mother of God, chase Putin out, chase Putin out, chase Putin out.'[70] Even prior to this performance, Pussy Riot had chosen their venues carefully. Previously it was the roof of Special Detention Centre Number One, which on the night of their visit was housing protesters arrested by police. Such choices uplight the piratical element of occupation rather than downplay it. On release, Pussy Riot performed again, this time in front of an Olympics logo at the Winter Olympics – despite having just been beaten up by Cossacks.

By contrast, buildings built for theatre can seem like the overfed adult next to the wild child. In such a proper theatre, the architecture's function-ality can easily mitigate or soften any disruptive intent. So-called 'radical' plays can easily blend into the visually pleasing walls without a hint of protest. Everything is just so; the event complements the space like a soft pudding in a bowl. There's a drink in the interval and perhaps a meal before. A doorman wishes you goodnight and taxis are not far away. 'Don't forget to keep the programme', 'Who was that funny actor again?' Brecht's observation of this trend led him to put it like this:

> Today we see the theatre apparatus being given absolute priority over the actual plays. The theatre apparatus's priority is a priority of means of production. This apparatus resists all conversion to other purposes, by taking any play which it encounters and immediately changing it so that it no longer represents a foreign body within the apparatus – except at those points where it neutralizes itself. The necessity to stage the new drama correctly – which matters more for the theatre's sake than for the drama's – is modified by the fact that the theatre can stage anything: it theatres it all down.[71]

Brecht's case, more argued than acted upon in his own life perhaps, is that 'theatreing it all down' should be staunchly resisted. The medium after all works partly on shock and surprise. Visitors to the theatre expect to be surprised and are happy to be so, but – and this is the key point regarding cultural conformity – only if the surprises are in the right place. Here lies an unspoken contract. Performers take a risk to break familiar, time-worn patterns. As Martin McDonagh has commented, 'The audience seems to be complicit in the dullness.'[72] When the reassuring frame of the proscenium arch is breached, punters get heated. This is what an outraged Quentin Letts, theatre critic, wrote in respect of the Dave St-Pierre Company at Sadler's

Wells in 2011 under the heading 'This Trashing of Manners is an Assault on Our Values':

> Luke Jennings, dance critic of the *Observer*, should sue Sadler's Wells theatre for assault. Last week he was watching an avant-garde show called *Un Peu De Tendresse Bordel De Merde*. Naked male dancers ran into the stalls, rubbed their crotches in people's faces, parted their buttocks within inches of women's noses and generally behaved like apes. There is a line between artistic shock and shocking art. The thuggishly nude show at Sadler's Wells proceeded to cross it. One of the dancers, spotting Mr Jennings, tried to steal his pen and notepad. Mr Jennings gripped tight to them.[73]

The surprises are all in the wrong place; the dancers have invaded the sanctity of the stalls and 'occupied' them. The audience's space has been besieged and this, it seems, even more than the nudity, is the principle crime – apart, of course, from the very real crime of attempted theft of a pen. It's one of the weapons of disobedient theatre: to ignore the written or unwritten rules of correct behaviour as laid down for certain spaces and buildings, precisely to avoid the core experience being 'theatred down'. Here however the shock of disobedience has prompted a critic to howls of outrage. It is in such howls that the unspoken nature of the contract between the theatre artist and the theatregoer (within a mainstream context) becomes most apparent. The affront was clear. The effect was shocking. We're on the brink of the law being invoked.

Elsewhere, the pop-up shop phenomenon has allowed opportunities for nomadic artists to occupy temporary sites. Improvisation, installation practice and live art have all benefited from the failure of capitalist economics to maintain a full roster of businesses inside their shopfronts. Into these yawning spaces theatre naturally flows. When Rideout constructed a replica prison cell and placed it in an empty shop in Wolverhampton Shopping Centre, passers-by were naturally surprised. They didn't expect to find a prison between a shoe shop and a phone shop. They didn't expect to be invited to sit on a prison bunk and discuss the offences of the ex-offenders in residence. Saul Hewish, co-director of Rideout, pointed out how the element of surprise works in favour of the interactivity in the Go To Jail project:

> The fact it takes place in a shopping centre is critical because it catches people off guard. It works as a provocation because it is unexpected – it's in the 'wrong' place. Some shoppers really struggled with what the cell 'was' because it challenged their notion of what one normally finds in a shopping centre. However, this in part is also what made it intriguing

and made them want to investigate further. It was also that for these visitors the cell provoked the greatest response, either because they were surprised by how claustrophobic and shocking it was, or because they felt it was not punishing enough.[74]

The experience of mounting Go To Jail demonstrated that, perhaps because of the unorthodox location, 'spectators' were more open to a participative exchange. They appeared more willing to let down their guard. They didn't arrive with their spectator head in place and they didn't hang their brains up in any cloakroom. As the project visited different UK locations, what was observable was the extent to which these visitors took the opportunity to confide personal secrets, personal traumas and unrealized desires to these 'prisoners'. It was almost as if the prisoner was the priest and the spectator the penitent. When the project was run within Kidderminster Town Hall in 2015, no day passed without visitors becoming quite unguarded in their revelations about their personal lives, often breaking into tears. It was unquestionably the siting of the opportunity and the gentle facilitation of the prisoners-in-role that made such responsiveness possible.

This is why there's such a strong case for occupation of alternative spaces, especially when theatre starts becoming about the demonstration of scenic or technological wealth. Arguably that time is now, given the recent arrival of *Spiderman: Turn Off The Dark*, the most expensive show in history at time of writing. Despite such wealth on display, what is inevitably lost is what makes theatre truly vital: responsiveness, the sharing of experiences, and the kind of storytelling that emerged in Go To Jail. Occupations then, while born in protest, rightfully return an emphasis on the agency dimension of performance, provoking reflection, conversation and a celebration of dissident thought.

6. Survival

Definition in this context: Keeping going despite the odds

How does the innovator stay independent when big fish are so hungry to consume young fish? How can she maintain creative integrity and survive? I talked to Lois Keidan about this.

> Integrity is a huge thing, but it's also important to know when and where it's appropriate to compromise. And I don't mean compromise in a selling your soul way, I just mean a sort of flexibility. I think a generosity really helps. And a sense of enquiry, an ability to take risks.[75]

Keidan's comment represents a more savvy, pragmatic and cold-eyed appraisal of the task of survival than pioneers of the 1960s were familiar with. Survival 'back in the day was easier', observed Keidan, 'when we could all sign on – it's much more difficult for artists now.' As Tash Fairbanks of Siren Theatre reiterated in the Argument Room: 'We would sign on – that was our Arts Council grant.'[76] To achieve longevity today takes a little more juggling. Creative independence is achievable but may have to be won as part of a bargain with commerce, most likely by taking a job either within – or more probably outside – the arts industry. A degree of financial independence thus achieved, the performer is in a relatively strong position to work on non-commercial, disobedient work that doesn't need to generate a livelihood. When I spoke to students at Rose Bruford College who were shortly to start their professional lives, they were all clear on this one point: the reasonableness of promoting Weetabix one week to make their own crazy, disobedient shows the next.

The teacher and artist Michael Craig Martin always said to students: 'If you have an alternative [to the artist's life], do it.' This is because, he argues, artists only take the creative path because they have no alternative. It's likely they will simply make no progress in any other profession. Making art is an imperative for them. And it's not as if there are no disincentives on this path. For those making this life decision, the likelihood of student debt is a first, huge disincentive. Emerging from university with a £40,000 debt is already a weight of chains around the feet. It's unsurprising many skip training altogether and launch themselves directly into careers.

Keidan pointed out to me that there's a difference between the USA and the UK in this regard. To some extent in the UK we're advantaged because in the UK 'there has been this sustained financial investment in this area of work for some considerable time, so there's more programming and commissioning opportunities, more work in Higher Education'. There are greater opportunities to find administrative or producing work within the arts field. 'What's happening with the younger generation of artists is they refer to themselves as "the slashees". They are the artist slash producer slash whatever.'[77] The opportunity to make non-commercial work is achieved by working as producers or administrators or by teaching.

Working actors are no less vulnerable to economic pressures than independent performing artists. In 2015 Equity stated that almost half of its member responders were earning less than £5,000 a year. This is against a national average wage of £27,000 a year. In 2013 only around 12 per cent earned over £10,000. How many earned over £50,000? Around 2 per cent. In the same period, over 10 per cent of Equity members did no work at all. The average number of weeks worked by an Equity member would be in the region of fifteen. That means that the 'average Equity member' spent thirty-seven weeks cleaning the house and waiting for the phone in 2013.[78]

Of all the arts, the theatre is the sector most culpable in not paying performers. Most of the non-paying jobs are in fringe theatre. However, there's an argument that runs: the fringe is really a training ground, a springboard to greater things. So surely it's justified as a strategy to progress a career? The actor John Gorick pointed out to me the folly of this notion: 'You realize quite quickly that apart from the experience of being onstage and working with other actors, in terms of your career it's pretty useless.'[79] He observes that while there is an 'upper level' of fringe where you might get seen, there's usually not even a guarantee of a review. The benefits of fringe work lie therefore more in keeping your creativity alive and building your networks.

It's unsurprising that artists and actors need a second profession to support the first. The range of second careers is as wide as the Sargasso Sea. Gorick is engaged in property management. 'Because we bought property at the right time in London, we're actually quite well placed by comparison with other actors.'[80] He works in partnership with the actor Elke de Wit and they share the work between them, one taking on property tasks if the other is engaged in theatre. The performer Kelda Holmes argues that 'you have to have a job that you can put down if you get a part; it has to be flexible so you can go to auditions. You're effectively on a zero-hours contract.'[81] Holmes has been an aqua-aerobics instructor, a call centre worker, a life model and a bedside befriender in hospitals. The actor Divian Ladwa has taught martial arts and stage combat. Andrew St John is a driver. Rachel Blackman has clients who come for massage. Jenny Rowe takes on house cleaning. Sam Meleady sells wine over the phone.

You could argue that acting in commercials – although technically 'acting work' – is really a way to support your acting career. That is if you accept what Divian Ladwa told me – that they don't want someone to act, they want someone who 'looks right'. The pay can be good; several thousand pounds for a day's work for a 'featured actor' is not surprising. But the work is demeaning – what Bharti Patel describes as 'literally a cattle market. You're in for five minutes, they take some photos and you're back out.'[82] John Gorick reiterated: 'It'll be a cattle call and you're braced for that. I had one advert, it was for an Italian chewing gum brand – I walked in and they literally threw a bunch of keys on the floor and said "Right, those are a bunch of human bones, you're a zombie. I want you to sit on the floor and pretend to chew them".' Divian Ladwa was asked to be a goldfish and to 'flap around on the floor ... as the audition went on I got angrier and angrier'. But he admits that 'if they'd offered me the job I probably would have done it'. The experience, says Gorick, can be humiliating: 'You do feel like a meat puppet. You do have to expose yourself quite often rather ridiculously.' So how does he cope with that kind of treatment? 'You just have to say – "I don't care". If you're not prepared to enjoy auditions, you're going to be in trouble quite quickly.'[83]

Having got through the audition to do a commercial, however, 'they may decide they want you to stop being a goldfish and be an iguana instead', Divian Ladwa told me.[84] He went all the way to Israel simply 'to play a stereotypical Indian policeman'. What did it involve? 'I had to wiggle my head a lot.' He justifies the trip by saying that 'they put me up in a nice hotel, it was on the beach. Back in the UK it was February, minus two degrees. It was twenty five degrees in Israel.' I asked him about the broader ethical considerations of doing such work. 'I once auditioned for an organization that doesn't pay tax. And I have an issue with that. But I know that if I don't do it, I'm not earning anything. And I have chosen this profession.'[85]

Bharti Patel's line in the sand was drawn in response to a different offer:

> An agent was looking for someone to do an ad for an organization; nice fee, £5,000 for a couple of minutes. I said, 'How much? – bloody hell, for how long, for half a day's work?' So I asked who it was for. 'It's for the Conservative Party.' I said I didn't think I could do it. The agent kept saying, 'It's 5k! It's 5k!' She's also thinking about her 20 per cent. But I thought, if just one person voted Conservative because of me – no, I just can't do it.[86]

There are products Patel won't consider advertising: beauty bleaching creams designed to make a dark skin lighter. And beef. She mentioned her mother's line of thinking: 'If you killed the cow, you killed your livelihood.' However she has promoted online gambling. I asked also about a different topic – if racism had been an issue within the business of auditioning. Nothing sprang to mind – but in making a particular film she recalled the writer encouraged her to 'bang your fist on your chest, because that's what you people do'. Bharti insisted she'd never seen any Asian woman do that but the writer insisted, and then added 'lift your hands up to the sky'. Patel refused. In keeping with other actors, she's happy to forego creative control over the vehicle in return for control over her own performance. She expressed to me her preference for a strong role in a bad play over a small role in a good play because 'people will come and say it's a shame the direction or writing is not great but you were bloody good'. However, she also told me about how such a priority doesn't mean neglecting issues of fairness in an ensemble context; during the tour of a play when she discovered other actors weren't getting paid, 'I was in a great position to say – and did say – "I'm not going on tonight unless you go in there and tell everyone they're going to get paid". And pay the other actors is what the management did.[87]

It's not surprising then, because of unemployment and the cattle market treatment, as John Gorick says, 'Most of us are going around asking ourselves, "Is this the year when I pack it all in?"' Following the death of the actor Paul Bhattacharjee Michael Simkins wrote: 'The cruellest aspect of the acting business is not that it's unfair, but that it's merely indifferent. It gives everything to some and nothing to others; talent, ambition and virtue have little to do with it.'[88] What does have more to do with it is simply luck – speaking on *Desert Island Discs* Dustin Hoffman defined his getting famous as a 'freak accident'.

Whatever the level of prominence, there are always choices. Ladwa commented to me how political awareness is not evenly distributed across the spectrum. It was his observation that a political sensibility can be a brake on powering ahead in your career:

> When it comes to actors, you get different kinds. Some are in it for fame, some for money, some for attention. But when I think of those I know who've been doing it for ten, fifteen, twenty years and haven't become famous but are still plodding along – they are always the ones that are politically in tune, that will maybe go on a march or say, 'I won't buy Nestlé products'. And you do realize, yes I can choose to have some moral fabric.[89]

This is not to suggest a certain amorality is crucial to a successful career. After all, Orson Welles said that, after he had become successful, 'having a theatre and putting on plays is FUN. But working for the cause of human liberty is the most serious job I can do today.'[90]

For the creative artist with a political conscience, the moral dilemma can rear its awkward head at any time. When it happens, the choice can be stark: either stay in the fold, or put your principles first. Within the adjacent field of comedy, Mark Thomas met such a dilemma while working for Channel Four, after which he decided to leave. There had been a series of disputes, one of which concerned the channel's reluctance to support a campaign concerning corporate accountability. Others who have walked away from employment at a major media company on grounds of principle would include radio producer Charles Parker. I first met Parker in 1978 after he'd left the BBC where he'd made the famous *Radio Ballads* with Ewan MacColl and Peggy Seeger. What was radical about these programmes was that they were radio documentaries without any authorial journalistic voice. While this was unheard of at the time, MacColl quoted the Director-General of the BBC as saying this was 'the best radio he'd ever heard.'[91] MacColl's private opinion of Parker was low: 'He was an intolerable human being, and a very indifferent producer.'[92] The partnership of MacColl and Parker finally ended in 1976 when Parker walked out in search of more independence and started Banner Theatre with the aim of carrying on what he'd done within the BBC but on the stage. At time of writing, Banner Theatre is still going, still moving ahead, still using many of the same techniques, still reaching the same audiences, still allied to the Trade Union movement.

There are comedians too who have had regular run-ins with major corporations. One of these is Jerry Sadowitz, whose spikiness and refusal to compromise is likely to keep him forever from the London Palladium. It's a survival strategy of his own that, like him or loathe him, deserves grudging admiration. Here is an edited email exchange with a journalist from www. comedy.com.uk.

> **Journalist** Your tour publicity labels you 'The World's Most Offensive Comedian'. Would you say that label is accurate? If so, do you feel pressure to continue to live up to that image with the material you write and deliver? If you don't think it's accurate, why is it being used?
>
> **Jerry** Yes. No. Unapplicable.
>
> **Journalist** You've said in the past 'I've got a lot of ideas that I'd love to do for telly, but they never see the light of day'.
>
> **Jerry** Television is class driven and favours the ruling class, the middle class, homosexuals, paedophiles and those who are promoted by one of those groups. As for the commissioning editors themselves, they are unequivocal plonkers who know very little about anything at all. Their faces go completely blank when you present them with an original idea so I stopped submitting anything to them a long time ago. Worse, many of them are now women which means the art of comedy will be completely lost within the next five years.
>
> **Journalist** You don't want your audience to agree with what you're saying but would you accept that some people who do see you are agreeing with some of the 'hateful' things you do say? Are you therefore earning some money by 'pandering to various prejudices'?
>
> **Jerry** That's right, I built my entire career researching what the public wants, and then spoon feeding and pandering to them. What a fucking moron you are.
>
> **Journalist** To finish on a light note, can we ask you: what has been the happiest day of your life, and what did the day involve?
>
> **Jerry** Of all the stupid questions so far, this one is particularly annoying, and irrelevant, and when I meet you, I propose to write it down on cardboard and nail it to your face.

If we're to consider surviving, it's useful also to look at not surviving: giving up, abandoning the cause, switching direction or being pulled off the stage by unseen hands. Friends of his argue that composer and musician Cornelius Cardew was murdered for his principles. I first met Cardew at a political meeting organized by the Communist Party of England (Marxist-Leninist). He invited me to political meetings where I learned about Maoism and the works of Enver Hoxha. We eventually worked together to present two Brecht plays at the Roundhouse. Cardew was killed by a hit-and-run driver in London several years later. Rumours circulated, and still do, that he was killed by fascists or MI5 because of his politics and the way he used his role as an artist to campaign against the British state. Nothing was ever proved but questions remain.

Joan Littlewood retired from the scene before anyone could remove her. She had become increasingly exasperated at not getting the support she and many others thought she deserved from the Arts Council. She was notoriously reluctant to compromise, yet at the same time her project – initiated with Ewan MacColl – flowered within a bubble of questing uncertainty. Peter Rankin writes that 'the energy she could bring to not knowing what she was doing was dangerous'.[93] While constantly seeking new theatrical strategies, she was unmoveable on principles. Directing a show in Paris, she was informed that 'the government was not too happy about the King of the Belgians appearing as a character in the play'.[94] She was effectively told by Georges Wilson, artistic director of the Théâtre National Populaire, that she needed to change the play because keeping sweet with the government was going to ensure 'a large sum of money for improving the theatre'.[95] A more precise example of a biting-the-hand-that-feeds dilemma would be hard to find. 'Not a word will I have changed', she said. 'Take out the King of the Belgians and they can take the whole play off' was Littlewood's response.[96]

Nor was commitment to the spirit of defiance restricted to the content of shows. With her company Theatre Workshop, Littlewood had travelled the UK and Europe often poverty-stricken, lacking even the income to provide daily meals. Yet come the onset of the Second World War, the company put in place a unique strategy that helped both its survival and its longevity. Rather than simply disband for the duration, the company set tasks for themselves to be completed as long as the war lasted. The company divided up the world's dramatic literature between them so that when peace came, they were in a better place to start all over again. One member was given Chinese Classical theatre, one Jacobean theatre, another a set of plays all dealing with marriage. As Ewan MacColl recalled:

> During the war years we were prepared to study like hell. We had an educational programme worked out in 1939 as soon as the war started. We hand picked the people that were going to stay and make it their life's

work. And we shared out the studies. Everyone had their job, everyone had a profound study. And then the results were shared around at the end of every month, by post. When we came together after the war, we were the most highly trained group in these isles.[97]

It wasn't failure of organization or lack of intent therefore that finally drove Littlewood into retirement in France. Not according to Richard Eyre. As he put it to John Bury, Theatre Workshop's stage designer, it was rather success that broke the company up. Her actors kept getting drawn away to appear in the West End.

John Bury Yes, Joan was very fed up. Every time she got a company together, it got split, and those bastards in the West End, as she referred to them, were stealing all her little chickens. And after a bit she gave up. I hung on as long as possible, in fact I two-timed for a bit at the end to keep Stratford East running.

Richard Eyre Was she very bitter at the lack of support from the Arts Council?

John Bury Well, verbally, yes. 'Right bastards' she'd call them all. I think she provoked the opposition in that she would never give way to any artistic mentor. She wanted to be alone; she didn't want to be lectured or talked to or have it explained to her why she couldn't have any more money. When I first joined the company, I couldn't understand why we weren't the National Theatre of Great Britain.[98]

If Littlewood was starting her career today, would she get a better reception from the Arts Council? It's far from certain. There's still a profound strain of conservatism within funding decisions that are given cover by progressive-sounding policy statements that often belie the actual decisions made. The Arts Council's accountability is paper thin. It doesn't reveal more than the ratio of failed applications to successful ones and it discourages companies from publicizing their failures. There is no available database of rejected applications. Tales of strong applications that hit all the right buttons, yet fail, are numerous. Talk of personal bias is not unusual. Geographical bias is well attested, as in the House of Commons Select Committee Report, 2014.

In terms of survival, the relevant question must be asked: is it possible for a disobedient theatre that offers a radical proposition to sit easily with long-term funded security? Matt Adams admitted to me how relatively embedded Blast Theory is in the securities of the UK economic infrastructure. Companies such as Forced Entertainment, DV8 and Dreamthinkspeak have also become significantly reliant on this state support, balancing this with European co-financing. Meanwhile pioneering forbears the People Show, Bubble and Forkbeard Fantasy are no longer regularly funded – yet the People Show and London Bubble have survived despite the loss. Mark Long of the People Show has declared it a relief to be 'free of that restriction'.

There are different views about the benefits of regular financial support. To some it's a bulwark against dissolution that is essential. To others it's the hoped-for dream. In recent times the Birmingham-based company Kiln have made a series of striking pieces of work within which you might hear echoes of Lumiere & Son, so I was surprised to discover that one of the founders, Emily Ayres, had left the company. She explained:

> After nine years making independent theatre with a small theatre company, I felt increasingly frustrated by both a lack of artistic freedom and a lack of financial security – represented by the holy grail of funding: the NPO status. It seems harder and harder to make good theatre while working within the arts funding system – the order of projects and the planning, forecasting and producer-meddling seemed to shut down the natural processes of making work at the same time they pretend to support them.[99]

While acknowledging the funding that the company did get, she doesn't think that 'theatre is adequately valued by society any longer, financially speaking ... so I just wanted to be part of something a bit more real, more tangible. So I trained to be an English teacher, which is over-structured but equally creative.'

The remaining company declined the opportunity to present a different perspective. The future is uncertain and will remain so.

So here we are, anticipating the end of Part One, and a lingering uncertainty is hanging around the final paragraph like a homeless man outside a bank. However, as the above strategies indicate, there are nevertheless a huge range of pragmatic solutions to the challenge of biting or not biting the hand that feeds. To requote Craig Martin, those that must make creative work, must. Somehow. Someway. Possibly every day. And the world is – has been – and should be – grateful for that. It seems that some measure of instability is inescapable, especially when the artist is working in a small room away from the grand pavilions. Perhaps this is an honourable place to be. It's certainly a place where the practice of disobedience is more safely nurtured. Disobedience is very often rewarded in the long term, after all. So – finally – in the spirit of best survival, here are some 'tips for artists' from the artist Action Hero (a summary; the full text can be found in Appendix 2):

1. Make good art
2. See it as a political act
3. Find cheap rent
4. Set the agenda
5. Make friends
6. Call yourself an artist
7. Immerse yourself in the works of others
8. Be patient
9. Do it yourself
10. Talk your own language
11. Share
12. Recognize jealousy
13. Work hard (but know what work is)
14. See limitations as possibilities
15. Make the work you want to make
16. Get paid
17. Talk to artists who make a living and ask them how they do it

Part Two

In the Room

5. Principles in Action

What might be tactics for the rehearsal room that put into practice a notion of disobedient theatre?

This section of the book assumes a theatre-making context where the makers come from a mix of backgrounds: professional, community, student, or even whoever walks in the room. It's a more informal collation of notes and suggestions. The thread through most of the sections is the task of devising a show from scratch.

1. Method vs Intuition

The best narratives in drama pivot around a theme that has resonance for an audience. These are the stories that inspire people, perhaps even inspiring them to action. A devising process hopes to uncover what these stories might be. So, when there's a show to make, the big question is always: 'What should the show be about?'

Let's imagine a company setting out to make a show. Now it's very possible the company is already united in a conviction as to what the show should be about. Perhaps it should address disability concerns, employment issues, green politics, or the failure of government to provide sufficient numbers of crèche places for the good citizens of Worthing. But it may be no agreement is present. Everyone is fired up about bringing down capitalism but no blueprint for action can be agreed on. Nor can the subject matter for this play. It's an uncertainty felt by many playwrights too. According to Martin Crimp:

> If you're sitting down as a writer, like you're meant to do, and think to yourself 'What am I going write about?', part of you might think, 'Well that's an impossible decision to make because there are so many choices now – which include the nature of a globalised world'.[1]

So it may be constructive to ask a different question, especially bearing in mind the lessons from the earlier chapters on the value of starting 'at home': 'What personal experiences should we bring to bear?'

This means sharing life stories. It's a tactic that can generate some strong material. But sitting and chatting in itself can become wearing; how do you weigh one person's story against another? At some point, the work needs to move to improvisation or the trying out of ideas. Here comes a choice: do we proceed methodically or intuitively? Do we follow a step-by-step approach to generating material or follow our collective nose and see where it leads us? To be honest, any process of putting together a show will involve some mix of both. But there are companies that work largely intuitively. This includes Blast Theory, whose founder Matt Adams observes:

> Our work does involve going through various small showings and tests, but I believe we make our best work when we don't fully understand what we're doing. You can't be too schematic about it. You have to follow your nose and at some point you're going to come unstuck. But that's the pleasure of having made a body of work; it makes you more relaxed about this.[2]

Without such a body of work, a different approach may be more useful. This chapter will therefore look largely at working more methodically, going step-by-step. I've always been intrigued by systematic, methodical approaches to creative practice. At drama school we studied Laban's Movement Analysis as developed for actors by Yat Malmgren. The system aimed to define a range of personality types you could draw from when working out your character in a script. We were told that in *Twelfth Night* there are twelve primary characters with two variations of each of the six basic personality types or 'inner attitudes' (Stable, Mobile, Awake, Adream, Near, Remote) that made up the system. The play therefore contains the maximum number of different personality types given that number of characters. We were told by our teachers, Christopher Fettes and Yat Malmgren, that if you knew the personality type of the character you were playing, it gave you the key to unlock that character's movements, behaviour and inner life. I was seduced.

Much, much later I began to realize how many actors found such a schematic approach quite limiting. But nevertheless it was clear there were benefits from proceeding methodologically. It can, for example, help to facilitate a process of diagnostics within devising. This will help us to answer the question: 'What should the show be about?'

It means following a process not of trying to second guess what will have resonance for an audience but of first discovering what has resonance for those of us who are in the room. Joseph Chaikin wrote that Julian Beck 'said that an actor has to be like Columbus: he has to go out and discover something and come back and report on what he discovers.'[3] But discoveries can also be made in the room. After all, the world exists in us just as we exist in the world. Temporary companies are always reassured by the presence of a methodology. Clarity of method creates a sense of safety, a feeling of being anchored in a wider tradition that, you may reasonably claim, goes back to the Greeks and beyond, to shamans in buffalo skins.

It's true that if the company in this context is largely full of young people, there are themes we would expect to emerge – identity issues, sexuality issues, independence from family issues, etc. – but to assume these can be schematized and mapped in advance by a facilitator does a disservice to the uniqueness and complexity of any group of any age. The virtues of a 'blank page' approach, coupled with a way of working that moves step by step to assist the discovery of some resonant themes as well as giving ownership of the material to the group, offers real benefits. And for this to happen, the journey has to be made by everyone travelling together without a map. Nor should the facilitator have the map coordinates of the final destination hidden in a knapsack. What he or she should have, however – and most essentially – is a sense of what a journey comprises.

'What Should the Show be About?'

It's a question deserving to be answered capably and intelligently – and without prejudice, whether you're in a South London youth centre or Jenin refugee camp. Especially if you are in Jenin refugee camp, because of the focus that theatre company will hold for the community. As Nabil Al-Raee, the director of the Freedom Theatre, said while in London: 'It's important for us to ask: why are we doing this show now? Our audience is always asking: what are you wanting to say? Why are you doing that play?'[4]

But before the investigation commences, there is an important task: to set the boundaries of the constituency. Who's involved in informing what the show is? It may be those in the room – or it may be a wider community. Chris Goode's project Open House at West Yorkshire Playhouse in 2011 invited all-comers to drop by the rehearsal room and join the devising process. And not only that, as it turned out. Goode writes: 'The "professional" ensemble that arrived on Monday morning numbered five; the combined cast of Friday's final show, sixteen.'[5] Other companies operate similarly. Claque Theatre, in common with Fluxx and Welfare State, leave the rehearsal room entirely and go out and consult widely in the community. In Claque's work, 'public soundings' are made via special workshops and encounters set up to identify a theme. This might be as simple as director Jon Oram talking to someone in a pub or in another case running a workshop with Somali women within shouting distance of the Barbican, which, interestingly, none of the women had ever visited. In all, Claque's process takes around eighteen months.

Once the constituency is defined, the detective work can begin.

Whether there has been external research or not, playfulness should still be the keynote of early work in the room. It's the view of Andrew Morrish, the Australian improviser and teacher, that playing in an abstract way can, despite the apparent foolishness of the task, lead you towards material of significance. And my view too; it's a key hypothesis within this methodology. But Morrish insists on an important condition: the actor must commit to whatever dramatic action emerges, irrespective of its apparent meaning. And that can feel odd. It feels odd because it can involve doing something for longer than would be thought useful or reasonable. Marina Abramovic writes about this process of meaning-emergence thus:

> In workshops with students I ask them just to open the door and close the door, as slowly as possible. You don't go in and you don't go out, you just do this for one hour, for two hours or for five hours. Then the door stops being the door and becomes something else.[6]

Five hours of door-closing seems a tad long for our context. However, interestingly, this kind of process is not dissimilar to that required in therapy where the patient is commanded to give attention to what emerges in the empty space created by the visit. In *The Psychopathology of Everyday Life*, Freud writes that 'what happens is that, with the relaxation of the inhibiting attention – in still plainer terms, as a result of this relaxation – the uninhibited stream of associations comes into action.'[7] Or as Keith Johnstone writes in *Impro*: 'If I pay close attention to my mental processes I find an amazing amount of activity.'[8]

It may be assumed by some that this process has nothing to do with politics or disobedience. However, the notion that activist material can only be arrived at via a top-down, ideological process of defining 'correct' issues is mistaken. There is little more powerful than raw material arrived at via a process of asking, 'What is most important to my self-determination and my progress in the world?' when this question is asked by those disadvantaged by the great march of capitalism. The answers to this question represent the essential fuel of devised theatre.

My own preferred sequence of activities when devising starts with building a sense of company solidarity. Once that is in place, the process moves like this:

1. Engage the group through play, using games and exercises that will generate raw material.
2. Examine and reflect on the material generated.

3. In a process involving everyone, select the most vital material out of what has emerged.
4. Play more formally and concentratedly with that selected material, i.e. elaborate it.
5. Marshal that new material into a shape for performance and rehearse it.

When teaching this process I sometimes refer to the image of a fish (see Figure 1).

The beginning of this journey is not far from John Wright's process which he shared with me as being 'just straightforward, unconscious play. Which is a bit like doodling or something.'[9] It may be just doodling but of course there is a higher purpose: to deliver some key material perhaps in the form of an image, a story, a scene or a relationship. Or perhaps even just a game that can be used in performance. 'The skill in "finding a game" becomes clearer as soon as you try and play it in front of an audience', Wright observes. Any selected raw material found in this way, if it carries resonance for the group, will then give support and context to any weaker material. Exercises like Abstract to Concrete can also be useful in this process of discovery.

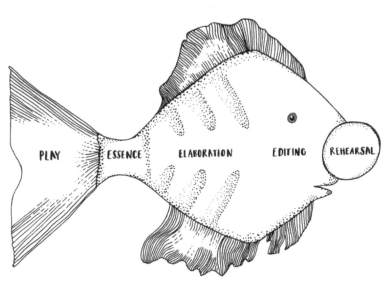

Figure 1 The Devising Process: starting with Play, finding an Essence, Elaborating this, Editing that material and moving towards Rehearsal

Abstract to Concrete

For a single performer. She starts randomly doing an abstract movement until it settles into a repeating pattern. Then she starts to look for what this abstract movement might be if it was an action in life. She plays with it and adapts it until she finds what kind of (concrete) action she's doing. Once a decision is made, the action can be perfected. An extension to this exercise might be to find another performer and for the two of them (wordlessly) to find a bridge between their actions so they can be fused into the one action.

Another particularly useful tool in the business of discovering resonant images is that of projection; allowing participants to project onto the work something of themselves. It's a misunderstood but valuable tool.

2. A Note on Projection

In the orthodox interpretation of the psychological act of 'projection', one person typically 'projects' on to another some negative aspect of themselves – possibly a character trait which the projecting person doesn't acknowledge. 'Oh, she's so dismissive of everyone', says the dismissive person. It's what Freud describes as 'a special psychic mechanism' whereby an attitude is 'projected from our inner perception into the outer world and is thereby detached from our own person and attributed to the other'.[10] In Freud's thinking this tends to be associated with an 'unconscious hostility'. However he also writes that other 'ideational and emotional processes' can also be 'projected outwardly and are used to shape the outer world'.[11]

We know there is a strong impulse within the brain to 'make sense' of what it sees. So faced with inadequate information, the brain will tend to 'fill in the gaps'. As watchers we are led seductively to these spaces of incompleteness. Our curiosity is aroused.

It's possible to construct exercises which invite our company members to fill in the gaps. This is achieved by deliberately putting forward very partial or opaque narrative information. The minds of the watchers then instinctively 'project' on to the blank spaces with their own imaginings. Such projections carry something of the current preoccupations of the watchers, which take this opportunity of the blankness to rise to the surface. When this happens, we learn what is seeking to be expressed. We can then go to the next stage and ask these watchers to verbalize what might be the stories suggested by the 'inadequate' material. Then what we do is grant a legitimacy to these projections. If the observer sees the story of George and the Dragon, or a love triangle, or the court of the Marquis de Sade, or a field of crying policemen, the material can be taken as that.

The exercise I developed that does this most effectively is Narrative Images. The exercise works because the makers of the comic strip have no sense of ownership of it.

Narrative Images

The group divides into a number of sub-groups each with roughly the same number of members. An optimum sub-group size would be six or eight.

Each sub-group is tasked with creating a sequence of still images like a cartoon strip. This is created by Player A making the first image, B the second, C the third and so on. At no time do they discuss the content or meaning of the images. The images are created using other members of the sub-group. In each case the sculptor places him/herself into the image once the others are placed. Each image follows the last on the basis of 'What happens next'. Preferably around six or eight images should be made in total so each player makes perhaps two images each. Talking is allowed but it should only be about who stands where, what the gestures are, etc. It mustn't deal with content. Finally the sequence of images is learned by the sub-group enabling the sequence to be performed uninterrupted; Image 1 then Image 2 then 3, etc.

Each sub-group performs for everyone else. The audience is invited to determine what each story is about; its theme and/or dramatic action. Given that the authoring sub-group have not agreed any interpretation themselves, any interpretation offered is justified and recorded.

Any observer is as entitled as the makers to interpret the sequence. In his book *Why Is That So Funny?* John Wright recalls being entranced in his youth by a similar process of projection:

> We had an art teacher ... who was called Miss Rose. She was a potter ... and would slam a piece of clay down on the bench.
>
> 'What does that remind you of? Come on. What do you see? Make a choice', she'd say.
>
> 'It's a hat, Miss', someone might say.
>
> 'OK, yes, I can see a hat there. It's a hat. Excellent ... Then we make it bigger', she'd say.[12]

By engaging a whole group in projecting and elaborating, we can discover themes or stories that are wanting to emerge. We start to identify something of the group's 'inner world' of thought and feeling. There is often a reluctance to acknowledge any depiction of the inner world. So there's jokes about it, perhaps mockery, perhaps even derision. However, the greater extent to which the members of the group have aspects in common, such as age, class, geography and disposition, the more their projections will tend to be similar and the more easily will they be welcomed. Such connections have the quality of what the group analyst Morris Nitsun calls 'resonance near'. As a result, the group are more likely to find consensus over which particular images or stories have resonance.

Other exercises which encourage projection would include this one:

Crying Woman, Laughing Man

This exercise is an improvisation which is triggered by an ambiguous image. The players are invited to project their own interpretation onto what is happening.

One player, it could be of either gender, sits on a chair and simulates crying. There is a chair alongside Other players are invited to make a choice about what is happening, to come into the scene and extend what is happening there. Usually the performer will make a weak choice, coming in and simply comforting the person and asking what's wrong. Almost any other choice is preferable. My favourite performance in a workshop context was by the actress Sophie Partridge who rode her wheelchair alongside the crying woman and sat with her while holding some papers. She then proceeded to 'read the papers' and laugh out loud at what she 'read' there.

A variation is a laughing man or a woman staggering about holding her head. In each case the group is invited to 'fill in the gaps', to 'make sense' of what is happening.

3. Working with Images

It's possible that the core material required to move the process on might be a relationship, a location, a theme or an image. The use of imagery can't be faulted. If it is an image it shouldn't be conceived too literally; it needs to contain some measure of ambiguity or mystery. The artist Deborah Jones talked to me about her search for such an image.

When I'm going out to do a project, a commission or a residency, it's important for me to have a central image that will hold it and anchor the work – and if I haven't got that, I feel I'm drifting around. If it doesn't turn up, it's really scary. I have to just wait for it and look for it.[13]

John Fox of Welfare State insists that such a central image or story should be able to be 'mythologized'. He told me that out of perhaps a hundred stories collected for a project, only two or three would fit the bill. He gave me an example of one that did:

> A local councillor did a lot of work to try and save the pier at Morecambe. The night she got elected the pier was set on fire by arsonists. She told a story about a taffeta dress she had as a child which she wore as she walked from Lancaster to Morecambe to go to the beach. Her brother pushed her in a puddle and the dress was ruined. She said, looking at the fire, it was like her taffeta dress being set on fire. It was a lovely story and able to be mythologized.[14]

The Sculpture Speaks

Performer A sculpts Performer B into a shape. If necessary the shape can be demonstrated or described if physical contact isn't appropriate. Performer B asks him/herself whether or not the shape provokes any emotion or sensation. If not, then another shape is found. If it does, then Performer B can adjust the shape to facilitate a stronger feeling. Then B has to find a phrase that feels appropriate to the shape. Once found, this is spoken. Performer A or C can then ask questions of B to elaborate what is going on; where he or she is, what's going on.

Blind Drawings

In a devising context, the players are asked to take 5 large A2 clean pieces of paper. Instruct them to draw on each an image of what is happening on stage during the five principal scenes of the play-to-be-devised. Instruct them to do this blindfold or with eyes closed. Encourage them not to be literal or representational but rather to express the feelings or perhaps the movement qualities of the different scenes. Ask them to ensure that the numbers 1, 2, 3, 4 or 5 are included on the back of the correct page.

Once completed, ask the group to arrive at a consensus as to which is the preferred number 1, 2, 3, 4 and 5 from all those images available for selection. You have then a visual score for the piece to be devised. Only at this point should there be a discussion about the 'meaning' or 'interpretation' of the selected images.

Exercises like The Sculpture Speaks or Blind Drawings use different approaches, with the same aim of generating raw material.

Sometimes however the process stalls. There are too many themes or no key images. A weariness sets in. It's for the facilitator to break the deadlock either by making proposals or by confronting the group with key choices. Deborah Jones was working with a project that concerned 'values', especially those that were to some extent beyond our human abilities to realize. While looking at the gardens where the project was to take place, she saw some statues that set off a chain of thought. She was able to take this to the group as a proposal:

> How do we today invite gods down into our homes? How do we have our values and bring these into our everyday life? The image I found for that was the lightning conductor. There was this lightning conductor that came down the Obelisk – that was the image for me, one of something up there in your mind or your dreams or your heart – how do you ground that?[15]

These are some examples of key anchor images from shows I've been involved in creating. In each case the identification of the image made possible some more focused work in follow-up, elaborating the image's secrets.

- An abandoned house, good for kids to play in (dangerously): project with young offenders, London
- The killing of an animal by ten-year-olds: young people's theatre, Greenwich
- A comatose woman who watches TV all day: show for Bradford Festival
- Women secluding themselves from men in the European countryside: fringe show, Brighton
- A dog reared to attack others: prisoners in therapy, HMP Dovegate

4. Working with Improvisation

There are of course many ways to generate material. One way I've used is via structured improvisation. In other words, the impro is given a frame, perhaps the location or the characters or the action of the piece, but there are also gaps to be 'filled in' by the improvisers during the playing. To take an example, in this scene one character is due to visit another – and to bring a problem to this meeting. But it's important the 'problem' is not fixed in advance. This is the gap to be 'filled in'. Probably their relationship will be fixed. So during the playing of the scene, the problem will be defined by the visitor. It's important, essential even, that the problem is not determined in advance.

The Visit

Player A 'visits' Player B. Their relationship is defined in advance, for example brother–sister, close friends. One or other is charged in advance with being the player who during the improvisation will either 1) make a confession or 2) introduce a problem, the solving of which requires the other party's help. Subsequent improvisations (scenes) can flow from this one.

The facilitator role is significant throughout this process. It's never one of being an unthinking servant to others' creativity; however it does involve giving priority to those images and stories which appear as being closest to the group.

Let's imagine that, in this case, the group has hit on some images which they've found and want to develop further. One is an image of someone who's lost a dog in the park. Another is a young woman peering into a derelict building where several people are sitting around a fire. The group has decided that these are the images the group wants to work with. They have agreed to sacrifice other material which doesn't 'fit' with this imagery.

selection

5. The Art of Elaboration

Arguably elaboration is how *commedia dell'arte* performers found their mojo back in the Middle Ages. The trainee performer would first choose a character, Arlecchino, Colombina or Pantalone, and then, rather than rehearsing, would simply watch the established performer working, before taking over the role and developing an interpretation in front of the audience. So how precisely did they evolve their craft onstage? What were the techniques? Colin Ellwood confided his theory:

> It's what I would call the Michael Jackson effect. The classic thing with Michael Jackson was to grab his crotch. So people would ask him, 'Why do you do that?' and he gave some reason. But if you look at the film, you see him grab his crotch and the audience goes wild. So of course he does it again. It's reinforcement. It was the same with *commedia*. Performers went into market stalls to find out what holds people's attention.[16]

Hence the value of always working with spectators, even in the rehearsal room; this replicates the player–audience relationship. It also enables the activist dimension of the work to be always present. How does this elaboration connect with our given theme/image/objective? What holds the audience's attention? What material engages and provokes? Observing the actor–audience relationship helps to answer these questions. It also helps to bridge the gap between 'rehearsing' and 'performing'.

To take another example of learning from the audience, Billy Connolly's stand-up routines were evolved initially in the breaks between songs. They got longer and longer until eventually the chat took over from the songs. Michael Rosen draws from the same approach. He's known as a poet who works with young people. Contradicting the stereotype, he says a lot of his poems are in fact elaborations that

> have come from stand-up. From improvisation. My poem *The Chocolate Cake* came from me just improvising a little bit then a little bit more – and seeing the laughter in the children's faces in the room. And thinking I could add a little bit here and some exaggeration here and some gesture there and then at some point or another I've gone, hey, I could write this down. And that approach has come about in part from reading Billy Connolly's monologues and Lenny Bruce's – and before that Joyce Grenfell's.[17]

So given this image of someone who has lost her dog, first there's an option of elaborating it by simply *intensifying the moment*. To do this, another actor might be asked to play the dog to see if this helps build a sense of connection. There might be games with the dog, perhaps even an imagined conversation between dog and master. But perhaps this should be mistress? If this character was played by a female performer rather than by a male, the two images selected by the group could be easily linked. Let's imagine the group makes this decision. The actress might then be asked to try out a range of games or exercises that build a connection. If successful, it means that when the dog disappears, the business of attempting to find it has more poignancy. (It also might be possible to bring in a real dog to join the process – Chris Goode in his show *The Forest and the Field* enlisted the services of a cat, a different one every night!)

Alternatively the moment could be *elaborated through time*. There is an exercise of Keith Johnstone's called What Happens Next? which personally I've always found rather clunky but works in other hands.

Moving backward in time, it would be possible to stage a scene with significant others in the girl's life – a husband or partner perhaps? Perhaps one of these is the real owner of the dog and charges the young woman with its

What Happens Next?

The player or players on stage complete an action within the scene – for example call out for the dog – then turn to the audience and ask, 'What Happens Next?' Someone calls out a response (if several responses, the facilitator might want to mediate and choose one) and the suggestion is acted out. Once completed, the question is posed again and again the suggestion is acted out.

care. Moving forward in time, when the girl returns to the dog owner, there's perhaps a confession scene for the girl. Perhaps she got too stuck into her book and didn't notice the disappearance. This throws the emphasis of the narrative onto the relationship, which can only be useful. The dog owner's response is vital in determining the future direction of the drama. Another way to move forward in time is to have the dog, rather than being found, returned to the girl by a stranger – this is a classic device for the start of a romance. Or the stranger might introduce her to a cause, a tribe or a social movement.

Or we could *replace some of the elements of the scene* with other elements that are dramatically stronger. There's something clumsy about an actor playing a dog, so instead of a dog, perhaps what is lost is a bracelet. But the group decided previously on 'lost dog'. Would this compromise this earlier decision? The group needs to decide. If the group is comfortable, then the story starts to be about a gift and the implications of losing it. A further, perhaps even more interesting, jump would be to have us explore what happens if the bracelet has been stolen. This then opens up some different options: the pursuit of the thief, crime, disparities of wealth, poverty, even drug addiction. It might also open up possible connections with the other chosen image – that of homeless men around a fire.

Alternatively, the material could be *moved into a different style*. Let's imagine a more storytelling approach with use of direct address to the audience. The bracelet owner tells the story of the day her favourite, beloved item was borrowed without permission and then lost by her daughter. A performer playing a homeless man steps forward and tells how he found the bracelet – or how he took it – and then subsequently sold it for a substantial sum of money. How this was spent: badly, wisely? If badly, perhaps it was spent on drugs. Who was responsible? The mother? The thief? The dealer? This leads us to several themes: personal responsibility, addiction, disparities of wealth and homelessness – suitable themes for a company wanting to progress a piece of activist theatre.

This Is My Brother

This starts with two players. Player A introduces the other as 'my brother' (or sister/wife/partner). Then Player A goes on to say something about that brother. Perhaps a story from childhood and a current preoccupation of that brother. Then the brother says something both about another character played by Player C who in turn introduces another character. And so on. The purpose is to build up a social world with a range of characters all connected with each other. Then the audience might be asked which of the relationships should be examined further. This relationship is then taken as the subject of a sequence of improvisations.

A social world

There is a standard exercise I developed, which can be used in a similar way to progress stories and launch improvisations. If this woman/dog/bracelet story is going to be part of a longer show, which we presume it is, any short scene has to earn its place in it. It quite often happens in a devising process that the best material isn't at the centre of the stage. Phelim McDermott talks about 'a signal that you can choose to ignore or you can amplify it' then 'taking that thing from the edge and cooking it up'.[18] What might be an example of this? It might be a character that was seen only briefly; perhaps it was the moody girlfriend of the bracelet thief. Perhaps we should learn her story. Or returning to the other image selected by the company, it might be the gambling that was taking place in the ruined house when the girl peered in.

Tim Etchells told me of how Forced Entertainment might operate in this way, albeit within a different style of performance – seeking out elements of improvisation worthy of elaboration:

> Since about *Marina and Lee* [an early show] a practice emerged that was about doing a lot of free-form improvisation where you'd have half an idea … and you'd just let it run for half an hour and see what happened. And then you'd select from that one little riff or routine that you thought had something in it. Then you'd start talking about 'What are the rules of that?' and 'How does this actually work?'[19]

Another way to elaborate the material might be to ask: does this material lend itself to *any particular dramatic genre*? The loss of the dog or bracelet might lead us to detective story structures. The acquisition of sudden wealth leads us into folk tales such as the one about the boy who is given magic beans but doesn't realize fully their value. What of the homeless figures around a fire? An elaboration of their stories might lead us to migration issues and refugees. In turn this suggests a Boccaccio-style form of story-telling and/or a promenade style of performance. The audience might be invited to move around the space and eavesdrop on a number of different conversations between different groups of migrants seeking refuge. Something is emerging here about wealth disparities and the vulnerability of those at the edge of society; those who are vulnerable to the casual mistakes of the wealthy. Do members of the company have relevant personal experiences that could be recounted? Or do they have friends with such stories? But to enable further elaboration of this material, and to move on to the devising of a narrative structure, there probably does need to be a decision about style.

6. Some Notes on Style

For reasons discussed earlier, an activist theatre tends to eschew a fixed naturalism, preferring more direct contact with the audience than that tradition allows. It might be assumed that a diagnostic approach (starting with nothing, discovering the theme and the story) leads inevitably to naturalism by default. But this doesn't have to be the case. There is an argument that devising is in fact better facilitated with an abstract vocabulary because it frees up performers to be more imaginative. They're not held in check by any attempt to be 'honest to life' or 'true to themselves'. The American director Joe Chaikin even suggested that the imposition of a socially realistic vocabulary is against the natural momentum of the work:

> The theatre … seems to be looking for a place where it is not a dupli-cation of life. It exists not just to make a mirror of life, but to represent a kind of realm just as certainly as music is a realm. But because the theatre involves behaviour and language, it can't be completely separate from the situational world, as music can.[20]

This is the point made earlier: theatre is a less abstract medium than dance or music. But that doesn't mean it can't engage and employ abstraction. In the work of reducing complex material into simple elements, abstraction is necessary. Such reduction is similarly a function of poetry. Boal describes this approach as being about developing material that 'belongs to two worlds at the same time, the world of reality and the world of fiction'.[21] He talks about 'operating in the language of image' and many of his diagnostic exercises are directed towards identifying features of oppression, using this non-verbal language. Nor does this approach imply that the process remains forever in abstraction; that would simply render a piece of dance

or movement. Shifts between vocabularies strengthen the muscularity of the
stage language as a whole.

From Abstract to Concrete and Back Again

As in the exercise Abstract to Concrete, the performer starts abstractly,
develops a repetitive movement then passes this to another player
who develops this movement further until it has a 'concrete' or 'literal'
expression. This is then passed to a third to make it abstract again (it's best
if the third player hasn't witnessed the earlier stages of the exercise). And
so on.

Theatre has a peculiar propensity for its unfolding action (or inaction) to
have meaning in two separate spheres simultaneously. With contemporary
television and film increasingly presenting 'what you see is all there is',
theatre offers doubleness. It offers realism and allegory both. Much medieval
theatre operated only allegorically and audiences expected no less. What
Shakespeare and his contemporaries did was bring a degree of psychological
realism into theatre vocabulary without sacrifice of allegorical content. It's a
tradition we're still within:

> Many of his characters are dual: they are human beings and allegorical
> figures at the same time. When we try to analyse, completely, a
> Shakespearean character by psychological means, we run into trouble;
> because the allegorical aspect will not yield to this interpretation.
> Scenes, too, that are psychologically baffling, may be allegorically lucid;
> and when so considered, they fall into place.[22]

In working non-realistically we're looking for the myths of the group to
emerge: a composite of images or stories that tell us something about
that group/us/people around us/our time/our context, which will provoke
and animate an audience. We're looking for imagery that speaks to our
immediate concerns: the everyday fluff of stuff but also what's beyond; what
carries universal resonance; the big, dark, giants of themes that never go
away.

A decision about style means a decision about vocabulary and in turn
about which elements of stagecraft are included: film, abstract movement,
personal stories, locations or direct address, for example. Whatever style is
chosen, it becomes important then to maintain consistency throughout the
piece.

7. Where the Attention Is

I don't say he's a great man. Willy Loman never made a lot of money. His name was never in the paper. He's not the finest character that ever lived. But he's a human being, and a terrible thing is happening to him. So attention must be paid. He's not to be allowed to fall into his grave like an old dog. Attention, attention must be finally paid to such a person.

Death of a Salesman, Act One

But a decision about style is only one part of the challenge. There's also the task within each scene of giving greater or lesser value to different aspects of that scene. One aspect of this is the commitment of the performer and where he directs his or her attention. As Stanislavski observed while watching a 'visiting star in Moscow':

I felt clearly that his entire attention was on the stage and the stage alone, and this abstracted attention forced me to be interested in his life on the stage, and draw closer to him in spirit in order to find out what it was that held his attention.[23]

Holding the Audience's Attention

This is a challenge exercise for a single performer. The aim for that performer is to hold the audience's attention for as long as possible. Initially, no props are allowed. Version One: no words, Version Two: with words. If a spectator ceases to be interested in what the performer is doing, this can be indicated by spectators holding up a hand. The hand may be withdrawn if the spectator finds an interest again.

Ask any performer to walk onstage and hold the audience's attention without speaking; immediately you can see what actions succeed or fail.

Consciously working with attention gives the performer a powerful tool. It was one of the distinguishing features of Brecht's theatre writing: the directing of the audience's attention to particular aspects – often economic – of the transactions between characters, as here in Act One, Scene Two of *The Threepenny Opera*:

Mac What have you got in your hand, your Reverence?
Jake Two knives, Captain.
Mac What have you got on your plate, your Reverence?

Jake Salmon, I think.

Mac And with that knife you are eating the salmon, are you not?

Jake Did you ever see the like of it, eating fish with a knife?

By endowing an action on the stage with significance via the direction of the audience's attention, it potentially creates a shift in the spectator's mind: the action insists on observance.

Three Ways to Play a Scene

This can be used on any scene. In this example (The Old Woman's Jewels), two performers (or characters) weigh up the values and virtues of stealing from an old woman. Having been let into her house by virtue of their confidence trick, she has gone to make them a cup of tea. The scene is played first as a crime drama with the emphasis on danger to the old woman and the moral culpability of the thieves. Next it's played with the emphasis on moral dilemmas. If the woman is rich, is not the theft justified? Finally it's played as a folk tale in which (for example) the two young men have been lured into this house. The jewels are fake but the large pot on the stove is real.

Our imaginary theatre company has, by the decisions it's made to date, called for certain social issues to be given attention. Now the details of these need to be worked out scene by scene. Willy Loman should not be allowed to fall into his grave like an old dog. An exercise such as Three Ways to Play a Scene enables a clarity of focus to be achieved around what precisely is the function of the scene. Is it to make the audience think? Is it to shock them? Is it to make them observe something about business or economics with which they are not familiar? Is it for them to share the dilemma?

The 2016 play *Minefield* (Royal Court Theatre) about the Falklands/Malvinas War, by placing emphasis on the psychological impact of the war on the soldiers, brought issues of class to our attention in ways that conventional histories would likely have avoided. By using real ex-combatants onstage, we were allowed to understand just how they had been manipulated. Their realization of this fact was all the sharper for being spoken from the stage by the former soldiers directly.

It's my argument that there are two primary ways in which an audience will engage with what is happening onstage. The first is by the spectators becoming curious about what will happen next. The other is by becoming curious about why things are happening as they are. The best scenes operate with both questions hanging in the air. The first of these questions is concerned with 'what'. What will happen next? The audience wants to know the answer to this question because there's something at stake. Our fears or hopes for another person have been triggered. Will he or she survive? What will be the outcome? The second is concerned with 'why'. Why is what we're looking at happening? What's the story behind it?

Understanding which question is paramount for any scene helps to structure and organize the scene. If, for example, there is an object used in the scene, what is the function of this object in respect of these questions?

Attending to the Object

An object is placed on a table and the table put on stage. A single player has to tell a story about this object. Another player then tells a different story about the same object. Perhaps a third does the same. Which is the story that most engages? What is it about the object that is most valuable to learn? What is the function of the object in terms of the hoped-for impact of the show?

(The Victoria and Albert Museum held an exhibition entitled 'Disobedient Objects' in 2015 which showed how everyday objects had been repurposed for political dissent through history. This book's title was informed by that exhibition.)

This is an exercise that sets up the second of the questions: Why is what is happening, happening?

The Backstory

Two performers decide in secret (a) their relationship and (b) an incident that took place recently which dented that relationship. Then they pick a situation where it's possible for this fracture to the relationship to be hidden. For example, it's a master (or mistress) / servant relationship which has recently broken down: the servant has resigned. However, they have to perform one last task, which is to show off some newly designed clothes to potential buyers – the audience. (The conflict over the resignation therefore is played as sub-text during the scene and not referred to directly.)

It appears characteristic of contemporary drama that many playwrights are more frequently utilizing question two – why are things the way they are – than question one – which is simply about good storytelling. Witness plays such as *Blasted, Chimerica, Attempts on Her Life* or *My Night With Reg*. Perhaps this contemporary preference reflects our greater need for theatre to help us understand an ever-complexifying world. We are less concerned with 'What happens next?' than with 'What the hell's going on?' We're more requiring of playwrights to explain the world to us. A disobedient theatre might well share this preference but, rather than supplying answers, shifts the focus of attention to where answers can be found – for example, in the testimonies of victims and witnesses. Take, for example, alongside *Minefield*, the plays *Queens of Syria* and Chris Goode's *Stand*, all verbatim pieces about class, war and activism respectively that project questions into the audience for their consideration.

A further possible step by which to engage the audience actively is to enrol the audience as active participants in an enquiry into how and why significant social events took place. Lucien Bourjeily's show *Vanishing State* might represent one example. Here, the audience becomes part of the action in drafting the Middle Eastern borders at the end of the First World War.

Finally, before moving on, just to avoid any over-solemnity that might be creeping into our imagined devising process, here's an exercise that helps to sharpen up performers' attentiveness, perhaps to run after a tea break (there are many variations out there).

The Numbers Game

The group sits in a straight line of chairs all facing the same way. The chairs are numbered off 1 to (however many players/chairs there are). Note that the numbers apply to the chairs not the players. The purpose of the game for the players is to move up the line to sit in Chair Number One. There's a player in that chair already who has to try and stay there. The action of the game is the passing of focus between the players. This is done by a player standing up, giving the necessary few words and sitting down again. So (for example) John in Chair One stands and says 'One to Five' (Five being the number of another chair). The occupant of Five has to stand and go 'Five to Eight' and so on. The focus keeps getting passed until a mistake is made. A mistake might be that someone misses their turn, fluffs a line or gets a number wrong. Then that person vacates their chair and goes to the end of the line (chair with the largest number). From the point of the vacant chair downwards, all players then move up one. A new player stands up and starts passing the focus again. The game can be played either for a fixed time period or until everyone is tired of it.

Focus

8. Attitude

Once attention is paid, attitude must be found. It's all very well to direct the spectator's attention to an aspect of the scene, but what is the performer's attitude towards that event/object/action? Should this be evident? Furthermore, what kind of function does the company want that material to play within the larger scheme of the play as a whole? What kind of resonance is sought for that moment? The orthodox, 'obedient' convention is to avoid attitude altogether and stay in neutral. This way some potential of the scene remains unrealized. It's often one reason behind the ineffectiveness of political theatre when performed by those who have no interest in politics.

One way to understand what attitude is, is to consider what it isn't – when a performer operates without attitude. John Wright talks about the neutral mask as one means to trigger such a state of neutrality:

> Neutrality is moving with no story behind your movement. If you watch somebody walk across the room, and if you can use an adjective to describe how they're walking – for example, you might say that someone looks determined, anxious, carefree, or distracted – then there is an inflection, or colour to their movement that clearly isn't neutral. If someone were to insult you, and knock you to the ground, and you simply got up, without comment, and walked away again – without a flicker of response – if you were in 'Neutral' we'd only see the bare facts of the action. There'd be no story, no colour, no emotional reaction.[24]

Attitude then is the colour that enters in to dispel neutral. It signposts anger or determination or regret. But attitude can also be deliberately suspended for the greater purpose of the performance.

No Attitude

A game for two performers in which Player A has to maintain neutral and Player B has to attempt to bring him/her out of it. For example, B throws him or herself to the ground, calling out for help. Performer A has to respond and play the scene but without showing sympathy or disgust or any other attitude. B then starts singing the praises of A or starts disparaging the Queen. Again, Performer A has to play the scene while remaining in neutral. Performer B again switches to another scene. It may be useful to have a Performer C who acts as referee and time keeper.

To be able to suspend attitude-taking in this way is a useful skill. In particular it can be used within performance to deliberately provoke an audience; it capitalizes on a rule of thumb, as defined by Tim Crouch: 'The less we do onstage, the more the audience is allowed in.'[25] Arguably this withholding of attitude was the tactic for Franko B, who prior to 2013 often performed naked. He used self-wounding as a performance strategy. Susan Hiller has described how he 'makes his way towards a spotlight; he is already bleeding from both arms simultaneously.'[26] He is deliberately withholding any attitude towards what is happening to him in order to provoke the onlookers to find their own. Hiller observes that the 'mixture of powerful reactions is overwhelming – disgust and compassion certainly, but most of all powerlessness.'[27] So the show is 'completed', as it were, by the responses of the spectators.

This is not the same as performers evading the challenge of finding attitudes as part of their character work. Within the kind of improvisation practice that explores character, relationships and story, the improviser has a responsibility to find attitudes constantly: to the other performer, to a previous event, to the 'room' (or castle or shop or jungle), to an object on the table, to a spoken word, all of which are part of the performance event. If the improvisation fails, it's often because the performer has become nervous about committing to an attitude, fearful this will burden the other players and inhibit their creativity. In fact, the opposite is true; they will welcome a strong attitudinal statement because the attitude is itself part of the raw material they can work with. 'Here is the book you lent me' is never so powerful as 'Here is the book you lent me – I liked the implicit message – I could go out with you on Tuesday?' The impro teacher Mick Napier puts it like this:

> At the top of an improv scene, in the very beginning, take care of yourself first. Simply, selfishly take a position in the scene … It doesn't even have to involve words. It's just, what is your deal? What's going to be your deal in the scene?[28]

Performers skip attitude-creation for many reasons; often it's laziness. You can find this vacuity in porn. The performer comes into the room with a pizza or bag of tools – the signifying apparatus is predictable – meets another performer and they go about their business. The industry convention forbids them doing more; displaying affection is taboo. As Caitlin Moran describes it, 'the vast majority of porn out there is as identikit and mechanical as fridge-freezers rolling off a production line'.[29] She laments the absence of people 'who actually want to fuck each other'. Instead we get two people moving inexorably towards coitus with all the eroticism of dump trucks getting into position.

It is attitudes that brings improvisation work alive. Here are two exercises where the rules of the exercise prompt the players to find attitudes without preparation.

Objects with a History

A game for two players. The first, Performer A, has a number of props hidden from Performer B. The items are presented by A to B in turn. B's task is to find an attitude to each one along with a reason why that attitude should be taken. For example, a toy bear is remembered with affection because it belonged to a sister who passed away. A knife is treated with contempt because B associates it with his father who used to threaten him with it.

Discovering the Room

Two players enter the space. Each takes contrasting attitudes towards the space. For example, Performer A loves it, the other finds it dirty and unacceptable given their status. Then character C enters and asks them what they think about the room. At which point both A and B present attitudes to him/her that are the reverse of what they just expressed to each other.

One reason why attitude-finding (or the conscious withholding of attitude) is so important is that attitudes are signifiers of emotion, and emotion is the fuel of performance. Emotions, however, are to a great extent beyond manipulation or choice; they can't be instructed to appear. They arrive or not as a result of the performer being in the midst of a scenario which prompts emotion. Attitudes, on the other hand, can be chosen. The performer can, first, choose to express the felt emotion honestly so there's transparency. Alternatively, the performer can choose to conceal the felt emotion.

To take an example, the giving of a gift will usually inspire an attitude of gratitude, and this would normally be shown. But should the gift be given by a master to a slave, there are different implications. The attitude it inspires may not be gratitude, it may be contempt. However, the slave may choose to show gratitude. The displayed attitude therefore conceals the true attitude. Within a context of a dramatic improvisation, one way to explore this set of conflicted feelings is by use of direct address to the audience. The 'true' attitude is expressed not to the other characters but to the audience. It's quite easy to set up improvisations in which this technique is employed.

The Jewellery Sale

This is a structured improvisation that allows the technique of direct address to the audience to be explored. Performer A explains to the audience that this necklace he or she is holding (a real necklace is needed for this) is really worthless. But still, the plan is to make money out of it from a gullible customer. Performer A then calls out Performer B who is told the truth about the necklace. However, because B is in the employ of A, B has to make a sale of it to Performer C. C has to be persuaded that the piece is worth, say, £200 (really it's only worth £10). Performer C then arrives. The 'sale' commences. At any time any of the three characters can step away to use direct address to the audience, giving a 'more true' account of their feelings than is being shown to the others.

Power relations

By using a technique in which the 'true' attitude is expressed to the audience rather than the other characters, power relations become more apparent. In the story of the stolen bracelet, if the bracelet is owned by the girl's father, his expressed attitude on hearing the news may be one of 'it's not a big deal'. Behind this, however, may lie a father's fury. It is this attitude of anger that he expresses to the audience along with an expressed intention to punish his daughter at a later date.

In the history of dramatic literature, we can see the technique of direct address employed by the Roman playwrights and then subsequently by Shakespeare, Molière and Brecht. The 'gap' between true desires and attitudes spoken because of social duress or personal ambitions becomes apparent. Shakespeare understood that a character adopting attitudes and sharing these with the audience was an essential part of the drama; it might even be the drama:

> **Malvolio** I will be proud, I will read politic authors, I will baffle Sir Toby, I will wash off gross acquaintance, I will be point-devise the very man ... I will be strange, stout, in yellow stockings, and cross-gartered, even with the swiftness of putting on.[30]

Other Shakespearean characters share similar intimacies with us, sometimes with tragic rather than comic ends:

Hamlet My tables – meet it is I set it down. That one may smile, and smile, and be a villain.[31]

The game of onstage characters concealing their true intentions has great potential within a theatre practice that takes social injustice as a theme. The gap between the presented attitude and the true attitude can say something about oppression, class or economic relationships, as for example in Brecht's *The Exception and the Rule*. Here, the Merchant and the Coolie (who is employed by the Merchant) are lost in the desert in a quest to find oil.

Merchant Pitch the tent. Our flask is empty, there's nothing left.

The Merchant sits down while the Coolie pitches the tent. The Merchant drinks secretly out of his bottle. To himself:

He mustn't notice that I still have something to drink. Otherwise, if he's got a spark of understanding in his thick skull, he'll do me in. If he comes close, I shoot.

He takes out his revolver and places it on his knee.

If we could only reach the last water hole! I'm nearly strangled with thirst! How long can a man stand thirst?[32]

Here we see how suspicions bred in class attitudes led to these two men being unable to deal honestly with each other. They are both stuck in the attitudes of their class. This is how we are led to the death of the Coolie at the hands of the Merchant, who erroneously mistakes the Coolie's good intentions as malevolent. It's by virtue of the direct addresses that the audience gains access to the interior thoughts of both men. It can see the tragedy coming.

Here are some further exercises that enable the stresses and contradictions of power relationships.

The Boss

A nominated player, Player A, steps forward and addresses the audience. A second player waits to the side. Player A explains that he/she works for someone. This someone is a terrible person to work for; wages are bad, the conditions are dreadful and there's bullying in the workplace. Player B steps forward. This is the boss. The boss engages the employee in conversation, acknowledging the presence of the audience. Asks what the employee was talking about to the audience. The employee lies, saying that he/she was only speaking of what a wonderful person the boss was to work for. The boss gives the employee a task to carry out in the space. The boss sits down to observe the employee carrying out the task. The employee takes whatever opportunities are available to talk to the audience without the boss hearing. As for the boss, he/she takes the opportunity to explain to the audience that he/she is looking for a chance to sack the employee.

The Reputation

An exercise for three players. Player A comes out and talks enthusiastically about Player B. It's as if Player B has almost god-like status. Player B appears and Player A is delighted. Player A continues to rhapsodize. Player B asks for a favour and Player A rushes to carry this out while Player B retires (task might be cleaning the room or preparing food). Player C appears and begins to inform Player A of 'the truth' about Player B. Player A is astonished, incredulous but believing. Player C leaves. Player A continues with the task but less enthusiastically. Player B returns. Player A confronts Player B with the truth. Player B admits this truth. They improvise the conclusion of the exercise.

In devising or impro work, any influences on a character's behaviour need to be identified as being rooted in other characters, i.e. within the world of the drama. This is very different from the kind of convention where attitudes are presented without any apparent root cause. They are presented simply as 'god-given', perpetuating the idea that they are beyond man's influence to change. It's necessary for any theatre that has a socially progressive role to acknowledge that there's little value in presenting 'justice' or 'honour' as motivating ideas unless within the world of the play there's a visible source that inspires these convictions. Brecht puts it like this:

> The 'historical conditions' (forces operating in the play) must of course not be imagined (nor will they be so constructed) as mysterious Powers (in the background); on the contrary, they are created and maintained by men (and will in due course be altered by them): it is the actions taking place before us that allow us to see what they are.[33]

To take an example, in the case of 'honour killings', it should be clear that any character onstage advocating such killings holds a position of authority within the family and that this authority is in part dependent on the perpetuation of the honour ideal. There is no 'absolute principle' that exists independently of the desires of men or women, just as there is no 'god' whose name can be taken as an unchallengeable authority. To take an example within playwriting, it is significant that in *Death of a Salesman* all the characters are present that will finally nudge Willy Loman towards his suicide: his wife, his sons, his boss and crucially Uncle Ben, his older, more successful brother. He does not commit suicide while arguing an abstract idea (or ideal), he does so while recalling the words of his family.

The Ghost

A structured improvisation for three players, two men and a woman.

Scene One – Man A and Man B. Man A is expecting his date to arrive at any minute. Problem is, his date is the ex-girlfriend of his dead friend. Man B is in fact the ghost of the dead friend who is taking Man A to task for asking her out. Man B – the ghost – can only be seen by Man A.

Scene Two – the Girlfriend arrives. Man A tries to woo her while he is constantly berated by Man B.

It is clear that Man A's timidity and fearfulness around romance has its source in anxieties over what feels like a betrayal of his friend.

women as property yuk!

9. The Use of Restrictions

Another way to explore how social pressures impact on individual psyches is to place restrictions on actors' freedom of expression. By doing this, we create a simulacrum of the way in which social conventions force people to be dishonest with each other, much in the way of the Merchant and the Coolie. This approach takes a different route from the 'Say Yes to Everything' philosophy of impro, which tends to create a rather uniform parade of external attitudes. By contrast, restrictions placed on the performers enable subtext to be generated, thereby giving depth to any staged encounter. And this complexity is what we want from theatre. It was Stanislavski – perhaps not a natural ally here – who wrote that 'spectators come to the theatre to hear the subtext. They can read the text at home.'[34]

Examples of social restrictions impeding a character's free expression are numerous within dramatic literature. To take just one, Franz Wedekind's play *Spring Awakening* shows how religious strictures in Germany imposed repression on its teenagers. The imposition of 'correct attitudes', for example the forbidding of any conversation about sexual desire, enforces this repression:

Melchior We'll go down together. I'll take the basket. We'll go straight through and be at the bridge in ten minutes. If you lie down – put your head on my arms – your thoughts can wander anywhere.

Both lie down under the oak.

Wendla What did you want to ask me, Melchior?

Melchior Yes ... Someone told me you often go and visit the poor. Take them food, and clothes and money. Is that your own idea, or does your mother send you?[35]

The felt inability of either Melchior or Wendla to speak their true feelings leads ultimately to disaster. Melchior finds he's unable to cope with the stresses of silence and loses self-control entirely, physically attacking Wendla. To replicate the kind of dramatic tension that's so evident here can be achieved relatively easily in the workshop room. For example, the improvisers are allowed only to lie about their feelings. Or else they are forbidden from eye contact. Or perhaps they are allowed to speak only by using metaphor. The performers, working hard to fulfil the restriction, create a jagged, halting, repressed atmosphere. It's not necessary then to order the actors to 'create a claustrophobic mood' or 'act as if you're horrified of sex'; the restrictions will do this on their behalf.

10. Shifts in Attitude

When in drama the attitude of a character changes, the force of the moment is largely conditional on the extent to which the attitude has been previously invested in. When Coriolanus realizes he's made a mistake in his treatment of the citizens or Lear recognizes his own cruelty towards his fondest daughter, the drama within that turnaround is achieved largely by the 360 degrees of shift:

Lear This feather stirs; she lives! if it be so,
It is a chance which does redeem all sorrows
That ever I have felt.[36]

In the rehearsal room, the same applies. Often actors will resist investing sufficiently in attitudinal consistency in the way that a playwright knows is necessary. Should our young woman character strike up a relationship with the group of homeless – as a result of looking for her dog (or bracelet) – it may be useful for her initial attitude to be one of contempt. This allows for any subsequent shift in attitude – towards sympathy perhaps – to have more impact. Sometimes an improviser will stick to the first-found attitude, claiming she would have 'lost her character' if that shift had been made. It's a position founded on a false premise. It proceeds from the misunderstanding that 'character' is a fixed quality, like a talking doll that says certain phrases when you pull a string. In fact behaving 'out of character' simply extends the spectator's understanding of who/what that character is.

In drama we are not seeing ordinary people engaging in the regular business of everyday life, which is, of course, the habitual. We are seeing people in exceptional circumstances, and thus we are seeing them behaving uncharacteristically. As George Eliot says in *Middlemarch*, 'Unwonted circumstances may make us all rather unlike ourselves.'[37]

Working with attitude is one way for radical theatre makers to establish a uniqueness. By working out from first principles what distresses or annoys them in the world, what hopes they have for the future, what needs to happen to change things, it's possible to build shows that help to expose the inner workings of our society. Clarity of attitudes assist this. It's achieved by taking nothing for granted, not least the banal homilies that underpin the final scenes of so much mainstream theatre: 'all is well', 'love will endure', 'the family is sacred' and so on. Shows which re-examine such 'god-given truths' invite a reassessment of what we accept as normal and, therefore, acceptable.

11. Tension

Performers have a dependency relationship with tension; it's their drug of choice. But it needs handling in small doses. As our imagined company moves closer to performing to a public, this issue becomes increasingly significant. Johan Huizinga wrote that 'The element of tension in play ... plays a particularly important part. Tension means uncertainty, chanciness; a striving to decide the issue and so end it.'[38] It's essential then to the business of performing. A failure to manage that tension and the actor's psyche ceases to operate efficiently. For at a certain point, as argued by psychologists, further 'increases in arousal lead to decreases in creativity, originality and variability of behaviour.'[39] As a result, the performer freezes.

The American actor and director Joe Chaikin confirms this, writing that 'I feel myself straining and pushing when it's not intended. I'm overeager to

be "understood", which is already a form of tension.'[40] There are also reper-
cussions externally; those around the tense colleague become uncertain
performers themselves. The unease spreads like treacle on the floor. The
impact of an over-heightened tension on a personal level is evident. This is
the impro teacher and performer Jimmy Carrane:

> Let me tell you, I was scared to death to be part of that [improvised]
> show [*Armando* at iO Chicago]. I was intimidated by the A-list impro-
> visers who were in it. I am not kidding you, the first six months I must
> have played someone who was scared in every scene because that was
> what my natural state was.[41]

Relaxation Exercise

My own approach to preparing a group to perform – and there are countless
in the world of impro especially – is to take the performers through a
sequence of activities in which 'focus' or 'attention' is the currency. But if
this is too long a process, then clapping games or throwing small bean bags
offer quicker alternatives.

Stage One: the group walks around the space and everyone tracks inwardly
to notice tensions and emotions in the body. Not to alter how things are
but simply to observe what's going on internally. Then the facilitator – on a
clap – calls for everyone to adopt a different walking shape, to notice how
tensions and emotions in the body may alter with a new rhythm or posture
or shape. Each new clap, a different walking shape.

Stage Two: the group walks around and turns their attention outwardly to
the space, the room or the stage. They are invited to follow their curiosity
to explore the space and the objects in it. To be as children and simply
explore the tactile sensations and sounds that can be discovered. Secondly,
they are invited to imagine the room is a stage (if it isn't); where do they
feel most comfortable on that stage, where least comfortable? After finding
these positions, perhaps they are questioned about these choices.

Stage Three: the group walks about but turns their attention to the others
in the group. To use their peripheral vision to observe them. Then to pick
one person and walk as they walk. Then eye contact is encouraged but
as soon as this is made the two players freeze and scream and run away.
After a while the instruction is changed; if eye contact is made then the
two players swoon and fall to the ground. The third instruction is for them
to point, laugh and run away. Variations on these instructions can also be
found.

[handwritten margin note: exploring the room]

When tension spreads in a company, the ensemble spirit can only diminish; shared goals and aspirations start to fracture. But the answer to all this isn't just 'Relax, dammit!' It's about transferring the tension out of the performer onto the stage. The Canadian director Robert Lepage puts it like this:

> Where should emotion be, in the theatre? In the soul, in the chest, in the heart of the actor? Or should it be in the room of the audience? Often the emotion stays with the actor and the spectator remains a spectator of someone else's emotion. 'Look at that actor', we say, 'he is so moved'. But he is not moving.[42]

The art of creating dramatic tension therefore begins with learning to create it between the players so it exists in the space. It moves from the body of the actor to its place on the stage. This means creating a situation where something is at stake – a situation to which more than one player/character is contributing. So there could be a number of different outcomes to the scene. And these possible outcomes need to impact on one or more of the characters positively or negatively. Somebody will win, somebody will lose. What might be lost? Perhaps reputation, wealth, love, friendship or integrity. Less experienced improvisers will tend to resist being put in a situation where they might be seen to 'lose'. They think that falling prey to that kind of vulnerability onstage should be avoided. But the truth is, the opposite is the case; the showing of vulnerability is what draws a spectator in. Audiences love a loser.

Raising the Stakes

There's benefit to practising the dynamics of dramatic tension so players get familiar with *putting something at stake*. These are some starter lines for two-person improvisations:

'If you tell Mary, that's the end of our friendship.'

'You sent me an email meant for someone else.'

'I've decided to become the Ultimate Fighting Champion.'

'You know what we said about being unfaithful.'

'I'm afraid the company is downsizing.'

Theatre traditionally tells stories of outsiders. It may be that in our imagined play, the thief's story is important, especially if the acquisition of the bracelet leads to the purchase of drugs and perhaps his overdose. Some dramatic tension will be achieved around the question of his survival. This may be heightened if he has migrant status. Turning to dramatic literature for comparable examples, *The Caretaker* by Harold Pinter offers an interesting case study. While there is admittedly – and very Pinterishly – a degree of mystery around the characters' motivations, the drives of 'need for shelter' and 'need for friendship' are nevertheless drawn clearly in the roles of Davies and Aston respectively. The older man Davies is grateful for the offer of a bed in what appears to be Aston's lodgings. These two characters and their respective needs seem to be compatible until a third party arrives when the old man is alone. This new man, Mick, avers that he is the rightful possessor of the bed given to the visitor. Davies refuses to give up the bed, creating a clear conflict. It's a situation of evident dramatic tension. The situation is intriguing because it sets up both key questions mentioned earlier: 'What's going to happen?' (narrative question) and 'How did this situation come to be?' (backstory question). In terms of what might happen next, there are some obvious possible outcomes:

- The older man admits defeat and goes.
- The older man is allowed to stay (but where does that leave the bed owner?).
- There's a fight; one wins, one loses.
- Aston returns to solve the problem.

It's a battle over rights to be in the space – a perennial topic for political theatre, whether the 'space' is a town, a country or a room. It's a brutal, elemental power play that critics argue says more about politics than Pinter's later work that is ostensibly about politics. What keeps the dramatic tension alive is a holding back from any outright conflict between the men, allowing a certain playfulness in the interaction.

Mick I hope you slept well last night.

Davies Listen! I don't know who you are!

Mick What bed you sleep in?

Davies Now look here –

Mick Eh?

Davies That one!

Mick Not the other one?

Davies No.

Mick Choosy. (Pause) How do you like my room?

Davies Your room?

Mick Yes.

Davies This ain't your room. I don't know who you are. I ain't never seen you before.

Mick You know, believe it or not, you've got a funny kind of resemblance to a bloke I once knew in Shoreditch.[43]

This is a play (or scene) structure that is relatively easy to co-opt into improvisation practice. Truth A is established before Truth B is introduced that conflicts with Truth A.

Here's an example of a similar structure that was developed by Fluxx for performance.

The Visitor

Two performers out of three are selected to play a close-knit couple – probably married, long-term partners or close friends. (When the company developed the model, the couple were selected from the players by the audience.)

Scene One – an establishing scene is played by the established couple. All appears well, they are devoted to each other (Truth A).

Scene Two – a visitor arrives, he or she meets the person in the couple with whom the visitor has no previous relationship.

Scene Three – the visitor plays a scene with the other partner. The visitor makes a demand or a threat that hinges on their past, close relationship (Truth B). This demand needs to put the existing partnership of the happy couple in jeopardy.

Scene Four – the newly informed person tells his/her partner about the visitor and the threat to their relationship.

Scene Five, Six, Seven? Further scenes follow, exploring this dilemma.

Of course all theatre employs dramatic tension. A disobedient theatre model does the same; where it differs is in the ways in which the tension is created (a matter of content) and in the ways in which the audience is implicated (a matter of form). Here, the dramatic tension is not presented as 'inevitable', 'timeless' or 'unalterable'. Rather, it's seen as rooted in the relations that human beings establish between each other, which can be altered. For practitioners, it's also necessary to understand the science of dramatic tension: what builds it, what maintains it and when it is necessary to release it (only to establish a new tension). We see in *The Caretaker* – a useful point of reference rather than a disobedient theatre model – first how a status quo is established; the offer of a bed is accepted, and then undermined; the integrity of the offer is thrown into question. We can see how dramatic tension is maintained via a certain playfulness in the drama. But this tension can't be maintained forever. Another tension – or game – needs to replace it.

One of the most dramatically tense scenes of recent world cinema was in Quentin Tarantino's film *Inglourious Basterds*. The film is set during the Second World War, in Germany. A number of Jews are hiding in a house in the country. The Jew Hunter has entered this house. The conflict is evident. However, rather than search the house immediately, the Jew Hunter sits and talks philosophy with the house owner LaPadite. The Jews are hiding under the floorboards of the same room. It's unbearably tense. Eventually however, the Hunter orders his soldiers to fire through the floorboards. Everyone is killed bar one. Only a girl escapes. It seems as if the Jew Hunter has in some way allowed her to escape. So just as one passage of dramatic tension is ended, another is set up. Will he pursue her? (narrative question). Why has he let her go? (backstory question).

Finally, here are some guidelines for facilitators who want to nudge the players into finding dramatic tension within the scenes they're playing. Some call this side-coaching.

Side-coaching for Building Tension

Coax players to 'do more of' what they're already doing.

Coax players to do what they're doing already but with more intensity and risk.

Ask one or all of the players to simply keep repeating the same key line.

Impose restrictions – 'Now you can't speak but keep playing the scene', 'Every line spoken has to involve physical contact', 'From now character John can only speak to the audience', 'Continue playing the scene without speaking', 'John, you can only use this phrase I'm going to give you'.

Remind the players of facts, routines or obligations previously established.

Give a direct instruction: 'Now you need to kiss him' or 'Find something to give him, a piece of jewellery perhaps'.

Remind the players of the existence of the audience.

Giving a direction about style: 'Keep playing the scene but as one written by Raymond Chandler'.

12. Establish, Transform, Shift

Moments in which tension is resolved and then recreated move the dramatic action forward. It's by such means that narrative is created. In David Edgar's *How Plays Work*, he talks about 'plot', a word for an aggregate of such moments. But arguably this is like talking about sausages while looking at pigs. When the pigs are dead, sliced and bunged into tubes, then we've got plot. Until then we're looking at sausage potential. Or as V. S. Naipaul puts it, quoted by David Hare in *The Blue Touch Paper*: 'Plot is for those who already know the world; narrative is for those who want to discover it.'

It's possible to look more analytically at how dramatic tension is created. One way to do this is to imagine two improvisers walking onto an empty stage without prior agreement. They have to engage full frontal with the issue of plot/story/narrative. Only of course they can't. They have to define stuff first. They have to create understandings about who, where or what they are, or who they are to each other, or what activity they are about. They need a context, a world, a set of conventions. Then it becomes possible to progress action. It's the same in the workshop room as in the theatre; the watchers expect a map. This is the task that is often referred to as 'establishing'. It's a task that is best shared. Below, however, is an exercise where the task falls to just one player.

Performer complicity is essential for both the growth and development of any improvised dramatic action. Players need to work together to create a status quo to be shifted from, otherwise the shift moment has no meaning. It is possible to start an improvised scene with a shift moment, of course – 'I've decided to leave you' or 'I've decided I don't need a cleaner any more' – but a status quo is still implied.

Sten Rudstrom is a performer and teacher working on movement improvisation. He outlined to me Action Theatre's take on the different ways to progress action; it's based on Develop – Transform – Shift. (Action Theatre is an improvisational training process developed by Ruth Zaporah.) In this

Player A Takes the Lead

Two players on stage. One has the task of establishing conventions, the other the task of simply supporting and extending what is created. The key decision is whether the players create a location or not. Are they in Pharaoh's palace or are they here in this rehearsal room? Next decision is whether the players are 'themselves' or not. Is it Alan and Shira or Capt. Hegolin and Sgt. Pete? In this exercise Player A has to make all the decisions (B makes none) and in this way 'looks after' B so B, knows the style of play. In feedback, the key question to B is, *'Did you understand who you were, where you were and what you were doing?'*

system, 'Develop' is similar to 'Establish'. It's about defining the status quo onstage. This means the performers define a context or articulate some imaginative proposition between them as a stage reality. So they decide they are two goldfish jumping out of a bowl. Or two homeless migrants hiding in a house. Or they are simply themselves, recalling an incident. As Rudstrom puts it: 'Develop is: "I'm doing something and I continue to do it."'[44] In continuing to do it, more detail gets filled in. The dramatic image comes into focus.

'Transform' is a slower, more evolutionary kind of progression, usually coming once 'development' or 'establishment' is concluded: 'I'm doing something, and it slowly changes into something else.'[45] One of the goldfish starts to move along the table to get away from the other. The two homeless men prepare to leave the house, to take up the girl's offer to visit her at home. The two storytellers start to realize they are recalling the same story differently.

Develop – Transform – Shift

For two players; one performs, the other directs. The solo performer has to create a state of play – either a dramatic scene or an onstage game. Then it's to accept the director's instruction which will either be 'Develop', 'Transform' or 'Shift'. The first will always be Develop. There's a further option which is 'Start Again', to be used if the director feels the scene or game isn't working. Or possibly if the scene/game idea has been exhausted.

'Shift' is different again. Shift is more explosive. Shift is: 'I'm doing something, then I'm doing something else.'[46] It's a more sudden and abrupt reorientation of circumstances. Usually it happens as a consequence of an accumulating tension, as outlined earlier. One of the goldfish falls off the edge of the table. The homeless men are interrupted by the voices of policemen; they decide to make a run for it. They run from the house and a chase begins. One of the two storytellers becomes angry and accuses the other of corrupting the truth.

In polite society, a shift moment is when social fault lines become visible. A shift moment is usually hushed and a healing blanket thrown over the antagonists. It may be when buried secrets or resentments burst into the open. This is why, onstage, shift moments should be welcomed and their dramatic implications amplified. Especially in our theatre model, shift breaks the carapace of social etiquette and brings the demons out of the cupboard. Absurdist drama excelled in delivering sequences of heightened shift moments to cause a provocative effect. It was a Dadaist technique adopted in New York Happenings where the aim was to protest against the banality of life while celebrating artistic freedom:

> Four people rush in from the outside, two with pails of coloured water which they throw. The outer cloth and paper walls are billowing in and out, pushed by assistants who shout and scream along with raucous sounds over the loudspeaker. The plastic room is then drawn up again, and it becomes dark and quiet. Suddenly five to ten photo-flash guns explode. Two torches are set afire. A wild man, swinging down on the rope from above, drops into the crowd yelling, 'The Niighhht!'[47]

This Happening was performed during May 1961 at the University of Michigan.

In the workshop room today, however, in order to build narrative – and therefore intrigue, interest and mystery – improvisers have to move more slowly. This may feel banal to them; it may mean sticking with a resistance, an obstacle or a dramatic conflict beyond the point at which it seems dramatically polite to do so. But this is one obligation of long form improvising – there will be a pay-off in the end. The facilitator can always side-coach, advising the players not to rush, to live in the moment, assuring them a shift moment will come. Then when it does, everyone earns the pay-off, the loss of temper, the storming out, the passionate kiss, the sudden and heart-stopping confession, the collapse on the floor, the revelation of a shameful secret, the taking off of clothes, the demand for sex, the exposure of the villain, the offer of a fight, the uncovering of a previously hidden identity, the start of a new life, the ascent to the throne or the descent into hell.

In our story, there might be a scene between the thief and the girl, perhaps several. She's been well brought up and doesn't want to challenge him directly about the bracelet. But someone she spoke to says this guy was seen taking it. To try and gain his confidence, she sits with him, perhaps even shares drugs with him. Finally, impatient that her strategy is not working, she loses her temper and confronts him with the theft. Such would probably be a shift moment. The extent of the shift depends partly on his response, for a shift can affect just one person or several. When it's just one person, for example within a group scene, this moment can be particularly strong, in part because of the refusal of others to shift. Here's an example from *The Brig* performed by the Living Theatre, in which only one person visibly shifts. The dramatic situation is one of acute, heightened tension. The setting is a marine punishment block. One character shifts and the rest, despite the terror, remain physically unmoved. The effect of this technique is to heighten the appalling conditions of the men's incarceration and how the regime is victimizing the individual under the cosh.

Grace Prisoners, right face.

Tepperman Back to your manuals, and someday, if you are good maggots who clean under their short hairs every day, you may be free.

All prisoners except Six pick up their books and start reading. Six emits a terrifying scream and falls to his knees. The other prisoners near him jump with fright. All give him a probing glance. Then everyone returns to his reading. Tepperman runs into the compound, billy club in hand, and stands over the prisoner, who has buried his head in his hands and is weeping.

On your feet, Six.

Six I am thirty-four years old. For God's sake, let me out of this madhouse.[48]

The other cadets are powerless to help. And they won't – because if they did, they would become the victims alongside Six.

The Confession

An improvisation for three players that can either be played in a comic or more serious style. If comic, the police carry balloons or rolled-up newspapers. If serious, they use physical contact.

There is a suspect in the chair. The three policemen/women come in one at a time, each after a decent interval. The game is, the suspect has no idea what the crime is but will move towards making a confession at the end of the scene. In order to 'develop' the scene the first cop lays down some assertions that the suspect accepts to be true – about the suspect's movements on a certain day. The second cop comes in and uses a 'transform' role, pushing the suspect to accept some interpretations of this evidence. The third cop arrives and behaves in a more directly accusative way, as a result of which the suspect confesses to the crime in a 'shift' moment, elaborating further details not provided by the police.

Improvisationally it takes courage to shift. Or in certain cases, to not shift. Whichever the choice is, it needs to be a strong, positive choice so other players understand what everyone's respective positions are. These are non-shift positions that might be taken in an improvisation:

- 'I don't care that you've lost your home and your livelihood. I never liked you. In fact I'm quite enjoying your predicament.'
- 'Fine. You slept with another man. Good for you. I only wish I'd started sleeping around before you.'
- 'Dad, you're a bully. You only do it when mum's not around. I lost mum's bracelet. OK – it wasn't my fault, OK? I said I was sorry and it makes no difference.'

Scenes for Shifts

A woman confronts her man with a compromising letter.

An amorous bear goes to visit another bear to ask it out.

Two animal rights activists; one is a policewoman undercover.

A headmaster delivers an ultimatum to a teacher; resign from the post or be charged with professional incompetence.

Three gay friends arrive at their hotel; there's only two rooms each with a single bed.

A swimmer has come first in a tournament but taken drugs to do it; his proud, unknowing mother welcomes him home.

Player A explains secretly to the audience why Player B is a shit; however, Player B overhears this.

It is possible and often useful to set up improvisation scenes that have 'built in' within the design of the scene the possibility of a shift moment. Especially for those just coming to improvisation, such a scene construct has the 'establish' and 'develop' elements already largely taken care of. The set-up is completed. Of course many improvisers will still refuse the 'offer of the scene' but at least the offer will be clear and evident. Assistance can come from the facilitator who, having defined the situation, guides the players via side-coaching: 'Doesn't your father object to this marriage on religious grounds?' 'You said previously you always distrusted migrants. Now you're inviting one into your home?' It's important for the facilitator, however, not to inhibit the improvisers from defining their own shift moments, for they may feel carried towards a shift which the facilitator hasn't anticipated. For example, in the scenes listed above, the police spy may persuade the activist to keep quiet about the secret identity using seduction. The proud mother may be indifferent to the drugs revelation and it's the son who shifts in horrified response to her indifference.

In comedy, the technique of one character refusing to shift can be used to great effect. It's a popular way to end a sketch or comic film because it simultaneously collapses the narrative, which increases the impact. There's an example in the film *Some Like It Hot*. In the last scene of the film, the character Jerry, disguised as a woman, is trying to get rid of his suitor, Osgood, the man who thinks Jerry's a woman and wants to marry him. They're driving in Osgood's speedboat. All the objections Jerry raises to the marriage are plausible and in fact true: he smokes, isn't a natural blonde, has a dodgy past cohabiting with a saxophone player and can't have children. Nothing discourages Osgood. Finally in desperation Jerry rips off his wig and in a voice two octaves lower attempts the 'shift' by revealing his identity as a man. 'Well, nobody's perfect!' responds the beadily un-shiftable Osgood.[49]

Finally, here are some more abstract exercises that may help the group understand the concept of shifting.

Shift Circle

The group stands in a circle. A sound and movement is passed round the circle. Initially the aim is simply to 'develop' the sound and movement in order not to change it but to better define it. The aim is to try and have it repeated more or less exactly round the circle. The next stage is to explore 'transforming' the sound and movement. So as it passes round the circle, it's slowly evolves, element by element. It becomes longer or shorter, louder or softer, or more emotional in some way. The next stage is to explore 'shift'. It's more effective for the shift moment to take place in a context of the sound and movement having already been 'defined'. The aim now is for the group to feel the moment when the sound and movement should shift; one player then shifts, abruptly changing the sound and movement into something radically different. Everyone else now repeats this new sound and movement until another shift is made. It's important not to shift too often as this only reduces the impact of any one shift.

Follow My Leader

This involves group members being able to move around the room. The group assembles as a 'pack' or a 'bunch'. Everyone faces the same way. Somebody chooses to lead off and starts to move around the space using a consistent sound and physical movement. Everyone follows, staying close together, copying the same sound and movement pattern. This should continue for a while. When the moment feels right, someone breaks away from the pack with a contrasting sound and movement. Everyone immediately copies the breakaway leader, and follows that person round the room. In the second stage of play, phrases can be chosen instead of sounds.

A variation: it's possible after the exercise has been running for a while, for group members to be allowed to stay with the existing leader and not follow the breakaway leader. Then you may get two, three or four rival packs each 'competing' for members.

As our imaginary production moves towards finding its final shape, it may be useful for our rebel company to check it isn't defaulting either into orthodox theatre manners or into the actors' own stock mannerisms.

13. Anti-defaulting

Individual performers have their own defaults and often get trapped in them. It's unsurprising, because the lingua franca of theatre, behaviour, is so mutable. Instinctively actors find themselves developing a repertoire of gestures, postures and attitudes 'that work'. Something about these behaviours gets the audience's attention and, too, applause. But should the performer over time become trapped in these patterns, the capacity to respond uniquely to each new challenge diminishes.

When I was travelling in Nigeria with two friends in a doom-laden attempt to make a film about us being in Nigeria (!), we were arrested, stopped in our car and told to get out by two policemen carrying sub-machine guns.

Then we were told to get back in the car and the two policemen squeezed in as well. (They didn't have a car.) Our driver was told to drive toward the bush and very obviously away from the city where the police station would be found. It was a tight squeeze. The policeman on my right kept ratcheting his machine gun. When my Nigerian friend's attempt to bribe the police failed and the driver was told to step on the gas, I turned into my father. I demanded to know our captors' names, ranks and police numbers because later I was going to be speaking to someone high up about this 'very seriously'. The two policemen roared with laughter and put me on an additional charge of insubordination. Finally, in a remote clearing, after we'd prostrated ourselves sufficiently – and, crucially, upped our bribe offer to the max – they let us go.

My impulse under pressure of fear was to go high status – a default played irrespective of any likely success. And in fact it only made our situation worse. Such impulses tend to operate irrespective of our will or conscious intention, sometimes even without our awareness. They operate most strongly in times of 'fight or flight'. This is the sympathetic function of the nervous system operating out of balance with the parasympathetic. You can observe it as a fundamental activity in nature. It doesn't even have to be learned socially:

> The female leaves the water and crawls to a point on the beach safely above the tide line, where she digs a hole, deposits hundreds of eggs, covers the nest, and turns back to the sea. After eighteen days a multitude of tiny turtles come flipping up through the sand and, like a field of sprinters at the crack of the gun, make for the heavily crashing waves as fast as they can, while gulls drop screaming from overhead to pick them off.[50]

The turtles are primed to run even before they've had experience of being hunted. This is default behaviour operating to the advantage of the possessor. It's unsurprising then that defaults operate for performers just as for turtles or regular humans, especially in the open context of improvisation where fear of failure often lurks. It's not surprising therefore to see blocking, evasion, physical stasis, joke-hunting, over-accepting or refusal to progress story being displayed, especially in those who are new to the medium. These performer safety measures are resorted to like a child reaching for a familiar blanket. However, it's unwise for the teacher to grab the blanket away too quickly. Default choices aren't a sin or a curse or a failing; life has simply led to them. They can be a strength for any performer – even a cash cow. It's the management of them that counts. It's only when they operate unconsciously, impulsively, that they become traps. The improviser Mick Napier writes about how in comedy improvisers can rely on them over-much to their ultimate disadvantage. In his highly popular book, *Improvise: Scene from the Inside Out,* Napier writes about how there's a well of characters each improviser has and they use them because they know they will always get laughs. And they do – for a while. But soon the well runs dry. And at that point, the need for reinvention has become overwhelming.

For a performer in training, therefore, the point is not to expunge defaults in some zeal of purity, it's to increase the zone of awareness so the performer can make better choices. In this way performance is seen as an arena of choice rather than compulsion.

Included here are some exercises to help increase that zone of awareness.

Place on the Stage

Players are invited to walk on to a predefined stage area – either a conventionally organised proscenium arch or a round staging – and choose a preferred place. They are answering the question: 'What is your preferred place on the stage?' 'Where do you instinctively gravitate to?' From this it's possible to see who prefers the limelight, who the shadows. This can be followed up with the question: 'What is the place you tend to avoid. Why is that?' Now go there'.

The exercise can trigger a conversation about default choices as to the use of the stage.

Positive Censorship

The group is divided into sub-groups of three players. In each sub-group, two will improvise a scene and one will function as a director. A frame for the improvisation is chosen. For example, a wayward child returns to a parent or Adam and Eve contemplate their options with the apple. The director watches the improvisation, particularly observing any phrases, gestures or actions from either improviser that are repeated. Afterwards, the director points out these repeating tics to the players. Then the scene is run again but with the players specifically avoiding those phrases, gestures or actions. There's the possibility of the improvisation being run a third time with even tighter restrictions. For example, it's run without words or in gibberish or without physical contact. Such restrictions can more powerfully eliminate defaults. The aim throughout is to identify such defaults and for the performers to consciously 'switch them off' for the duration.

It's very likely the performer isn't even aware of defaults. So it's a matter of pointing out carefully and uncritically what the performer is doing, and asking, 'Are you aware you're doing this?' The benefit of involving all the watchers in this conversation is that it takes away any suggestion the teacher/facilitator is 'picking on' the individual.

A different approach is to employ anti-defaulting devices – sets of rules – to help shift performers out of their familiar patterns. This sounds like a veterinary procedure, but it has form. Jonah Lehrer argues how this works in poetry:

> Just look at poets, who often rely on literary forms with strict requirements, such as haikus and sonnets. At first glance, this writing method makes little sense, since the creative act then becomes much more difficult. Instead of composing freely, poets frustrate themselves with structural constraints. But that's precisely the point. Unless poets are stumped by the form, unless they are forced to look beyond the obvious associations, they'll never invent an original line. They'll be stuck with cliches and conventions, with predictable adjectives and boring verbs. And this is why poetic forms are so important.[51]

In theatre practice the same applies: you need structures for actors to wrestle with, in order that 'the difficulty of the task accelerates the insight process'. As discussed earlier, Keith Johnstone devised games that established fixed rules through which the actors were forced to funnel their creativity, for example by imposing verbal restrictions.

Verbal Restrictions

Players are given a scene or dialogue to improvise which must be completed using speeches of no more than one, two or three words in length. 'If every sentence has to be three words long, then the players must attend to what they're saying. Instead of "Come in", they'll have to say, "Come in please", or "'That you, honey?" This prevents beginners from leaving their mouths on "automatic" while their minds gallop off into the future. Rapport is noticeably improved.'[52]

Other useful restrictions would include: 'No swearing allowed', 'There must be a swearword in every sentence' or 'You never complete your sentences'.

Because the player's mind is taken up with dealing with the task or restriction – the form – content emerges less censored. This content represents a by-product for the performer (since she is focused on the restriction) but is a dramatic focus for the audience.

Defaults can also operate quite strongly within ensemble contexts. When Eugenio Barba came to Sadler's Wells in 2014, he talked about how hard it is for a company that knows each other as well as Odin members do, to wrench themselves away from familiar patterns: 'After a few years working in the same way, the actors develop clichés. What distinguishes a creative action is not the cliché but action that is not habitual.'[53]

Part of the secret, he said, lay in the casting. It would be relatively easy for company members to slot into roles that were familiar – the angry mother, the casual lothario, the embittered junkie – but it wouldn't advance the actor's development and it wouldn't surprise a regular audience.

Two and Two

Two players are chosen to be improvisers, another two as task-setters. The latter pair sit behind a table. This can be done as an exercise in front of an audience or without. The task-setting pair write a scenic idea on a piece of paper and pass it to the performers. It should be detailed enough to spark an improvisation without being prescriptive. It might give a location and a relationship or an activity and an event. 'Two burglars plan a robbery' or 'A man leaves his wife'. The improvisation happens.

The task-setters then create a new task, a new improvisation based on a challenge to the improvisers that will take them out of what appears to be a comfort zone. If the improvisation was very argumentative, the task might be 'Two architects dream up a new city'. If the pair have been physically passive, it might be 'A man meets a lion in the jungle'. If there is lacking any emotion or vulnerability, it might be 'A girl confesses to her boyfriend about something she did, which she now regrets'. The improvisers take the new instruction and act it out. Once this is completed, the task-setters set a third and perhaps final task, again basing the challenge on encouraging what appears to be absent in the playing of the last improvisation.

Tim Etchells, director of Forced Entertainment, has observed that his company has a similar challenge in devising new material – after all, the core company has stayed constant over many years. He spoke in the Argument Room about how having defaults as a group, at one level, is 'great because it saves you time. You don't have to say, "Don't mime going down some stairs" because you know we won't be interested in that.'[54] But he acknowledges how this tendency to have a set vocabulary can get productively dislodged by outsiders coming in.

> But also what's cool is when we invite new people in or we forget ourselves for a moment, and people do things that are on the 'banned list' occasionally that makes it in, and that shifts things … The vocabulary that you build up is a source of strength but it's also something that you do well to challenge from time to time, to bust it open and end up in a different place; that's how the work grows, otherwise you're trapped in a museum spiral of your own greatest tricks.[55]

That's Right, Bob!

I was introduced to this game by a travelling Canadian impro troupe. Two players, A and B, address the audience to tell a story of an adventure, a mission or a business initiative. The story might be one of success or failure. Player A begins. At regular intervals, the other player interrupts the first with 'That's Right, Bob!' (or Jane or Jo or Julius). The new speaker takes forward the last point being made, perhaps enlarging or giving the background to it. Alternatively the cue can also be passed over by the current speaker so the other is compelled to go, 'That's Right, Bob'. The aim is, by driving the story forward, each player is pitched by the other into a line of thought that would not otherwise be chosen. This can be done deliberately so that Player A gets B into trouble with a line such as 'We found the secret to making the bread rise without yeast, using – petrol!' at which point B is obliged to say 'That's Right, Bob', and take this idea forward, explaining it to the audience.

14. Transgressing

Arguably being a performer requires not just flexibility to avoid defaults but also a greater access to 'human-ness' than most achieve, and a greater willingness to make this quality transparent. Which means showing more, telling more, sharing more, externalizing more, being more impulsive, more sensuous, more sexual, more intuitive and more comfortable with risk. This is no less true when devising than at other times. In performance, the hope is that the performers will 'go further', not retreat into fearfulness. This is no less true while creating a performance for the town square as it is for a show involving a stolen bracelet. But there is always a voice in the performer's head trying to inhibit any of these things. Usually this resistance is based on fear or shame. Steven Pressfield's view is this:

> Resistance is fear. But Resistance is too cunning to show itself naked in this form. Why? Because if Resistance lets us see clearly that our own fear is preventing us from doing our work, we may feel shame at this. And shame may drive us to act in the face of fear. Resistance doesn't want us to do this. So it brings in Rationalisation.[56]

Directors will be familiar with the performer who rationalizes as a means to avoid a challenge. 'My character wouldn't do that', says the actor playing the thief when it's suggested he should break into the house of the girl (who's helped him). But the audience wants the performer to do that, to go on their behalf where they wouldn't go. To help with this, it may be useful to urge some separation between performer and character. This will enable the performer to become dislodged from familiar patterns and make more transgressive choices. Tim Crouch spoke to me about his playing of Malvolio in his play *I, Malvolio*, which offers an example of this:

> Malvolio is a lot of the time a very over-wrought character. I have a funny face, I have a funny voice, I have a costume. And the audience, especially a young audience, know that I'm just playing that. There's an understanding that this character exists outside of me, outside of you and I'm going to manipulate that character and pull the strings of that character. And I and the audience will have a great time picking at him and demolishing him. But he will kind of win at the end.[57]

Crouch observed that while working for the National Theatre as Education Associate,

> I used to remove actors from scenes and replace them with randomly selected inanimate objects, in classes. And the actor would stand out of the space and project lines on to those objects. And was allowed to move those objects not to represent physical movement but to represent emotion.[58]

Here's an exercise that's close in spirit to the tactics Crouch was adopting.

Toys

In pairs, players sit down around a small table. You'll need a random selection of household objects for this: brushes, plates, forks, hairbrushes, sponge, etc. A traditional story is given to each player to work with. For example, Romeo and Juliet, Cinderella, Little Red Riding Hood or Dracula. The pair have to tell the story with objects representing characters.

The story should be corrupted in order to take the transgressive opportunities offered by the remote control of the objects. There might be a third player sitting alongside whose role is to be a spectator and ask provocative questions: 'So could you make clearer what happens exactly when Cinderella and Prince Charming are dancing?' 'Has there been any history of drug-taking in the family of Little Red Riding Hood?'

The argument about distance versus immersion within character portrayal is an ongoing one. Here, in our devising process, given the activist disposition of the project, we're advocating an anti-immersion stance which is closer to that argued for by Brecht. It's also close to what Robert Lepage argues for here:

> There's a school of thought that if you want it to sound real, you have to make it sound like you would say it for real, like you were inventing the words, which is one conception of acting. But there's also exactly the opposite. Which is that this [the speech] has been written by someone else, who is not me.[59]

Let's imagine that our drug addict/thief character is called Zed; and there's a scene in which Zed visits the girl but she's not in, only her parents. Given the extent of his addiction, it's likely he went there with a view to financial gain. So we might expect the actor playing Zed to take some risks in the situation on his behalf, as it were. However, if the actor avoids any risk-taking, then after the exercise I might suggest a strategy that will help enable him to take this route next time around. I'll suggest he has three tracks operating, something like tracks on a digital audio file:

- the first is his performer thought-track;
- the second is his character thought-track; and finally there's
- the voice of the commentator.

When improvisation teachers talk about 'getting out of your head' they mean silencing this commentary track because it's probably saying things like 'Help!' and 'I'm shit!' The actor should generally pay less attention to this thought-track and more to the performer and character tracks. These are likely to be quieter in the performer's head. Here what's important is to build the performer thought-track because this will allow attention to be directed to the dramatic, political and social potential of the scene. It might be going 'We need to move this forward now' or 'I'm getting a signal my drug addict character is really frustrated. It would be appropriate to push this into a reprehensible action of some kind. Maybe I should steal something.' When this thought-track is activated, the actor has one eye on the stage action while the other is trained beyond the edge of it; monitoring the audience.

However, it's also useful to build up the character thought-track to enable a sense of a 'real' character with its own life – even though 'Zed' doesn't actually exist – and to do this without disappearing into it. This means staying aware of the audience while being prompted by impulses moment-to-moment. These might be impulses such as 'I'm becoming angry' or 'I need a fix'.

By establishing the idea of tracks, the improviser will be better able to distinguish the more useful impulses to act on. He or she will be able to distinguish between those thoughts to be acted on and those to be ignored.

One Step Further

A scene is defined for two or three players with their relationships also defined in advance. The improvisers play the scene. At any point the facilitator calls 'Freeze!' at which the players stop exactly where they are. The facilitator then 'resculpts' or instructs the players so that they physically are in a more compromising or compromised situation. The command is then given; 'Restart!' The players continue the scene, finding new dialogue from the new positions.

The Actor and the Bathplug

A scene is improvised between an actor and a domestic object such as a bathplug, a plunger or a broom. A second actor will 'play the part' of the object, saying the lines of that object and occasionally moving the object expressively within the scene. The first actor plays the scene straight, as if to another performer.

Despite this proposal for a degree of separation between actor and character in the playing, this doesn't mean that acting should be puritan in spirit. This is not an argument for avoidance of risk or passion. It shouldn't feed into the English tendency to be nervous around sex, nudity or violence. Rather it should be enabling of a playful, risk-taking approach to these very issues. Keith Johnstone devised many exercises to help actors get over their pasty, nervous selves. He reminds them that within an improvisation, to say you're going to impregnate the grocer's daughter, cut off her head and make soup from it, this is not actually what you're going to do in life. Actors do often struggle to understand the distinction, leaving them trapped in a Groundhog Day of super-politeness.

Yes, And

Two players stand a few feet from each other. The first says a line expressing a proposal that the two of them do something together. It should be relatively mundane proposal such as, 'Let's go for a walk' or 'Let's have a cup of tea'. The second elaborates this, starting the response with 'Yes, and - '. The first player responds similarly, again further elaborating the proposal. No response should comprise a 'list' of activities but rather a development from the previous suggestion.

'Let's go for a walk.'
'Yes, and we can steal a dog.'
'Yes, and we can hold its owner to ransom.'
'Yes, and we'll get £5!'
'Yes, and we can buy a big net to catch more dogs!'

'Yes, And' has become something of a classic exercise that helps actors jump into a more fantastical way of thinking, one that has an imaginative logic if not a realistic one. For those who don't know it: once the line is crossed and the improviser becomes accepting of transgressive material that's vulgar, inappropriate, crazy or violent, it's surprising how easily it's embraced. Sometimes it just takes that nudge, no more than a reminder of what acting actually is – a foolish enterprise, really.

15. Foolishness

Underlying several of these tactics, anti-defaulting and transgression in particular, is the spirit of foolishness. It sits underneath all of them, a lively, gregarious and generous state of being that welcomes contradiction and delights in the revelation of awkward truths. Arguably it's the godmother of all performance having its precedents in the Trickster myths of Anansi, Loki and Robin Goodfellow. So within this loose-limbed conversation about devising and ensemble, it feels essential to include a short section on foolishness in the rehearsal room before the conversation concludes.

Last Day of Life

This is a challenge for a solo performer. He or she sits or stands in front of the group. The challenge is to give an account of what you would do if you only had one day to live. Who would you speak to, spend time with, have sex with, get killed? It's understood that you couldn't be held responsible for anything you do. The exercise can be enhanced by the presence of an onside provocateur who interjects questions periodically; 'Is that all?', 'More detail!', 'That sounds dull!'

While it may well feel like a digression, and perhaps it is, it's a digression worth the journey. After all, foolishness is perhaps the quality most respected and valued by improvisation companies across the world. It embodies the positive, the creative, the insightful and the altruistic. It operates not for profit but for delight. Understanding and working with foolishness, however, is not always straightforward. It takes more than a rebellious head. One reason for this is that as adult citizens we've internalized a need to corral our waywardness, which is why so many good folk, disenchanted with the over-regulation of their wilder impulses, seek impro classes to let fly a little. Here the core attitudes of trust, commitment, spontaneity and exuberance are cultivated using what is now a vast and ever-expanding range of games and exercises.

A particular value of many exercises that are dedicated to foolishness is that they devolve authority from the teacher or director to the conventions of the exercises themselves. In other words, everyone in the room is equally eligible to comment on the extent to which the exercise is being fulfilled. This mitigates against the more authoritarian atmosphere that you find in some director-led rehearsals where 'good' or 'bad' judgements appear to depend largely on the director's personal view.

This concept of foolishness is at the heart of the impro project as developed by Keith Johnstone, Viola Spolin, the Compass Theatre and many, many American and UK companies. However, it's important to note that foolishness is not simply mucking about; it's a discipline that depends very much upon acuity of mind and generosity of emotion. Nor is it a discipline that can be practised in isolation. It's not possible 'to fool' in one's bathroom in front of the mirror, or alone on a beach. It's a discipline that requires an audience for its exercise. So, you might think, it can't be 'rehearsed', and this is true. Lending itself uniquely to improvisation, fooling instead insists on each moment being unique. However, in a workshop or rehearsal context, there always is an audience when the group size numbers two or more – and a learned ability to fool can only complement a devising process.

In the practice of this discipline, the fool requires a subject–object relationship to be in place. The fool requires a target, be that an audience, a prop, the room, a story or perhaps another performer. To fool is 'to fool with'. The 'with' establishes the relationship between the fool and the object of the fooling. This recognition is useful because it undermines the idea that foolishness is just messing about without any purpose or function. Fooling is about fooling in relation to something. It's therefore different from clowning, which is more dependent on routines and comedy that is generated from failure.

'To fool with' means:

• Accepting offers unconditionally
• Playing with them
• Working abstractly (not being drawn into literalness)
• Maintaining contact with others
• Being less concerned with any end result than with the moment-by-moment playfulness; it's a 'time-less' activity
• Working without judgement but with emotion

In a workshop therefore it may be useful to identify what delivers the 'with' element. This takes the pressure off the performer. Exercises involving fooling with objects provide an easy way in. Such exercises can move on to explore fooling 'with the space' or 'with the audience'.

Jonathan Kay, one of the UK's leading fool teachers, has developed a methodology for teaching foolishness that is unique to him. It's one that is uniquely powerful. It isn't necessarily a model to follow uncritically because the approach may not work in the same way for other teachers; however his experience, learned over decades, means there are few reasons not to study his approach, if possible as a pupil. Other teachers such as Kevin Tomlinson, a former student of John Wright, have likewise built up the kind of foolish knowledge that only decades of study can deliver.

Kay often starts the first day of any workshop the same way: 'The first thing to do is get everyone on the same level. It doesn't matter how good or

Fooling With Props

A table with an assortment of props, some literal, some abstract. Two or three players stand around the table. Any player goes first, picks up a prop and uses it in a way in which it's not intended. For example, a toothbrush becomes an animal which is placed on the arm and stroked. The next player picks a piece of string and begins to whip herself with it, recounting sins. And so on.

To extend the exercise, once a player has defined the object and its use, another comes in to reinforce the game. For example, the animal is admired and there's speculation on whether it was stolen. A player finds another 'whip' and also begins self-admonishment. Their conversation discloses a shared act of disobedience within a monastery.

bad they think they are.'[60] This means that everyone has to jump up in turn; they get two minutes onstage, unsupported. 'They can choose whether to do an exciting two minutes or a dull two minutes.'[61] But the exercise doesn't end until two minutes is up, even if that person never leaves the chair. But at the end of the two minutes, 'everyone gets an uproarious standing ovation. And whatever they've done, that's when they realize – if they hadn't before – that it was something. Because the clap makes it into something.'[62]

Gang of Fools

This is based on The King Game that is attributed to Keith Johnstone. The teacher/facilitator takes the role of a gang leader who is looking for new gang members. But this is a foolish gang and only the most foolish will be accepted. The gangmaster sits at one end of the room – or at a distance away from the players. Any player can then get up and present him or herself for acceptance into the gang. The presentation can be physical, verbal, musical or of any kind – but it must be foolish. Each player makes an offer of some kind, a promise or the demonstration of a skill, which in the normal world would not be valued. The gang master may question or engage with the player but will quickly or slowly make a decision: either to wave the player in or to 'kill' them by clicking two fingers. In which case the player falls down dead and another player steps up. The teacher/facilitator will be looking to 'kill' those who are evading the foolish challenge.

Then Kay introduces some of the concepts behind his approach. He empha-sizes the importance of understanding the difference between an idea and an offer: 'An idea is something you think about intellectually, you toss about and squash. Mainly people are going after ideas. But when you jump up, whatever you see, smell, touch – these are offers. You don't have to make an idea out of them.' By not turning them into ideas you stay in the playful world, what Kay calls 'the inner world'. 'Ideas are useful when you're sitting down but they're not useful when you're in the world of offers, they get in the way.'[63]

Kay's distinction between 'offer' and 'idea' might be thought of like this: a performer picks up a prop, for example a piece of wood, and sets it down so it's a boat on the river. The performer then plays a 'going down the Amazon' routine, resisting any temptation to segue into any other reality. This would be an example of turning an offer into an idea. Whereas to simply play with the wood as an offer would be to place it down, endow it as a boat, walk off the boat as if walking on water, hear a sound from the audience, react to this, and in response, perform a Christ-like miracle. This way the performer does not remain, as it were 'trapped' within a scenic conceit.

This is one of the challenges for beginners: learning to avoid the impulse to define what's happening too closely. Instead the learning is all about being comfortable with ambiguity, uncertainty and unresolved tension, hence the value of playing early short games, which require simple bursts of imagi-native, uncensored exuberance; games which encourage an imaginative expansiveness.

'Let's ...'

One member of the group calls out 'Let's ... (do something / be something / enact something)'. Everyone agrees, calling out 'Yes, Let's (do that thing). Then everyone does it and continues to do it until someone else calls 'Stop! Let's (do something different)!' At this, everyone agrees again and again performs the thing. The game continues in this way.

Keith Johnstone writes of the value of master–servant and other status games to encourage the foolish disposition. His writing indicates how in these games the foolish conceit needs to encircle both servant and master, fool and king. He encourages students to play both roles as a means of 'accelerating the skills'.[64] By switching between parts, that necessary detachment from any one role is encouraged. The performer is not the servant, is only playing the servant. The performer is not the king ... etc.

The Blind Servant

To make the relationship more interesting, the servant wears a blindfold. Then the king gives the servant some tasks to do in the space. They must be doable, perhaps involving fetching a glass of water, moving chairs around, bringing a book to read, etc. In order to administer justice, the king has a rolled-up newspaper. This is used to hit the servant every time the servant makes a mistake. Which, let's face it, is likely to be often. Possibly the king prefers not to move from his or her chair so for each punishment, calls the servant to come over. If by chance the servant reaches a point of rebellion, he or she may rip off the blindfold and refuse to serve further. This would be a shift point, for sure.

What beginners find particularly difficult is suspending their judgement on proceedings. An indication of their difficulty is evidenced by feeling awkward when laughed at. Yet laughter is the warm fertilizer that encourages foolishness to extend out into the world. Nor are these exercises for foolishness irreconcilable with an activist position. Look at the example of the Clandestine Insurgent Rebel Clown Army whose routines are self-evidently foolish, their target often the police line in front of them. This is what they 'fool with': the hierarchical state structures of which the police are the embodiment:

> Police in black riot gear stand shoulder to shoulder. Their clear, body-length plastic shields form a wall across the city street. Visors are down. Heavy boots and hulking full-body armor add to their imposing appearance. They are poised to preserve public order ... The police are confronted by a disorderly gaggle of men and women in chaotic facepaint, second-hand military gear, and clownish, garish pink and green frills. Far from being intimidated, the CIRCA folk seem overjoyed to see them, and hail them as friends and playmates. The clowns scrub the policemen's boots with their feather dusters. They breathe on the shields to fog them up, and then polish them ... Finally, one trickster, aptly named Trixie, kisses one of the police shields. Her kiss is so enthusiastic and vigorous that she smears her clown makeup and lipstick all over it. She then goes from shield to shield, all the way up the phalanx-line, kissing and leaving a smeary mark on each one. The police stay in formation.[65]

16. Ownership

After this essential digression, it's meet to return to our devising project and
to conclude with some observations about ownership. It can be argued, and
I would, that one of the afflicting ills of much theatre is the dysfunctional
relationship that exists between the performers and what is performed. Not
that the latter often lacks grace, insightfulness, pertinence or the means to
make us wonder at the extraordinary pageant of the world; rather there is more
often than not a lack of a sense of ownership of that material by the performers.

It's not entirely inappropriate to apply a Marxian analysis to mainstream
theatre work. Actors for their part don't (usually) own the means of
production. They are the resources (usually) acquired by a capital-owning
producer in order to achieve production. Through their endeavours (usually)
they create a surplus value which may be monetary or reputational. But these
benefits will largely accrue to the producers, the significant director or the
leading actor or some combination of these. Those banging in the nails
at the edge of the stage are unlikely (usually) to influence the production
without an Eric Clapton clause. Eric Clapton cannot contractually enter into
any show involving other musicians or bands without his agency having
a measure of control over the whole event. Actors, lacking this, will help
to create a great show – but that may be the end of their association with
it. They are however, for good or ill, usually familiar with this tradition of
directorial autocracy such as Nicholas Ridout describes:

> The actor is paid to appear in public speaking words written by someone
> else and executing physical movement which has at the least been
> usually subject to intense and critical scrutiny by a representative of the
> management who effectively enjoys the power of hiring and firing.[66]

Or as it happens in practice: 'So many directors waste time trying to work
out in rehearsal how to move people round the stage, others let the actors
feel their way around, but Trevor has planned it all already.'[67] That's David
Weston in his account of working as Ian McKellen's understudy in Trevor
Nunn's *King Lear*.

This tradition of theatre making, by placing supreme confidence in the
director, runs a certain risk: the director imposes a vision on the ensemble
against their inclination. In a context we would define as one governed by
ideas of ensemble, it's less likely to happen. But before progressing further,
it's probably wise to ask: what is ownership?

Here's one interpretation: it's a sense of connectedness between the
performers and the dramatic material, a pride of the former in the latter, a
sense that the material was 'made by them'. To illustrate: in my early career

of devising shows I several times found myself confronted by revolution. Usually a revolution against me as the director. The group, a mix of professional and community actors, would reach a point about three-quarters of the way through rehearsals and declare: 'Chris, we don't want to do this show. It doesn't say what we want to say.' And I would be knocked off my perch. Besides, we were three days off performing. I'd bluster, call an end to rehearsals, go home and hunt for my copy of *The Empty Space*. What I realized only later was that by launching this putsch, the group was engaged in a necessary act of taking ownership. They were triggering a crisis, unconsciously perhaps but still intentionally, in order to prepare for walking out onstage. It was a crisis to be passed through almost as a rite of passage to emerge emboldened the other side. And interestingly, what I found when we reassembled was the changes demanded were largely symbolic. Very few were requested but they were endowed with significance. I was reminded of when Augusto Boal, exasperated that a woman spectator wasn't happy with how her suggestion was being acted out by the actors, invited her to come onstage and act them out herself. She acted these out in almost exactly the way they had been acted previously; but now she was doing it herself. So it felt different. Boal called this new kind of performance Forum Theatre. The group I was working with also felt different once I had accepted the need for change and the script was fractionally altered. This renewed sense of ownership fortified the actors to walk out onstage.

It became clear that at some level I'd withheld ownership. In more recent times I would hope to avoid this by adopting a number of strategies during the course of the process:

- Sharing certain decisions about content while maintaining the integrity of the dramatic frame.
- Proceeding step-by-step achieving shared ownership of the process incrementally.
- Being more willing to try out others ideas which I didn't initially value.
- Leaving more material in the frame than it was possible to contain and allow the group to request an edit.
- Having a systematic methodology that involved 'checking in' with the group periodically as to how the process was going.

In a devising context, it might be thought ownership best achieved by working autobiographically. Such a route does have evident merit in many contexts. The director Jeremy Weller has worked extensively with young offenders and homeless people. He conducts a quite rigorous process that enables a use of personal stories to transformational ends, meaning the participants get some insight into their own lives as a result:

Autobiography

By encouraging people to present a public performance of their own experiences, however disguised or edited, the company hopes to create the opportunity for them [the participants] to step back from their daily lives and see themselves, as it were, from a distance – as others might see them.[68]

Such an approach of externalizing previously submerged experiences has clear benefits for the performers, and too the audience, which is drawn in by the integrity of the performing.

However, it's also possible to take individual stories and thread them together to achieve a woven tapestry within which the individual stories are embedded but not visible. There are exercises to enable this process such as Chinese Mime or Common Elements.

Chinese Mime

All bar two of the players are sent out of the room. The remaining Player 1 tells his or her story to Player 2. Then another player comes in and Player 2 now enacts – performs the story soundlessly - to Player 3. Then the next player, number 4, comes in and the exercise is repeated. The final player, rather than enacting the story, tells what he or she thinks is the story to the rest of the group.

Variation: Player 3, rather than enacting, tells verbally what is thought to be the story. Player 4 enacts, then Player 5 story-tells, and so on.

Common Elements

This exercise assumes everyone has a story to share perhaps on a theme already agreed. The group divides into pairs. Each pair has a large piece of paper. In each pair Player 1 tells his or her story to Player 2. While it is being told, Player 2 writes down what might be scene titles for this story: Confrontation, Escape, Theft, Shelter, etc. – if possible one key word for each section of the story. Roles are then reversed and Player 2 tells a story while Player 1 writes the key words. Then all the key 'scene titles' from all the pairs are shared. Then any common titles are pulled out and put to one side. This is how we learn what kinds of scenes these different stories have in common. Put into sequence (there may be gaps) this list of scene titles offers a narrative shape for the play.

then merge pairs into groups
montage

A different route to ownership is offered by working with myth or folk tale. This cupboard of stories has no back on it. Tales can be selected and shared out to subgroups for each to interpret dramatically. Tales such as Little Red Riding Hood, Frankenstein or Bluebeard are given to each subgroup to interpret dramatically in its own way. Then it's a matter of seeing which stories catch fire in the presentations. If a tale does catch fire, the wider group instinctively starts to invest in it through its comments and praise. There grows a sense that this folk tale 'belongs' to that group.

17. Casting

Another aspect of this process of achieving ownership lies in the casting. For an activist theatre, the business of building the company itself is likely to be very different to any procedure that involves a casting director. It's almost certain that some affinity with the aims of the project will be a precondition of membership. This approach might be typified by Breach Theatre Company, whose director Billy Barrett told me that when casting their show *The Beanfield*, about the breakup of the Stonehenge Free Festival, 'It was more important that people were emotionally and politically connected with the issue rather than they could give a flawless performance'.[69]

However, there's still the work of casting roles. It's observable that performers, whether professional or community, will likely have a natural momentum towards performing certain kinds of roles. These aren't necessarily default preferences, although they might be, but they are preferences that need to be acknowledged. One has a natural affinity with the disrupter, the charmer, the teacher, the seducer, another with the sulk, the clown or the leader. Possibly that individual with an affinity for a certain character should be encouraged to play that role. Alternatively there may be good reasons to consciously cast against a particular talent. Either way, what's hoped for is for the performer to start 'owning' that role. It's quite likely that performer will start to grow a little inside it. It's part of the directorial or facilitative skill set to manage this process.

If no natural symmetries offer themselves, it's possible to discover affinities between performer and role via a different route; by imposing restrictions or using masks. With mask work, role can emerge in a way that surprises everyone in the room, especially the wearer. There comes the possibility almost of being 'instructed' by the mask, which is a kind of ownership. The performer Kelda Holmes said this of her experience while performing in an improvised show – *Night, London* – at the Tristan Bates Theatre. Her onstage task was to find another performer on the stage, her long-lost brother, a task which she achieved unsighted. 'For me that was about being in tune – the bucket was my mask'.[70] In this case it was the restriction applied, the mask, that prompted a sense of liberation and 'in-tune-ness'. It allowed a degree of ownership to be found through discovery of a character persona. On this subject, Keith Johnstone observes:

> Once students begin to observe for themselves the way that Masks compel certain sorts of behaviour, then they really begin to feel the presence of 'spirits'. It's true that some actors will maintain that they always remain 'themselves' when they're acting, but how do they know? Improvisers who maintain that they're in a normal state of consciousness when they improvise have unsuspected gaps in their memories which only emerge when you question them closely.[71]

The issue of 'possession' is hotly contested between advocates of mask work. Keith Johnstone has consistently advocated for the use of the mask as a means to introduce trance states. John Wright, on other hand, resists any suggestion of the performer 'becoming possessed', but does acknowledge that a certain impulsiveness enters in for the mask-wearer that would not be present otherwise. Given that a close study of Mask is largely outside the scope of this book, it makes sense only to recommend as starter texts both John Wright's and Keith Johnstone's seminal books that touch on this subject.

What does emerge from this brief examination of ownership however is this paradox: a greater sense of ownership of 'role' may be best achieved through some abandonment of individual personality.

18. The Price of Ownership

In the context of community and education work where artistic control of the project involves granting 'ownership' to a particular group, the exercise has to involve handing over power. It is to the discredit of many UK projects that the implications of this bargain tend to be avoided. It is often advertised as happening – 'Work With Us To Make YOUR OWN Show!' – the bait to catch the wavering fish – but the reality is often different. Turning disenfranchised young people into independent artists takes considerable time, patience and commitment. The assumption it can be achieved by walking them into a drama studio is like assuming you can change vegetarians into carnivores by walking them round Norfolk.

I recently ran a drama session for an education institution in Bradford, working with teenagers who had multiple issues; some were refusing to go to school or were refused by the school, others had mental health or drug concerns. They were fifteen strong. The young people came in the room and within the first ten minutes over half of them had announced they were not going to participate. If it hadn't been clear before, it was now: they had been compelled to attend. I would love to boast by the end of the session they were all asking about Equity membership. But that would be a brazen lie.

After a chaotic first half in which a few theatre games were tried and aborted, I tried a different strategy in the second. I asked for two volunteers to sit on the chairs onstage. I then asked the 'audience' to determine who these characters might be. I was told they were two crack heads. I allowed the two girls who'd volunteered to choose whether to accept this designation. They did, fortunately. On the audience's prompting we introduced other characters: a drug dealer, a policeman, and a parent. It was at that point I took one of my better decisions: I invited the most opinionated of the spectators to become the director of the piece. The young man accepted. But in giving away power, I was taking something of a risk. As it proved.

The young man started to run the dope-scoring scene, became dissatisfied with it, stopped it, sent the actors offstage and started it again. He started the same scene three or four times. The drug dealer came and went. The policeman came and went. There was shouting and falling about and anger and blame and reference to a fire in a warehouse and previous deals that had led someone to overdose and die. The girls fell out with each other and with the parent and with the director and requested to go home. The scene was never finished because the idea of closure itself, of dramatic shape or conclusion, was largely unfamiliar. So instead we slid inexorably towards a film-making template where the 'film' was never completed. Moments of dramatic action were bookended by shouts of 'Action' and 'Cut' (or in this case – '[expletive deleted] start again!').

It was going well and I was pleased with my decision. Then the fight took place. The guy playing the policeman and the guy playing the drug dealer took the opportunity to introduce some realism. 'Stand back, Chris, or you might get hurt', said one politely as they squared up. The staff member, I noticed, was staying firmly in her seat. The 'director' was joining in. I was already writing the news article in my head: 'Teenager Stabbed in Drama Workshop – "I just was trying to give them ownership", says Drama Teacher.' Very luckily, as is often the case in young offender institutions, the lads knew how to manage combat without actually killing each other. Before long they were sitting down next to each other discussing where the drama should move next. That's what I like to think anyway. I have some pride.

That giving away power comes with an element of risk is a point insufficiently understood by civic institutions whose declarations in favour of creative engagement often conceal either ignorance (at best) or deceit (at worst). In 2015 a promenade play called *Homegrown*, devised and created by young people in East London and which addressed the issue of Islamic radicalization, was cancelled by the producers the National Youth Theatre within days of opening. Unsurprisingly the NYT used the time-honoured excuse of 'artistic standards' as justification, evidently concealing issues of politics and control. The NYT put out a statement saying: 'After some consideration, we have come to the conclusion that we cannot be sufficiently sure of meeting all of our aims to the standards we set and which our members and audiences have come to expect.'[72] That this justification hid another truth became evident after a Freedom of Information request led to the release of an internal email that referenced the director/writer team as having an 'extremist agenda'. It wasn't as if the team hadn't been accommodating. As the *Homegrown* writer Omar El-Khairy wrote in the *Guardian*:

> The cancellation came after local government intervention led to us being thrown out of our original venue [a school], and after police had suggested security measures that included reading drafts, attending rehearsals, planting plainclothes officers in the audience, and carrying out daily sweeps of the venue by a bomb squad.[73]

The cancellation led to no less than 115 young people being told that the show they had devised over several weeks, they could not perform.

The story clearly bears out some of the points made earlier in this volume about the civic and institutional resistance that exists to suppress theatre the content of which is deemed subversive, insurrectionary or simply problematic. That the creative team had successfully engaged so many young people in a theatre exercise – on a subject absolutely contemporary and important – is only to be commended. That they used an innovative form of production – the audience were to be able to walk around listening to characters in conversation – is also praiseworthy. This choice of theatre form is significant because it begins to put the event out of reach of any artistic control that might exerted by the producers. It's not surprising then that both sides emerged subsequently with quite different versions of what happened about the 'script approval' that had been sought by the NYT. And what of the content of the production? Let the last word on that belong to the director Nadia Latif. The reader may decide on the extent of its subversive nature:

> It's a kaleidoscopic look at communities, cultures and conversations about Islam in Britain and the radicalisation of young people. We're trying to say these kids are becoming radicalised in a nation that's rife

with phobia – whether that's homophobia, sexism or Islamophobia. This doesn't happen in a vacuum. Sexism doesn't not happen to brown people. We're trying to say these are universal problems. The artists involved had a lot of opinions and the show was partly about working through those within the national narrative. We were making the play in a particular political climate, and we wanted the audience to make up their own minds.[74]

It's a show description that carries some aspects of our migrant thief/innocent girl storyline. Perhaps that too would run the risk of censorship. It still seems to be the case that whoever controls the field of play may well attempt to control the play.

19. Disobedient Theatre

Throughout this book I've tried to argue that the practice of theatre is one inseparable from the business of being provocative. Yet there are shows and companies who do more than this; they harness the art of provocation to concerns over social justice and human rights. It's these artists and companies that are most likely to hit trouble, as we've seen. The paradox is that often it's this quality of 'disobedience' that can be found less in the hearts and minds of the makers than in the eyes of those who would throw rocks in the road to impede their progress. While it's true there are some theatre makers who do set out to upset, disturb and scandalize just for the hell of it (and sometimes one reasonably asks, 'Why not?'), others are merely raising issues important to them or their communities. Yet because of this struggle for legitimacy of expression and its concomitant civic fear of disturbing a perpetually maintained soft parade of niceness, many of these artists are having to spend more time fighting their corner than making the art. Perhaps this is inevitable. Despite this, the view from the field of play is still encouraging. Artists and audiences are coming together in some innovative ways to make pioneering work crack open some of our prejudices about how art can function, as examples in this book have hopefully demonstrated. Experimentation in unlikely locations being encouraged. Peer support networks are helping. There is some de-professionalization which is leading to exciting collaborations between theatre artists and others from different professions or none. Performance is (almost) everywhere. So to help fuel this spirit of optimistic advancement, I offer this volume as a small contribution, both to the heavy ideological lifting, as well as to the small but vital work of fitting the wheels to the van.

Appendix 1 – Beginnings

The playwright or performance artist is in the bar after the show. A spectator comes up. They chat. And here it is; *that* question. 'Where do you get your ideas from?' A wan smile, an inward sigh and a struggle to be honest that will probably fail. A better question would have been: 'So what prompted you to pursue creativity when so many other children abandon theirs?' Here are some answers to that bar room question from my contemporaries, artists who can be found at different points along the disobedience spectrum.

Roland Muldoon – 'I wrote the school shows. *The Goon Shows* were an inspiration; surrealistic, knockabout fun. And the school allowed me to do it. The schools were a lot better in a way then. I was always over the top. Without considering what I was doing, I would get up in front of the class and improvise. On any old subject, talk about anything. There was a little coterie at school of those of us who could improvise. And say funny things. My favourite thing was when someone came up to me and said, "You're a cunt", I'd say, "Yes, I am. And – what are you?" My mum was a Tory, my dad was a Liberal. My sister was Labour and my brother became a Tory. So we were unusual on our council estate. We were very volatile, politically. I followed the Kerouac trail and went to Devon then Bristol where I worked on a building site. Then heard about the Old Vic Theatre School. Being from a working class background I hadn't seen much "proper theatre". But there was a group called The Alberts, very famous early fringe group – they used to appear in concerts. Bruce Lacey was an Albert. They did *An Evening of British Rubbish*, taking the piss out of what it was to be British, wearing pith helmets and union jacks – I was quite influenced by them. And then while I was at Bristol, I saw a production of *Ubu Roi*, the Jarry piece, it had a very cartoon style and I thought, "Uh-oh."'[1]

Oreet Ashery – 'I was born in Jerusalem. Quite early I did a lot of walking in the streets. Quite a lot of things I did when I was young fed into my practice later on. So walking in the streets, I was very very aware of the territories. Because we lived on the borderline between Jerusalem on one side, the Palestine villages – and on the other side was very religious Jewish neighbourhoods, extreme Orthodox areas, almost like ghettos. As a girl I was very aware of not being supposed to be there. And crossing over to the territories and being perceived as a female. Quite early on I was very aware of my gender and body. In the orthodox neighbourhood, I remember falling off my bicycle once and all the women coming to me and saying, "You have to run away, the men will be coming out of the synagogue and they're going to see you with shorts and t-shirt." They couldn't tend to me, they just had to get me out of all the little streets. I started wearing my dad's clothes when I was about sixteen, just to go to town, for protection – I didn't know anything about gender politics, it was just unconscious. I remember one time hitch-hiking to Accor where they had an early performance festival – there was a performance artist and a soundtrack, Laurie Anderson's *Superman* – it really really affected me, someone carried someone wrapped in bandages – it didn't fit with anything else. It was a really big experience.'[2]

Chris Goode – 'I liked using constructed events that I could control to engage with other people. At the age of seven I organized a sports day which today I think about as being one of my first acts as a director because it was all about bringing people together. I had a feeling that if I could control the frame in which I was meeting people and they were meeting me, I could control what otherwise would be horrendously chaotic, noisy and violent. I had a next door neighbour friend – we had a role playing thing going on – we were in a Space Detectives thing and for him that was about a moment-to-moment experience of being a Space Detective, but for me I had thirteen episodes of this thing plotted. I had a precociousness that made me think I could hold people by being entertaining. One formative experience was a school play I organized at the age of fifteen. It was quite radical and political, very left-wing (*The Ragged Trousered Philanthropists*), it had been done at the Riverside by Stephen Daldry and it was unusual for a school play. Suddenly there was a really different model for making and it was attached to a different political language to the one I was used to. That was big. Doing theatre was a way of being able to be in a room with people – I spent freshers week at Cambridge writing a play that I could then present to the Drama Society at its first meeting. I look back now and see myself as an "accidental renegade".'[3]

Nick Kent – 'I suppose my theatrical awakening was funnily enough, two different things; the film *Z* about the Greek Colonels and also meeting Gemma Jones who was passionate about that. I just realized that good art could be political and change peoples course. And also to some extent the play *Sizwe Bansi* at the Royal Court and then meeting John McGrath.'[4]

Alecky Blythe – 'The first play I experienced took place in my second-form Speech and Drama class. It was my favourite class, run by the formidable Mrs Blythe. Tall and elegant, and an actress in her youth, she injected into her teaching the same passion and theatricality that I imagine she must have put into every part. One particular week (in my second-form Speech and Drama class) we were treated to a performance of a Joyce Grenfell monologue from *George, Don't Do That!* by one of the older girls, who was in need of a group of seven-year-olds on whom to rehearse. I sat cross-legged on the floor along with my classmates and listened in wide-eyed wonder. I found myself completely transported to Grenfell's world of naughty children and truly believed I had become one of them. This to me seemed quite different from the poetry recitals I had heard in class before, as this time, even though I was still just listening, I was actively engaged in listening rather than passively, and that was how the spell was cast. When I later discovered that some people made a living out of this magic called "make-believe", I knew that was what I wanted to do with my life.'[5]

Matt Adams – 'I remember a couple of things in quick succession when I was about 13. I won an audition into a professional production of a Children's Music Theatre. And it was a time in my life when things were quite difficult so it was great to jump into something like that. I wanted to do it, but in a plucky, middle-class kid, I'll give it a go type way – but the really significant thing was going to see a production of *An Inspector Calls* by J. B. Priestley at the Wolsey Theatre in Ipswich. It was the realisation that theatre could unmask social and political and familial hypocrisies. And pretences. That was like a real bombshell to me, to actually go to a place where was stripped out the pretensions of a middle class family – I was completely gobsmacked by that. That was the moment I became set on the idea that theatre was something I wanted to do.'[6]

Kathleen McCreery – 'I saw the most wonderful play that the Teatro Campesino did in California, about the Vietnam war. There was a Chicano boy who was drafted and at the beginning of the play, a figure in a monks role with a calavera, a death mask, they told you that the boy was going to die. So there was no question of suspense. The question was how, when, where and why. It was told in two languages, Spanish and English. They had a wonderful scene between a mother writing a letter in Spanish and her son answered in English. Finally they had a scene in Vietnam and death comes out with the calavera and raises the rifle and the boy dies. But before he dies, he has this realisation that he understands that the people he is asked to fight are people just like himself, that he shouldn't be there. It was so simply done yet so powerful. And they tapped into the cultural references of those people. There were hardened farm hands there, standing, weeping. They did this on the back of a flatbed truck. At the end they came out and said, this was a play but it's happening and if there are any boys here subject to the draft, come and see us. And immediately half a dozen young men went up and they gave them advice on how to avoid the draft. Which meant travelling, going up to Mexico or to Canada, as my brother did.'[7]

Simon Callow – 'I am standing in a queue in a London street on a cold dark November night in 1953 with my Uncle Maurice and my grandmother. I am four years old and howling with all the considerable power of my infant lungs. My fingers and toes are frozen and I don't know why we're here, lined up with all these other people. The bright lights on the front of the building are getting closer as the queue shuffles forward. I howl louder and louder, not in the least mollified by assurances that I'll love it when we get inside. We pass through the front doors and into a sort of a hallway and then on into a vast room with rows and rows of seats covered in red velvet. At the end of the room is a huge curtain, with gold tassels and braid in figures of eight down the sides. I am more upset than ever, only wishing to be back home in familiar suburban Streatham. Then music starts and the lights go out. Terror. The great curtain goes up, and there before me is the inside of a big house filled with beds and children and their nanny, who happens to be a dog. And my jaw drops and I immediately stop howling. And then a boy in a green costume flies in at the window, looking for his shadow, which turns out to be in a drawer, and a fairy flickers around the stage, and soon all the children fly out of the window as the music surges up. And my eyes open so wide it hurts, and I don't want to go back to Streatham; in fact, I never want to go back to Streatham again. I want to fly out of the window, I want to fight pirates and rescue Indian maidens, I want to clash swords with Captain Hook, I want a winkling fairy of my own. And I want to do it to the roars of approval and disapproval that well up from the hundreds of children in the theatre that evening.'[8]

Lois Keidan – 'I think there was an early moment that piqued my interest at the Liverpool Everyman. Because of those times, it was a very politicized space in terms of what they were doing shows about. But it was also about how they were doing it. It was the first time I'd experienced this removal of the fourth wall involving the audience and it felt very anarchic and exciting. I was only moving into my early teens. That wasn't what necessarily what I wanted to do, it was just experiencing that there was a different way of doing things that had an attitude, being a Scouser, that was exciting for me, knowing there was something that wasn't the RSC. I didn't think I wanted to do this until after university. I remember my sister taking me to see Lumiere & Son – Circus Lumiere – and being blown away by that. Then being aware of politicized work coming out of Eastern Europe – aware of people like Joseph Beuys and some of the politics around that. So there were lots of different moments. There wasn't a single epiphany moment, just a momentum.'[9]

Mike Bradwell – 'At the Edinburgh Festival Theatre Conference in 1963. Joan [Littlewood] had famously declared that "all drama is piss-taking and we are all here to take the piss" which had impressed me enormously. Also I had joined the Young Communist League and Youth CND at the age of fourteen, and I had heard that she was both a pacifist and a communist. I had seen her groundbreaking production of *Oh What a Lovely War* in the West End and knew something different was going on. The actors had a quality I had never seen in rep. They were real. They could dance and they could sing and they talked to the audience not at them. They seemed to own the show and could move from comedy to tragedy at the drop of a hat, and I wanted to know how they did it.'[10]

Julia Pascal – 'I was brought up by grandparents in Manchester, my father was an Irish Jew and I heard a lot of Yiddish and Romanian. I think the foreignness of it, the displacement of it, and not feeling English was not pleasant as a child. I knew I was 'other'. My father was a Zionist. He had been a religious Jew then the Holocaust happened and he turned against religion. There being a place where Jews could be safe began to obsess him. In Manchester I was exposed to music and ballet and the Hallé Orchestra and I fell in love with all that. I wanted to be a dancer, I was obsessed with it. Then when I was about twelve, this shifted into theatre. I was praised for my acting. I was not praised at home because girls were not expected to achieve educationally in my shtetl. I think in terms of dance, I became heavy and I wasn't at ease with my body. Besides I don't think I would have been a good dancer. More interesting were the influences around me when I was growing up: circus, Punch and Judy, a working-class ethic, Hylda Baker, George Formby – the importance of working-class theatre, the vulgarity, the muscularity of it were huge for me. So there was a mixture of the high art – the Hallé Orchestra – and this working-class, much more vibrant voice of the people going on.'[11]

David Gale – 'I had no theatre background. I studied at university, I did English Lit – then I went to film school, I thought I wanted to be an underground film-maker. I noticed that some of my classmates didn't want to be underground film-makers. And didn't they do well? But I was asked to go to some theatre workshops. I didn't know what a theatre workshop was. This was New York La MaMa Company recruiting to try and form a London group. This was very exciting. I could not believe that showing off could be so rewarding. Well, I knew it could be rewarding because I'd been doing it for so long but in a more casual way. And that ideas could be framed in such a way as an aspect of the profession. The audition went on for a year. At the end of it, I decided I didn't want to be in the company. But during that time I did meet Hilary Westlake.' [12]

Mark Borkowski – 'Theatre is about changing people's lives. It's about exciting people. That's why I do this job. For me, as an individual with Polish roots, my greatest theatre experience was seeing *The Dead Class* by Tadeusz Kantor. This was in the 1970s, and I schlepped over to Riverside Studios to see it. Why? I was curious to discover what it was about. So I went, and I just couldn't believe what I saw. For days, there were images of that show in my mind. I thought: well, I'm touched by that, and I could easily never even have seen it. How less rich my life would have been!'[13]

Geraldine Pilgrim – 'At that time, when you were young, you had to make a decision whether to go to art school or drama school. And I discovered at that time a place called Oval House. And the Oval House in South London at that time was absolutely extraordinary. I used to go there after school and have workshops with the experimental theatre groups of those days. But then I went to art school. I was the shy one at the back who thought a lot. I decided to concentrate on fine art. I went to Bradford because I wanted to leave London. Through a complete fluke, on the day that I arrived, everything changed. I met a tutor called John Darling, one of the great unrecognized figures of alternative theatre. He gave me a book, which was *Theatre* by Edward Gordon Craig. It changed my life.'[14]

Mike Kenny – 'The first thing that blew me away was a show I saw on a works outing for my mum who worked at Littlewoods. We went to see *Hair*. Because of where I grew up – the Welsh borders in 1968 – having not seen much theatre all my life, this was the theatre equivalent of taking acid. It had rock music, actors crawling over the seats, nudity, it was about the Vietnam war and you were invited onto the stage at the end. So it broke all the rules of the time. I felt, I want to do that. At the time I had no idea how to get near anything like that. I was a working-class boy in Oswestry. No chance, really.'[15]

Appendix 2 – How to Make a Living as an Artist, by Action Hero

Some of this advice may appear contradictory. It may also be wrong and/or uncertain. That's because I live in THE WORLD.

1. Make Good Art

This is always the first step. What 'good' means is of course subjective but I can't be arsed to go into that. Many artists attempt to legitimize themselves by setting themselves up as a company, or making a fancy website, or creating an infrastructure around them, but the only thing that will ever legitimize you as an artist is the art that you make. So start with that (see point 8).

2. See It as a Political Act

I have always viewed the attempt to make a living as an artist as a deeply political act. For me, being an artist is about playing a role in a philosophical shift that pre-empts political change. The act of being an artist and being paid for it shifts how we think about value, how we think about labour and how we view ourselves as human beings. There may be people (other artists included) who will see the desire to make a living as a somehow less authentic way of being an artist. This is bullshit and you must ignore it. Its important that you make a living making the art that you make, not the art that gets you paid or the art that other people want you to make, because then its no longer a political act. Stick to your principals, make the art you want to make and then make a living from it (see point 4).

3. Find Cheap Rent

The easiest way to make a living is to make sure a very small amount of money counts as a living. The first year I quit my 'other' job (van driver) to go full time as an artist I earned just over £5,000. This requires making many sacrifices and letting go of certain romantic notions about what it means to be an artist. For example, the arty parts of town are the most expensive to live, London is the most expensive city. Driving a VW campervan might make you look like an artist but it will also make your living costs too high to be an artist in the first instance. The hardest challenge on the way to making a living as an artist is the point at which you make the jump. There is a point where we must leap into the unknown and stop earning money from our other jobs and its hard to know how/when to do this. Reducing your living costs pragmatically allows you to reach this jumping off point much sooner and you're a lot lower to the ground should you not quite make it. After you've jumped off is the time to start thinking about campervans and arty parts of town but not before.

4. Set the Agenda

There is no model. You are in charge of designing the model for how your art will make you a living. Many people will tell you that in order to make a living you have to 'get real' and 'diversify' or whatever. Don't listen too much to these people. Start with the art, then design a way to make it pay. This will mean forcing the agenda in lots of ways. When we started out we were told we wouldn't be able to make a living because the only way to make a living was via regular funding from the Arts Council which was about to be removed as an option. We didn't give up and it turns out they were wrong. We found a way to do it without regular funding partly because we demanded it was possible (see point 2).

5. Make Friends

Otherwise known as networking. If you don't like someone, don't be their friend (like real life!).

6. Call Yourself an Artist*

It took me years to summon up the courage to call myself an artist. This is just wrong-headed. Call yourself an artist immediately.

*or theatre maker, or director, or jazz poet or whatever it is you want to self-define as

7. Immerse Yourself in the Work of Others

A very simple step but vitally important. Go and see as much work as you can. Go to all the shows in your local theatre, all the exhibitions in your local gallery, go to music gigs, read novels, travel and see art in different countries, watch TV and films, see as much as you can in as many different formats. Be a massive geek about it. Good artists who say 'I never see any other artists' work' to make themselves look cool and authentic are BIG FAT LIARS.

8. Be Patient

It's massively rare, if not totally unknown, for artists to pop out of nowhere with beautiful art. The culture of 'next big thing' and artists 'breaking through' is a falsehood. It takes a long time to learn how to make art and you will make lots and lots of bad art before you make anything good. So take your time, make the bad art, be honest about where you're at. If you've just left university its unlikely you can make world-beating art. Place yourself in different contexts, go and see the world, do some living (see point 7), make lots of work and grow your practice slowly. Be patient with yourself.

9. Do it Yourself

No one is going to do it for you.

10. Talk Your Own Language

Artists shift the way we think about the world. That includes shifting the way we think about the artworld. Don't feel like you have to talk the language of the funders, or the venue programmers, or other artists, or even your audience. Talk your own language.

11. Share

Small pots of money and limited opportunities makes for a seemingly competitive environment but don't be fooled. You will be stronger and you will make better art if you share. Share information, share knowledge, share ideas, share successes and failures, share your fears and your worries. Set up an artist collective and share resources.

12. Recognize Jealousy

Art jealousy is a useful tool. If you feel jealous of another artist it can help you acknowledge what it is you want your art to do. But make sure you know your jealousy comes from an appreciation of the work of that artist*. Don't resent other artists their successes.

*Sometimes artists make shit work and do make a living and that can make us jealous too. There is clearly a shortage of good art (because it's v. hard to do) so continue trying to make good art as your priority. Don't be fooled into thinking you have to make shit art in order to make a living. Seeing shit art can help you make better art so thank them for it, don't resent them.

13. Work Hard (But Know What Work Is)

You need to be a bad-ass maniac to make a living from your art. The task will consume you. It is a mountain of graft. But don't perform your hard work for other people's benefit. don't feel like you have to prove yourself by working too hard. Learn what work can look like if you're an artist. Emailing is not the only kind of work. Conversation can be work, going for a walk can be work, sitting down and thinking can be work. There are some assumptions about what constitutes work that as an artist you can be responsible for changing (see point 2). It's also important to know that you are not a worse artist if you aren't working. Taking three months off to go to Asia or taking the day off to watch the whole of *Friday Night Lights* on DVD could be the best thing you ever do for your art (see point 8).

14. See Limitations as Possibilities

Making a living as an artist is hard to do. Making art is hard to do. There are lots of limitations. But limitation is an important tool in the creative process so you can use the fact that its hard to your advantage. Limitation will impose structure and rules on your process which can actually facilitate more freedom of thought elsewhere. Don't believe the 'starving artists makes better art' bullshit (peddled by people who should know better) but it's OK to have some hurdles (and hurdles are one thing you can count on).

15. Make the Work You Want to Make

Don't let ANYONE tell you what kind of work you should be making. EVER.

16. Get Paid

Some places might want to put on your art. Some of these places will be institutions that pay salaries to their staff and receive income from subsidy, ticket sales, philanthropy and pre-existing assets. Some of them will be artist-led projects run on alternative models, exploring the different kinds of value we might place on art. You need to recognize which is which. Don't let yourself be exploited by not getting paid. If there is a system that is paying people enough to live and your work is needed by that system, you deserve to be paid enough to live too. There may be people who try and convince you otherwise. Do not listen to these people.

17. Talk to Artists Who Make a Living and Ask Them How They Do It

I've been making a living solely from Action Hero for five years (ish). I count this as one of my proudest achievements. But five years is not that long and the sands shift every day. I talk a lot to other artists who make a living to help me find ways to navigate the tricky territory and find new models all the time to allow it to continue. Some artists have been doing it for twenty years or longer. They are good people to talk to. It's not easy but I keep trying because I believe we should expect that artists can make a living from their work. We don't have to if we don't want to of course. But it should be possible (see point 2).

Notes

Introduction

1 *Globalisation – the Human Consequences* by Zygmunt Bauman, Introduction.
2 Quoted in *King Came Preaching: The Pulpit Power of Dr. Luther King*, p. 87.

Part One – In the World

1. Some Principles

Defiance

1 *Avant-Garde Theatre* by Christopher Innes, p. 6.
2 *Talking Theatre* by Richard Eyre, p. 287.
3 Ibid.
4 Women's Theatre episode, www.theargumentroom.net (accessed August 2016).
5 Interview with the author.
6 Ibid.
7 Ibid.
8 *Brecht, A Literary Life* by Stephen Parker, p. 103.
9 The Reith Lectures, Grayson Perry, 19 October 2013. www.bbc.co.uk (accessed August 2016).
10 Rabea Turkman, speaking in film 'Freedom Theatre' presented Toynbee Studios, 22 May 2015.
11 Nabil Al-Raee, speaking at Toynbee Studios, 22 May 2015.
12 Interview with the author.
13 Ibid.

Provocation

14 *Theatre in the Expanded Field* by Alan Read, p. xvii.
15 Interview with the author.
16 *Theory of the Avant-Garde* by Peter Bürger, p. 72.
17 *The Forest and the Field* by Chris Goode, p. 82.
18 *Guardian*, 19 March 2016.

19 *The Cheviot, the Stag and the Black, Black Oil* by John McGrath, p. x.
20 Interview with the author.
21 The quote has no findable source but is, I suggest, typical of Curtis's approach.
22 *Great Moments in the Theatre* by Nicholas de Jongh, Location 2191 of 5506 (Kindle edition).
23 *Independent*, 19 January 1995.
24 www.ruraltouring.org/latest/choose-wisely-this-season-a-voluntary-promoters-perspective-on-new-directions (accessed August 2016).
25 *Guardian*, 11 April 2015.
26 *Artificial Hells* by Claire Bishop, p. 26.
27 Ibid.
28 *No Go The Bogeyman* by Marina Warner, p. 6.
29 *Theory of the Avant-Garde* by Peter Bürger, p. 80.
30 Interview with the author.

Transgression

31 *Politics, Prudery and Perversions* by Nicholas de Jongh, p. xiii.
32 *Playwrights at Work* by George Plumpton, p. 191.
33 Interview with the author.
34 Ibid.
35 *Guardian*, 15 March 2010.
36 *Guardian*, 28 September 2014.
37 ABC RN Breakfast, www.youtube.com.
38 Ibid.
39 Ibid.
40 Ibid.
41 Ibid.
42 Ibid.
43 *In-Yer-Face Theatre* by Aleks Sierz, p. 105.

De-identification

44 *As You Like It* by William Shakespeare, Act 4 Scene 1.
45 *The Art of Living: An Oral History of Performance Art* by Dominic Johnson, p. 92. The author identifies the concept of the 'third mind' as being invented in the 1960s by Burroughs and Gysin.
46 www.bryonykimmings.com (accessed August 2016).
47 *The Revolutionary Theatre* by Leroi Jones (Amiri Baraka), July 1965. An essay commissioned by the *New York Times* but not printed. First published by Black Dialogue.
48 The Busted! episode, www.theargumentroom.net (accessed August 2016).

49 Ibid.
50 *Primitive Mythology* by Joseph Campbell, p. 240.
51 *Mandala* by Joseph Campbell, p. 197.
52 *Group Psychology and the Analysis of the Ego* by Sigmund Freud, p. 45.
53 *Four Archetypes* by Carl Jung, p. 69.
54 *Dancing in the Streets* by Barbara Ehrenreich, p. 14.
55 *Group Processes* by Rupert Brown, p. 11.
56 Ibid.
57 *The Comedy Improv Handbook*, p. 41.
58 *The Revolutionary Theatre* by Leroi Jones/Amiri Baraka.
59 Bernardine Evaristo speaking at Oval House, 6.12.13.
60 *Turbulent Voyage* by Larry Neal, p. 237.
61 *The Contemporary Ensemble: Interviews with Theatre-Makers* by Duska Radosavlevic, p. 48.
62 Interview with the author.
63 Vice News, www.youtube.com (accessed August 2016).

Equality

64 www.theargumentroom.net (accessed August 2016).
65 *Encountering Ensemble*, ed. John Britton, p. 8.
66 Stanislavski, quoted in *Encountering Ensemble*, p. 8.
67 *The Contemporary Ensemble: Interviews with Theatre-Makers* by Duska Radosavlevic, p. 49.
68 *The Life of the Theatre* by Julian Beck, p. 46.
69 Richard Katz in the Busted! episode, www.theargumentroom.net (accessed August 2016).
70 Ibid.
71 Ibid.
72 Gillian Hanna in the Busted! episode, www.theargumentroom.net (accessed August 2016).
73 *The Stage*, May 2016.
74 *Punishing the Outsiders* by Philippa Burt, p. 124.
75 *Obedience, Struggle and Revolt* by David Hare, p. 25.
76 *Talking Theatre: Interviews with Theatre People*, p. 292.
77 www.beescope.blogpost.co.uk (last accessed August 2016).
78 *The Contemporary Ensemble*, p. 101.
79 *Organizing Genius* by Warren Bennis, p. 198.
80 Ibid., p. 208.
81 *Encountering Ensemble, Building Chartres in the Desert*, p. 230.
82 *Covering McKellen: An Understudy's Tale* by David Weston, p. 228.

Prefiguration

83 Interview with the author.
84 www.ietm.org (accessed August 2016).
85 Interview with the author.
86 The Co-Authorship episode, www.theargumentroom.net
87 Private email.
88 *The Forest and the Field* by Chris Goode, p. 235.
89 https://orgsync.com/9859/events/1415858/occurrences/3210648 (accessed August 2016).
90 *Performance and the Community*, ed. Caomihe McAvinchey, p. 91.
91 Evaluation Report by prison inmate submitted to Rideout, 2014.
92 *Theory of the Avant-Garde* by Peter Bürger, p. 50.
93 The Political Theatre episode, www.theargumentroom.net (accessed August 2016).

2. Tactics

Animation

1 *Dorothy Heathcote on Education and Drama: Essential Writings* by Cecily O'Neal, p. 21.
2 *Community Education in Social Justice*, ed. Cameron White, 2012.
3 I'm not able to locate this quote – however, I'm confident that even though it flows from folk memory rather than accurate recording, it is typical of her approach.
4 Mojisola Adebayo, quoted in *Performance and Community*, p. 64.
5 *Dancing in the Streets: A History of Collective Joy* by Barbara Ehrenreich, p. 24.
6 *Orson Welles: Hello, Americans* by Simon Callow, p. 388.
7 Ibid.
8 *Tactical Performance*, p. 100.
9 *Carnival Art, Culture and Politics: Performing Life*, ed. Michaeline Crichlow, p. 145.
10 *Tactical Performance*, p. 121.
11 *Guardian*, 15 December 2011.
12 www.improveverywhere.com (accessed August 2016).
13 Ibid.

Adaptation

14 Interview with the author.
15 Ibid.
16 Ibid.

17 Sarah Derbyshire writing in the *Guardian*, 1 October 2015.
18 *Mindfulness for Health* by Burch and Penman, p. 70.
19 Interview with the author.
20 Ibid.
21 'But is it art? The artist and participatory practice', People Dancing International Event 2014, www.youtube.com (accessed August 2016).
22 Ibid.
23 Interview with the author.
24 Ibid.
25 *The Social Animal* by David Brooks, p. 249.
26 Interview with the author.
27 Ibid.
28 *Adapt* by Tim Harford, p. 248.
29 Ibid.
30 Ibid.

Responsiveness

31 *Games for Actors and Non-Actors* by Augusto Boal, p. 66.
32 Ibid., p. 84.
33 Interview with the author.
34 Ibid.
35 *Dancing in the Streets* by Barbara Ehrenreich, p. 99, quoting Stallybrass and White, *The Politics and Poetics of Transgression*, p. 176.
36 Interview with the author.
37 www.b-arts.org.uk (accessed August 2016).
38 www.weareimprobable.tumblr.com (accessed August 2016).
39 *The Forest and the Field* by Chris Goode, p. 70.
40 www.thestage.co.uk (accessed August 2016).
41 The Co-Authorship episode, www.theargumentroom.net (accessed August 2016).
42 *Theatre and Architecture* by Juliet Rufford, p. 48.
43 Wil Alsop, *Independent*, 25 January 2011, www.independent.co.uk (accessed August 2016).

Immediacy

44 *Different Every Night* by Mike Alfreds, p. 24.
45 *Theatre and Politics* by Joe Kelleher, p. 39.
46 www.culturebot.org/2012 (accessed August 2016).
47 *Essays on the Blurring of Art and Life* by Allan Kaprow, p. 18.
48 Andy Field, *Guardian*, April 2009.
49 *Do It! By Jerry Rubin, Takin It To The Streets*, Bloom/Breines, p. 280.

50 Interview with the author.

51 Ibid.

52 Ibid.

53 Ibid.

54 *Shoot an Iraqi – Art, Life and Resistance Under the Gun* by Wafaa Billal, p. 11.

55 Ibid., p. 14.

56 Ibid., p. 89.

57 Ibid., p. 93.

58 Ibid., p. 101.

59 Ibid., p. 157.

60 *No Innocent Bystanders: Performance Art and Audience* by Frazer Ward, p. 125.

Un-timing

61 *Montaillou* by Emmanuel Le Roi Ladurie, p. 280.

62 Ibid.

63 *The Medieval Stage* by E. K. Chambers, p. 24.

64 *The Making of the English Working Class* by E. P. Thompson, p. 397.

65 *The Rainbow* by D. H. Lawrence, p. 292.

66 *Out of Now: The Lifeworks of Tehching Hsieh* by Adrian Heathfield, p. 21.

67 *Tactical Performance* by L. M. Bogad, p. 37.

68 *The English Year* by Steve Roud, p. 15.

69 Ibid.

70 *Dancing in the Streets* by Barbara Ehrenreich, p. 105.

71 Interview with the author.

72 *Eyes on Stalks* by John Fox, p. 158.

73 Leroi Jones, *Negro Digest*, April 1966, p. 22.

74 The Radical About Impro episode, www.theargumentroom.net (accessed August 2016).

75 *Thinking in Time: An Introduction to Henri Bergson*, p. 65.

76 *Out of Now: The Lifeworks of Tehching Hsieh* by Adrian Heathfield, p. 352.

77 Email to the author.

78 Hans Ulrich Obrist, https://mitpress.mit.edu/books/out-now-0 (accessed August 2016).

79 *Out of Now: The Lifeworks of Tehching Hsieh* by Adrian Heathfield, p. 32.

80 Ibid.

81 Ibid.

82 *Shamanism – Archaic Techniques of Ecstasy* by Mercia Eliade, p. 108.

83 http://www.electricscotland.com/history/folklore/folklore5.htm (accessed August 2016).

84 *The Hero with a Thousand Faces* by Joseph Campbell, p. 84.

85 *The Origin and Function of Culture* by Geza Roheim, p. 38.

86 The Theatre and Audience episode, www.theargumentroom.net (accessed August 2016).

3. Transmission

Voice

1   Interview with the author.
2   *The Element: How Finding Your Passion Changes Everything* by Ken Robinson, p. 16.
3   *The Talent Code* by Daniel Coyle, p. 32.
4   *Guardian*, 11 November 2015.
5   *Guardian*, 22 August 2015.
6   Interview with the author.
7   *Talking Theatre*, ed. Richard Eyre, p. 118.
8   'Remembering Andrea Dunbar', WOODDDDDDDYAMOVIES3, https://www.youtube.com/watch?v=p3thxr8XUxk (accessed August 2016).
9   Ibid.
10 Ibid.
11 *Joan Littlewood: Dreams and Realities* by Peter Rankin, p. 129.
12 www.improfestuk.co.uk (accessed August 2016).

Contrariness

13 *The Naked Civil Servant* by Quentin Crisp, p. 1.
14 *Keith Johnstone: A Critical Biography* by Theresa Dudek, p. 23.
15 *The Fool in European Theatre* by Tim Prentki, p. 20.
16 *Impro* by Keith Johnstone, Introduction by Irving Wardle, p. 9.
17 *Impro for Storytellers* by Keith Johnstone, p. x.
18 Quoted in *The Fool in European Theatre*, p. 177.
19 Interview in *British Comedy Guide*, www.comedy.co.uk (accessed August 2016).
20 *Dancing in the Streets* by Barbara Ehrenreich, p. 88.
21 Ali G as played by Sacha Baron Cohen, www.youtube.com (accessed August 2016).
22 *The Applied Theatre Reader* by Tim Prentki and Sheila Preston, p. 1.

Resonance

23 *Guardian*, 16 May 2015.
24 *Man and his Symbols* by Carl Jung, p. 20.
25 *Taking on the Empire* by Roland Muldoon, p. 101.
26 Interview with the author.
27 Theatre Museum Canada, www.youtube.com.
28 Private interview with Ewan MacColl conducted by Frances Rifkin and Dave Rodgers.

29   *Guardian*, 23 July 2013.
30   *Improvisation and the Theatre* by Keith Johnstone, p. 109.
31   Interview with the author.
32   *Talking Theatre* by Richard Eyre, p. 126.
33   Interview with the author.
34   Ibid.
35   *Playwrights at Work* by George Plimpton, p. 263.
36   Interview with the author.
37   *Playwrights at Work* by George Plimpton, p. 231.
38   Interview with the author.
39   *San Quentin News*, 28 November 1957, quoted in *Theatre of the Absurd*, p. 20.
40   *In-Yer-Face Theatre* by Alex Sierz, p. 100.

4. Survival

Affinity

1   Interview with the author.
2   Ibid.
3   Ibid.
4   Ibid.
5   Ibid.
6   Interview with Mark Borkowski in *Programme Notes: Case Studies for Locating Experimental Theatre*, p. 152.
7   Ibid.
8   Ibid.
9   *Performance and Community*, p. 94.
10   Interview with the author.
11   Ibid.
12   Ibid.
13   Ibid.
14   Interview with the author.
15   Ibid.
16   *Guardian*, 30 November 2015.
17   *Guardian*, 21 August 2015.
18   *The Beatles: Tune In* by Mark Lewisohn, p. 728.
19   The Theatre and Audience episode, www.theargumentroom.net (accessed August 2016).
20   www.hyperallergic.com (accessed August 2016).

Allies

21 Interview with the author.
22 *The Reluctant Escapologist* by Mike Bradwell, p. 234.
23 Ibid., p. 235.
24 The Busted! episode, www.theargumentroom.net (accessed August 2016).
25 Interview with the author.
26 *Taking On the Empire* by Roland Muldoon, p. 114.
27 *Guardian*, 30 November 2015.
28 Ibid.
29 The Volunteers episode, www.theargumentroom.net (accessed August 2016).
30 Interview with the author.
31 *Education for Socially Engaged Art* by Pablo Helguera, p. 34.
32 Interview with the author.
33 Ibid.
34 *Taking On the Empire* by Roland Muldoon, p. 154.
35 Interview with the author.
36 Interview with the author.
37 Ibid.

Agency

38 Interview with the author.
39 Interview with the author.
40 *The Art of Disobedience*, www.ietm.org, 2015.
41 Interview with the author.
42 Ibid.
43 www.unfinishedhistories.com (accessed August 2016).
44 www.unfinishedhistories.com (accessed August 2016).
45 *Taking On the Empire* by Roland Muldoon, p. 336.
46 Ibid.
47 Ibid., p. 342.
48 *Theory of the Avant-Garde* by Peter Bürger, p. 90.
49 *Taking On the Empire* by Roland Muldoon, p. 342.
50 *Guardian*, 8 July 2015.
51 Private conversation with the author.

Scale

52 www.unfinishedhistories.com (accessed August 2016).
53 www.strengthweekly.com (accessed 19 September 2016).
54 The Theatre and Audience episode, www.theargumentroom.net (accessed 19 September 2016).

55   Interview with the author.
56   https://www.youtube.com/watch?v=YP9viSaRLr4 (accessed August 2016).
57   The Live Art episode, www.theargumentroom.net (accessed August 2016).
58   *Guardian*, 14 March 2015.
59   The Volunteers episode, www.theargumentroom.net (accessed August 2016).
60   Ibid.
61   Ibid.
62   Ibid.
63   Ibid.
64   Interview with the author.
65   Interview with the author.
66   Ibid.
67   www.frieze.com (accessed 19 September 2016).
68   Ibid.

Occupation

69   *Imagine* by Jonah Lehrer, p. 251.
70   *Words Will Break Cement: The Passion of Pussy Riot* by Masha Gessen, p. 101.
71   *Brecht on Theatre*, p. 43.
72   *Observer*, 13 September 2015.
73   *Mail Online*, June 2011.
74   Private email.

Survival

75   Interview with the author.
76   Women's Theatre episode, www.theargumentroom.net (accessed August 2016).
77   Interview with the author.
78   www.equity.org.uk (accessed August 2016).
79   Interview with the author.
80   Ibid.
81   Interview with the author.
82   Interview with the author.
83   Ibid.
84   Interview with the author.
85   Ibid.
86   Interview with the author.
87   Ibid.
88   Paul Bhattacharjee Obituary, *Guardian*, 23 July 2013.

89 Interview with the author.
90 *Hello Americans* by Simon Callow, p. 3816.
91 Private interview with Ewan MacColl conducted by Frances Rifkin and Dave Rodgers.
92 Ibid.
93 *Joan Littlewood: Dreams and Realities* by Peter Rankin, p. 138.
94 Ibid.
95 Ibid.
96 Ibid.
97 Private interview with Ewan MacColl conducted by Frances Rifkin and Dave Rodgers.
98 *Talking Theatre* by Richard Eyre. Interview with John Bury, p. 257.
99 Private email.

Part Two – In the Room

5. Principles in Action

Method

1 http://d1wf8hd6ovssje.cloudfront.net/documents/Attempts_bkpk.pdf (accessed August 2016).
2 Interview with the author.
3 *The Presence of the Actor* by Joseph Chaikin, p. 54.
4 Interview with the author.
5 *The Forest and the Field* by Chris Goode, p. 95.
6 www.artpractice.sva.edu (accessed August 2016).
7 *The Pyschopathology of Everyday Life* by Sigmund Freud, Location 1444 (Kindle Edition).
8 *Impro* by Keith Johnstone, p. 80.
9 *Why Is That So Funny?* by John Wright, p. 39.

A Note on Projection

10 *Totem and Taboo* by Sigmund Freud, p. 4.
11 Ibid.
12 *Why Is That So Funny?* by John Wright, p. 163.

Working with Images

13 Interview with the author.

14   Interview with the author.
15   Ibid.

The Art of Elaboration

16   Interview with the author.
17   *Word of Mouth with Philip Pullman*, 19 January 2015, www.bbc.co.uk.
18   Interview with the author.
19   Interview with the author.

Some Notes on Style

20   *The Presence of the Actor* by Joseph Chaikin, p. 25.
21   *Games for Actors and Non-Actors* by Augusto Boal, p. 201.
22   *The Shakespearian Ethic* by John Vyvyan, Location 575 of 4558 (Kindle Edition)

Where the Attention Is

23   *My Life in Art* by Constantin Stanislavski, p. 464.

Attitude

24   *Why Is That So Funny?* by John Wright, p. 107.
25   Interview with the author.
26   *The Illustrated Man* by Stuart Morgan, http://www.franko-b.com/The_Illustrated_Man.html (accessed August 2016).
27   Ibid.
28   *Improvise: Scene from the Inside Out* by Mick Napier, p. 17.
29   *How To Be a Woman* by Caitlin Moran, p. 35.
30   *Twelfth Night* by William Shakespeare, Act 2 Scene 5.
31   *Hamlet* by William Shakespeare, Act 1 Scene 5.
32   *The Exception and the Rule* by Bertolt Brecht.
33   *A Short Organum for the Theatre* by Bertolt Brecht, p. 38.

The Use of Restrictions

34   *Stanisklavski for Beginners* by David Allen, p. 144.
35   *Spring Awakening* by Franz Wedekind, Act 1 Scene 5.

Shifts in Attitude

36   *King Lear* by William Shakespeare, Act 5 Scene 3.
37   *How Plays Work* by David Edgar, p. 51.

Tension

38   *Homo Ludens* by Johan Huizinga, p. 11.
39   *Handbook of Creativity* by Robert J. Sternberg, p. 140.
40   *The Presence of the Actor* by Joseph Chaikin, p. 22.
41   *Improv Therapy* by Jimmy Carrane, Location 222 of 795 (Kindle Edition).
42   www.youtube.com, Robert Lepage in interview, Theatre Museum Canada.
43   *The Caretaker* by Harold Pinter, Act 1 Scene 2.

Establish, Transform, Shift

44   Interview with the author.
45   Ibid.
46   Ibid.
47   *Happenings in the Theatre* by Jean Jaques Lebel, p. 49.
48   *The Brig* by Kenneth H. Brown, Act 2 Scene 2.
49   *Some Like It Hot*, dir. Billy Wilder, final scene.

Anti-defaulting

50   *Primitive Mythology* by Joseph Campbell, p. 30.
51   *Imagine* by Jonah Lehrer, p. 22.
52   *Impro for Storytellers* by Keith Johnstone, p. 155.
53   Eugenio Barba, speaking at Sadler's Wells, 22 April 2013.
54   www.theargumentroom.net (accessed August 2016).
55   Ibid.

Transgressing

56   *The War of Art* by Steven Pressfield, p. 55.
57   Interview with the author.
58   Ibid.
59   Theatre Museum, Canada, www.youtube.com.
60   Interview with the author.
61   Ibid.
62   Ibid.
63   Ibid.
64   *Impro* by Keith Johnstone.

65   *Impro* by Keith Johnstone.

Ownership

66   *Tactical Performance: Serious Play and Social Movements* by L. M. Bogad, Ch. 2.
67   *Stage Fright, Animals and Other Theatrical Problems* by Nicholas Ridout, p. 100.
68   *Covering McKellen: An Understudy's Tale* by David Weston, p. 30.

Casting

69   *Performance and the Community*, ed. Caoimhe McAvinchey, p. 130.
70   Interview with the author.
71   Interview with the author.

The Price of Ownership

72   *Impro* by Keith Johnstone, p. 152.
73   http://www.bbc.co.uk/news/entertainment-arts-33785904 (accessed August 2016).
74   *Guardian*, 13 April 2016.

Appendix 1

1   Interview with the author.
2   Interview with the author.
3   The Theatre and Audience episode, www.theargumentroom.net (accessed August 2016).
4   Interview with the author.
5   *Extract from My First Play*, ed. Nick Hern, p. 13.
6   Interview with the author.
7   Interview with the author.
8   *My Life in Pieces*, Simon Callow, p. 1.
9   Interview with the author.
10   *The Reluctant Escapologist: Adventures in Alternative Theatre*, p. 2.
11   Interview with the author.
12   The Live Art episode, www.theargumentroom.net (accessed August 2016).
13   *Programme Notes: Case Studies for Locating Experimental Theatre*, p. 152.
14   The Live Art episode, www.theargumentroom.net (accessed August 2016).
15   Interview with the author.

Bibliography

Abramovic, Marina. Available online: www.artpractice.sva.edu/follow-svaartpractice/in-workshops-with-students-i-ask-them-just-to-open (accessed August 2016).

Alfreds, Mike. *Different Every Night*. London: Nick Hern, 2007.

Allen, David. *Stanislavski for Beginners*. Newburyport: Red Wheel/Weiser, 2015.

Al-Raee, Nabil. *The Freedom Theatre*, Toynbee Studios, 2015.

Arguelles, Jose and Miriam Arguelles. *Mandala*. Colorado: Shambhala Publications, Inc., 1974.

The Argument Room. Available online: www.theargumentroom.net (accessed August 2016).

Bailey, Brett. 'Yes, Exhibit B is challenging – but I never sought to alienate or offend'. *Guardian*, 24 September 2014. Available online: www.theguardian.com/commentisfree/2014/sep/24/exhibit-b-challenging-work-never-sought-alienate-offend-brett-bailey (accessed August 2016).

Baraka, Amiri and Leroi Jones. *The Revolutionary Theatre*. New York: Black Dialogue, 1965.

Bauman, Zygmunt. *Globalisation – The Human Consequence*. New York: Columbia University Press, 1998.

Beck, Julian. *The Life of the Theatre*. Winona: Limelight Editions, 1972.

Bennis, Warren and Patricia Ward Biederman. *Organizing Genius*. New York: Basic Books, 2007.

Bilal, Wafaa and Kari Lydersen. *Shoot an Iraqi: Art, Life & Resistance Under the Gun*. San Francisco: City Lights Books, 2013.

Bishop, Claire. *Artificial Hells: Participatory Art and the Politics of Spectatorship*. London: Verso Books, 2012.

Blackwell, Louise. 'How to encourage thriving contemporary theatre companies'. *Guardian*, 30 November 2015. Available online: www.theguardian.com/culture-professionals-network/2015/nov/30/how-to-encourage-thriving-contemporary-theatre-communities (last accessed August 2016).

Bloom, Alexander and Winifred Breines. *Takin' It to the Streets: A Sixties Reader*. Oxford: Oxford University Press, 2015.

Boal, Augusto. *Games for Actors and Non-Actors*. Abingdon: Routledge, 2005.

Bogad, L. M. 'Carnivals Against Capital: Radical Clowning and the Global Justice Movement', in *Carnival Art, Culture and Politics: Performing Life*, ed. Michaeline Crichlow. Abingdon: Routledge, 2012.

Bogad, L. M. *Tactical Performance*. Abingdon: Taylor & Francis, 2016.

Bradwell, Mike. *The Reluctant Escapologist*. London: Nick Hern, 2010.

Brecht, Bertolt. *The Exception and the Rule*. California: Chrysalis, 1961.

Brecht, Bertolt. *Brecht on Theatre*. London: Bloomsbury Publishing, 2014.

Britton, John. *Encountering Ensemble*. London: Bloomsbury Academic, 2013.

Brooks, David. *The Social Animal*. New York: Random House, 2012.

Brown, Kenneth H. *The Brig*. New York: Hill and Wang, 1965.

Brown, Rupert. *Group Processes*. Oxford: Wiley, 1988.

Burch, Vidyamala and Danny Penman. *Mindfulness for Health: A Practical Guide to Relieving Pain, Reducing Stress and Restoring Wellbeing*. London: Hachette UK, 2013.

Bürger, Peter (trans. Michael Shaw). *Theory of the Avant-Garde*. Manchester: Manchester University Press, 1984.

Burt, Philippa. 'Punishing the Outsiders: Theatre Workshop and the Arts Council'. *Theatre, Dance and Performance Training* 5 (2) (August 2014).

Callow, Simon. *Orson Welles: Hello, Americans*. New York: Random House, 2011.

Campbell, Joseph. *The Masks of God: Primitive Mythology*. London: Penguin Books, 1976.

Campbell, Joseph. *The Hero with a Thousand Faces*. San Francisco: New World Library, 2008.

Carrane, Jimmy. *Improv Therapy*. Kindle, 2014.

Chaikin, Joseph. *The Presence of the Actor*. New York: Theatre Communications Group, 1972.

Chambers, E. K. *The Mediaeval Stage*. Massachusetts: Courier Corporation, 1996.

Coyle, Daniel. *The Talent Code*. New York: Random House, 2010.

Crisp, Quentin. *The Naked Civil Servant*. New York: Harper Collins, 2007.

De Jongh, Nicholas. *Politics, Prudery and Perversions*. London: Methuen, 2000.

Derbyshire, Sarah. 'Music education is out of tune with how young people learn'. *Guardian*, 1 October 2015. Available online: https://www.theguardian.com/culture-professionals-network/2015/oct/01/music-education-how-young-people-learn-exams (accessed August 2016).

Dudeck, Theresa. *Keith Johnstone: A Critical Biography*. London: Bloomsbury Academic, 2013.

Edgar, David. *How Plays Work*. London: Nick Hern, 2009.

Ehrenreich, Barbara. *Dancing in the Streets: A History of Collective Joy*. New York: Henry Holt and Co., 2007.

Eler, Alicia. 'The Artist is not Present but the Brand Sure Is'. Available online: www.hyperallergic.com/75766/the-artist-is-not-present-but-the-brand-sure-is/ (accessed August 2106).

Eliade, Mircea. *Shamanism: Archaic Techniques of Ecstasy*. London: Penguin, 1989.

Esslin, Martin. *The Theatre of the Absurd*. London: Bloomsbury Publishing, 2015.

Evaristo, Bernadine. 'Speaking at Oval House', *Unfinished Histories*, 2013.

Eyre, Richard. *Talking Theatre: Interviews with Theatre People*. London: Nick Hern Books, 2009.

Farrell, Joseph. 'Dario Fo at 90: So farce, so good'. *Guardian*, 18 March 2016. Available online: www.theguardian.com/stage/2016/mar/18/dario-fo-at-90-so-farce-so-good (last accessed September 2016).

Field, Andy. 'Invisible theatre: So real you don't even know it's happening'. *Guardian*, 30 March 2009. Available online: https://www.theguardian.com/stage/theatreblog/2009/mar/30/invisible-theatre-boal-acconci (last accessed August 2016).

Fotis, Matt and Siobhan O'Hara. *The Comedy Improv Handbook*. Abingdon: Taylor & Francis, 2015.

Fox, John. *Eyes on Stalks*. London: Bloomsbury, 2009.

Freud, Sigmund. *Totem and Taboo*. Massachusetts: Courier Corporation, 1998.

Freud, Sigmund. *Group Psychology and the Analysis of the Ego*. Worcestershire: Read Books Ltd, 2014.

Freud, Sigmund. *The Psychopathology of Everyday Life*. Worcestershire: Read Books Ltd, 2014.

Gardner, Lyn. 'Adrian Howells obituary'. *Guardian*, 24 March 2014. Available online: www.theguardian.com/stage/2014/mar/24/adrian-howells (accessed August 2016).

Gessen, Masha. *Words Will Break Cement: The Passion of Pussy Riot*. London: Granta Books, 2014.

Goode, Chris. *The Forest and the Field*. London: Oberon Books, 2016.

Guerlac, Suzanne. *Thinking in Time: An Introduction to Henri Bergson*. New York: Cornell University Press, 2006.

Hare, David. 'David Hare v the establishment: A memoir'. *Guardian*, 21 August 2015. Available online: https://www.theguardian.com/books/2015/aug/21/david-hare-v-establishment-memoir (accessed August 2016).

Hare, David. *Obedience, Struggle and Revolt*. New York: Farrar, Straus and Giroux. 2005.

Harford, Tim. *Adapt: Why Success Always Starts with Failure*. London: Hachette UK, 2011.

Heathfield, Adrian. *Out of Now: The Lifeworks of Tehching Hsieh*. Massachusetts: MIT Press, 2015.

Helguera, Pablo. *Education for Socially Engaged Art*. New York: Jorge Pinto Books, 2011.

Hemley, Matthew. 'Scrap artistic directors, urges Red Room boss'. *The Stage*, 13 May 2016. Available online: https://www.thestage.co.uk/news/2016/scrap-artistic-directors-urges-red-room-boss/ (accessed August 2016).

Hickling, Alfred. 'Gurpreet Kaur Bhatti: "I'm not scared"'. *Guardian*, 15 March 2010. Available online: www.theguardian.com/stage/2010/mar/15/gurpreet-kaur-bhatti-behud-behzti (accessed August 2016).

Huizinga, Johan. *Homo Ludens*. Abingdon: Taylor & Francis, 1949.

ImproFest UK. Available online: www.improfestuk.co.uk (accessed August 2016).

Innes, Christopher. *Avant-Garde Theatre*. Abingdon: Taylor & Francis, 2004.

Johnson, Dominic. *The Art of Living: An Oral History of Performance Art*. Basingstoke: Palgrave Macmillan, 2015.

Johnstone, Keith. *Impro: Improvisation and the Theatre*. Abingdon: Routledge, 2012.

Johnstone, Keith. *Impro for Storytellers*. Abingdon: Routledge, 2014.

Jones, Leroi. 'In Search of The Revolutionary Theatre'. *Negro Digest*, April 1966.

Jones-Hughes, Claire. 'The new flashmob – breastfeeding mothers come out into the open'. *Guardian*, 15 December 2011. Available online: https://www.theguardian.com/commentisfree/2011/dec/15/flashmob-breastfeeding-mothers-brighton (accessed August 2016).

Jung, Carl. *Four Archetypes*. New Jersey: Princeton University Press, 2012.

Jung, Carl. *Man and his Symbols*. New York: Random House, 2012.

Kaprow, Allan. *Essays on the Blurring of Art & Life*. Berkeley: University of California Press, 1996.

Kelleher, Joe. *Theatre and Politics*. Basingstoke: Palgrave Macmillan, 2009.

Kimmings, Bryony. Available online: www.bryonykimmings.com (accessed August 2016).

Latchford, Cate. 'Choose Wisely This Season'. National Rural Touring Forum. Available online: www.ruraltouring.org/latest/choose-wisely-this-season-a-voluntary-promoters-perspective-on-new-directio (accessed August 2016).

Lawrence, D. H. *The Rainbow*. Massachusetts: Trajectory Inc., 2014.

Lebel, Jean Jaques. *Happenings in the Theatre*, Les Lettres Nouvelles, Denoel, 1966.

Lehrer, Jonah. *Imagine: How Creativity Works*. Boston: Houghton Mifflin Harcourt, 2012.

Le Roy Ladurie, Emmanuel. *Montaillou, the Promised Land of Error*. New York: Vintage Books, 1979.

Letts, Quentin. 'Naked dancers jumping on the audience? This sort of trashing of manners is an assault on our values'. *Daily Mail*, 7 June 2011. Available online: www.dailymail.co.uk/news/article-1395061/Naked-dancers-jumping-audience-This-sort-trashing-manners-assault-values.html (accessed August 2016).

Lewisohn, Mark. *The Beatles: Tune In*. New York: Crown/Archetype, 2016.

MacFarlane, Robert. 'The eeriness of the English countryside'. *Guardian*, 10 April 2015. Available online: www.theguardian.com/books/2015/apr/10/eeriness-english-countryside-robert-macfarlane (accessed August 2016).

McAvinchey, Caoimhe. *Performance and Community: Commentary and Case Studies*. London: Bloomsbury Academic, 2014.

McGrath, John. *The Cheviot, the Stag and the Black, Black Oil*. London: Bloomsbury Publishing, 2015.

Moran, Caitlin. *How To Be A Woman*. New York: Harper Collins, 2012.

Mouffe, Chantal. 'Artistic Activism and Agonistic Spaces'. *Art and Research* 1 (2) (September 2007).

Muldoon, Roland. *Taking on the Empire*. Leicester: Unity Press, 2013.

Napier, Mick. *Improvise: Scene from the Inside Out.* Colorado: Meriwether Publishing Ltd, 2015.

Nightingale, Benedict. *Great Moments in the Theatre.* London: Oberon Books, 2012.

O'Hagan, Sean. 'Martin McDonagh interview: "Theatre is never going to be edgy in the way that I want it to be"'. *Guardian*, 11 September 2015. Available online: www.theguardian.com/culture/2015/sep/11/martin-mcdonagh-theatre-never-going-to-be-edgy-hangmen-interview (accessed August 2016).

O'Neill, Cecily, ed. *Dorothy Heathcote on Education and Drama: Essential Writings.* Abingdon: Routledge 2014.

Parker, Stephen. *Bertolt Brecht: A Literary Life.* London: A&C Black, 2014.

Perry, Grayson. 'The Reith Lectures'. Podcast. Available online: www.bbc.co.uk/programmes/b00729d9 (accessed August 2016).

Pinter, Harold. *The Caretaker.* New York: Dramatists Play Service, 1962.

Plimpton, George. *Playwrights at Work.* London: Harvill Press, 2000.

Prentki, Tim. *The Fool in European Theatre.* New York: Springer, 2011.

Prentki, Tim and Sheila Preston. *The Applied Theatre Reader.* Abingdon: Routledge, 2013.

Pressfield, Steven. *The War of Art.* London: Orion, 2003.

Radosavljevic, Duska. *The Contemporary Ensemble: Interviews with Theatre-Makers.* Abingdon: Routledge, 2013.

Rankin, Peter. *Joan Littlewood: Dreams and Realities.* London: Oberon Books Ltd, 2014.

Read, Alan. *Theatre in the Expanded Field.* London: A&C Black, 2013.

Ridout, Nicholas. *Stage Fright, Animals & Other Theatrical Problems.* Cambridge: Cambridge University Press, 2006.

Robinson, Ken. *The Element: How Finding Your Passion Changes Everything.* London: Penguin, 2009.

Roheim, Geza. *The Origin and Function of Culture.* New York: Doubleday, 1943.

Roud, Steve. *The English Year.* London: Penguin UK, 2008.

Rufford, Juliet. *Theatre and Architecture.* Basingstoke: Palgrave Macmillan, 2015.

Shakespeare, William. *As You Like It.* London: Penguin Books, 1955.

Shakespeare, William. *King Lear.* London: Ganymede Original Editions Ltd, 1963.

Shakespeare, William. *Hamlet.* Upminster: Swan Books, 1983.

Shakespeare, William. *Twelfth Night.* Philadelphia: J. B. Libbincott Co., 2001.

Sierz, Aleks. *In-Yer-Face Theatre.* London: Faber & Faber, 2014.

Silvestre, Agnes. 'Punchdrunk and the Politics of Spectatorship'. Available online: http://www.culturebot.org/2012/11/14997/punchdrunk-and-the-politics-of-spectatorship/ (accessed August 2016).

Simkins, Michael. 'Paul Bhattacharjee and Cory Monteith deaths: Is acting today just too tough?'. *Guardian*, 23 July 2013. Available online: www.theguardian.com/stage/2013/jul/23/paul-bhattacharjee-cory-monteith-acting (accessed August 2016).

Some Like It Hot. Dir. Billy Wilder. Mirisch Company, 1959.

Stanislavsky, Konstantin. *My Life in Art*. Abingdon: Taylor & Francis, 1952.

Sternberg, Robert J. *Handbook of Creativity*. Cambridge: Cambridge University Press, 1999.

Sylvester, David. 'One continuous accident mounting on top of another.' *Guardian*, 13 September 2007. Available online: https://www.theguardian.com/theguardian/2007/sep/13/greatinterviews (accessed August 2016).

Taylor, Paul. 'THEATRE/ Courting Disaster'. *Independent*, 20 January 1995. Available online: www.independent.co.uk/arts-entertainment/theatre-courting-disaster-1568886.html (accessed August 2016).

Thompson, E. P. *The Making of the English Working Class*. London: Penguin UK, 2002.

Turkman, Rabea. *Freedom Theatre*. Film, date and production company unknown.

Turpin, Annabel. 'Here's what happened when we asked audiences to set their own ticket prices'. *Guardian*, 8 July 2015. Available online: www.theguardian.com/stage/theatreblog/2015/jul/08/audiences-ticket-prices-arc-stockton (accessed August 2016).

Unknown. 'Audio Transcriptions'. Unfinished Histories – Recording the History of Alternative Theatre. Available online: www.unfinishedhistories.com/hidden/audiotranscriptions/ (accessed August 2016).

Unknown. 'Folk Lore in Lowland Scotland'. Electric Scotland. Available online: www.electricscotland.com/history/folklore/folklore5.htm (accessed August 2016).

Unknown. National Theatre Education. Education pack. Available online: www.d1wf8hd6ovssje.cloudfront.net/documents/Attempts_bkpk.pdf (accessed August 2016).

Vyvyan, John. *The Shakespearean Ethic*. London: Shepheard Walwyn Publishers Ltd, 2011.

Ward, Frazer. *No Innocent Bystanders: Performance Art and Audience*. New Hampshire: University Press of New England, 2012.

Warner, Marina. *No Go the Bogeyman*. New York: Farrar, Straus and Giroux, 1999.

Wedekind, Frank. *Spring Awakening*. London: A&C Black, 2013.

Weston, David. *Covering McKellen: An Understudy's Tale*. London: Rickshaw Productions, 2011.

White, Cameron, ed. *Community Education in Social Justice*. Rotterdam: Sense Publishing, 2014.

Windom Hayes, Floyd. *A Turbulent Voyage*. Lanham: Rowman & Littlefield, 2000.

WOODDDDDDDDYAMOVIES3. 'Remembering Andrea Dunbar'. Available online: https://www.youtube.com/watch?v=p3thxr8XUxk (accessed August 2016).

Wright, John. *Why Is That So Funny?* London: Nick Hern, 2006.

Wood, Catherine. 'Tino Sehgal'. Frieze. Available online: www.frieze.com/article/tino-sehgal-1?language=en (accessed August 2016).

Wroe, Nicholas. 'Frank Auerbach: "Painting is the most marvellous activity humans have invented"'. *Guardian*, 16 May 2015. Available online: https://www.theguardian.com/artanddesign/2015/may/16/frank-auerbach-when-paint-fantastic-time-lots-girls (accessed August 2016).

Index

The letter *f* after an entry indicates a page that includes a figure.